Ancient
America
Rediscovered

Ancient America Rediscovered

as recorded by

Mariano Veytia(1720-1778)

Including an Account of America's First
Settlers Who Left from the Biblical Tower of
Babel at the time of the Confusion of Tongues.

First English Translation

Compiled by
Donald W. Hemingway
W. David Hemingway

ISBN: 1-55517-479-5
v.2

Published by Bonneville Books

Distributed by:
925 North Main, Springville, UT 84663 • 801/489-4084

CFI Publishing and Distribution Since 1986
Cedar Fort, Incorporated
CFI Distribution • CFI Books • Council Press • Bonneville Books

Typeset by Virginia Reeder
Cover design byAdam Ford
Cover design © 2000 by Lyle Mortimer

Printed in the United States of America

TABLE OF CONTENTS

GLOSSARY AND NOTES OF TRANSLATOR

Artifice Spanish artificio. It is used to indicate the system of how the calendar works.

Infante A king's son who is not an heir to the throne.

Gentilism Spanish gentilidad. Refers to the fact of the Indians' being gentiles, or non- Christians, and also the time period before the conquest, as the Spanish supposedly brought Christianity to America and from that time on the Indians were no longer gentiles. I opted for this word rather than heathenism or some other synonym because I wanted to preserve the Spanish root word gentil, or gentile, a long with its irony, particularly in view of the Book of Mormon usage of the word gentile.

Century This is the usual translation of the Spanish siglo. Although the prefix cent indicates 100, here century refers to a 52-year period.

Quinary A five-day period, used to refer to the five days at the end of every year that were not a part of any month.

Septenary A period of seven, either days or years.

Hebdomad A seven-day week, as opposed to the thirteen-day week of the Indians.

Indiction Spanish indiccion. In the general sense it is the 15-year taxation period used in the Roman empire, but is used here to refer to the 13-year periods the Indians' centuries were divided into.

Triadecateride Spanish triadecaterida. It is not in the dictionary in either Spanish or English, but from the context it is clear that it refers to a period of thirteen, either days or years. When it refers to thirteen years, it is sometimes used interchangeably with indiction, above, but is always preferred when the emphasis is on the number thirteen.

Notes

1. Throughout the document Mexico does not refer to the area covered now by the country of Mexico, but a much more limited area, probably the region around what is now Mexico City.

2. Don (and the feminine equivalent Dona) is used throughout the source text as a title, rather than a name; the closest equivalent in English is

Mr. or Sir, but in most cases I haven't included it in the English and haven't translated it. An exception: I have retained it whenever it appears in the footnotes in English in the source text (see point 3 below). I have included and translated the title Father when it occurs in the source text, but not Fray, meaning Friar, except in one or two places where I thought it was helpful to include mention of the religious capacity of the person in question.

3. I have left the English in the footnotes exactly as it was in the source text, without correcting errors in spelling or punctuation, with the possible exception of places where the source text was mostly illegible, but could be figured out from the context.

4. In places where the two source texts differed, I indicated the discrepancies with square brackets. When it was just a matter of spelling, capitalization, punctuation, or paragraph formatting, I generally followed the book, "Historia Antigua de Mexico" unless the other text was obviously better.

5. For passages in Latin, I translated them into English when the meaning was clear to me, such as in scriptures where the reference was given at least partially I copied passages that I couldn't translate as found in the source text.

6. Names like Moctezuma (Montezuma) and Hernan Cortez have various spellings; I am not positive that I have been consistent in spelling them the same way each time, though in general I have followed the Spanish text.

Ronda Cunningham

Translator

FOREWORD

This book was originally written sometime prior to 1778 by Don Mariano Fernandez de Echevarria y Veytia. It is the first portion of his two volume work titled "Historia Antigua de Mexico" and relates to the origin of the native Americans.

Veytia was a Spanish gentleman, born in Puebla de los Angeles, Mexico, 16 July 1720, a descendant of Spanish royalty, a friend and associate of King Carlos III of Spain. He lived and wrote much while in Europe, serving as attorney for the Spanish Royal Councils and ultimately becoming Trustee Attorney General. Remembering his homeland he later returned to Mexico and continued in his extensive literary career. It is estimated he died in 1778.

Veytia's understanding varied considerably from many of the teachers and evangelists from Spain in America. Where many of the earliest Spanish priests considered the past of the native Americans to be of the Devil and ordered the records be destroyed, Veytia declared that the early American records were very detailed and valuable in revealing the "information of their history, the codes of their laws, the decrees of their nobility, the titles of their possessions, the rules of religion, the guidelines of their festivals, the calendars of their astronomical calculations" etc. These records were in the form of paintings, charts, monuments and diagrams. He learned to read them and understood that the figures on their paintings served native Americans as letters and characters as the ones we use serve us. Understanding these charts was taught them as reading and writing is taught us.

The writings of Veytia lay in the dust for many years after his death until 1836 when his "Historia Antigua de Mexico" was first published. This work of Veytia had come to the attention of the great gatherer of Mexican antiquities, Edward King Kingsborough (Lord), (1795-1837). an Englishman of royalty whose fervid belief was that the native Americans were of Israel (part of the lost ten tribes). Lord Kingsborough's work was published in "Antiquities of Mexico", nine volumes (1831-1848). Among his collections, in Volume 8, is found a portion of the historical writings of Mariano Veytia. This portion has been the basic material for this present volume. Chapters one through a portion of chapter five and chapters eleven through twenty-three were taken from Lord Kingsborough. Chapters five (last portion) through chapter ten and "About the Author" have been taken from Veytia's "Historia Antigua de Mexico", the latest edition being 1944. Lord Kingsborough did not include these chapters in his text because "the concluding portion of this chapter [5] and the five following chapters treat of the Mexican methods of computing time, of the division of the years into eighteen months of twenty days each, and of the various signs allotted to them. They are omitted here for the sake of brevity, and because a full explanation of the Mexican calendar will be found in the second book of Sahagun's `History of New Spain.'" We have included them here since the above cited copy may not be available to the reader.

Among other things Veytia tells of the coming to New Spain (Central America) of a great teacher of religion whom the natives called Quetzalcoatl (Quetzalcohuatl). He transcribed many of the teachings of Quetzalcoatl recognizing similarities to his own Christian doctrines and practices. Not knowing how such teachings could come to America he assumed St. Thomas of the original quorum of twelve apostles, as chosen by Jesus Christ in biblical times, taught in America.

President John Taylor, prophet and president of The Church of Jesus Christ of Latter-day Saints, 1880 - 1887, was acquainted with the works of Lord Kingsborough and noted in his "The Mediation and Atonement" (1882), page 201, that the great Christian teacher, Quetzalcoatl, mentioned by Veytia, was the resurrected Jesus Christ as described in the Book of Mormon.

Other LDS Church leaders have recognized the works of Lord Kingsborough. Elder James E. Talmage cited his works, Articles of Faith, 1952 edition, p. 506. Elder Orson Pratt discussed the writings of Lord Kingsborough in a lecture delivered Dec 29, 1872 and reported in the Journal of Discourses, Volume 15, pp. 259-260. Elder B. H. Roberts cited Lord Kingsborough, "Antiquities of Mexico" concerning "Crucifixion and Atonement Believed in by Mexicans." in his "Outlines of Ecclesiastical History," p. 72. He also refers to the writings of Veytia in "New Witnesses for God," Vol. 3. pp. 5, 6.

A copy of Lord Kingsborough's "Antiquities of Mexico" was in the LDS Church library in Salt Lake City for many years, possibly brought from England when President John Taylor returned from Church service there. It is now housed at Brigham Young University with a micro film copy at Salt Lake City.

Originally written in Spanish this portion of Veytia's history, for the first time of which we are aware, is now translated into English. The excerpt copied by Lord Kingsborough has been compared to and coordinated with the presently available Spanish edition of "Historia Antigua de Mexico".

Where there are variations in the two texts, the translator has inserted in brackets the variation and its translation. The word "Book" in these variations means the word or words are found in the book "Historia Antigue de Mexico." Footnotes in the Lord Kingsborough portion were written by Lord Kingsborough himself. Footnotes in the other portion are assumed to have been written by C. F. Ortega, publisher of the 1836 edition..

The translation was first done by Thomas Hemingway, a former LDS Guatemalan missionary and student at Brigham Young University, Hawaii Campus. This translation was done by Ronda Cunningham, who for twenty-two years worked as a translator for The Church of Jesus Christ of Latter-day Saints. She has also translated for the United States federal government. She was accredited in 1981 by the American Translators Association for translation from Spanish to English and in 1985 for translation from French into English.

Veytia presents a most interesting visualization of the people of ancient America in the earliest times, where they came from, when they came, as well as their religious beliefs and practices.

He followed and was well acquainted with the writings of Fernando de Alva Ixtlilxochitl (1578-1650). Translation of a portion of Ixtlilxochitl's works is found in "Ancient America and the Book of Mormon" Hunter, Milton R. and Thomas Stuart Ferguson, Oakland, California, Kolob Book, 1950 and in "Exploring the Lands of the Book of Mormon", Allen, Joseph L. PhD, Brigham Young University, Print Services, 1989. Another interesting collection of similar early writings is found in "Christianity in America before Columbus?" Hemingway, Donald W., 1988. (Available through Cedar Fort, Inc., 925 No. Main, Springville, Utah 84663)

A few interesting citations in this volume are:

1. The first families in New Spain came from the Tower of Babel at the time of the confusion of tongues – pages 40, 48, 49, 50, 192. (see Book of Mormon. Ether 1:33-43; 2:1-25; 6:1-13)

A. The first progenitor of those who came to america from Tower of Babel was commanded by the Lord to come to these lands (Mexico)-page 47 (see Ibid. Ether, Chapters 1,2,6)

B. Description of how the first settlers crossed the seas to New Spain—pages 50, 51 (see Ibid. Ether 2:16, 17; 6:4-12)

2. Origin and beginning of the whole universe was the work of a supreme and only God, the creator of all things—pages 41, 44 (see Ibid. 2 Nephi 8:13; Mosiah 4:9; Alma 30:44)

3. There was a great flood on the earth from which only

eight persons survived–page 44. (see Holy Bible, Genesis 7:11-13, 17-20)

4. Ancestors of early Americans had two arrows and used them to know if they were going to win a battle or if they should retreat–page 53. (see Ibid. 1 Nephi 16:10; Alma 37:38-40.

5. The suspension of the sun for a day was recorded–pages 55, 56. (see Holy Bible, Joshua 10:13)

6. Among the first settlers in America were giants–pages 56, 57, 137, 138-140. (see Ibid. Ether 1:34)

A. These giants were destroyed 107 years before the Christian era–pages 143, 144. (see Ibid. Onmi 1:20-22, Ether, chapter 15)

7. The world was divided into four ages or times- page 60, 61.

A. Creation to the flood–sun (or day) of water.

B. The flood to the hurricanes–sun (or day) of air.

C. Hurricanes to furious earthquakes–sun (or day) of earth.

D. The last age is to end with violence of fire-sun (or day) of fire. (see Ibid. 2 Nephi 26:5,6)

8. Great earthquakes were experienced the time of which was calculated to have been at the death of Jesus Christ—page 148 (see Ibid. 3 Nephi 8:5-23)

9. The coming of Quetzalcohuatl or Jesus Christ to New Spain- pages 152-156. (see Ibid. 3 Nephi 11: 1-11)

10. Some teachings of Quetzalcohuatl-page 163. (see Ibid. 3 Nephi chapters 11-27)

11. Doctrine of Godhead, virgin birth etc. was taught by Quetzalcohuatl—page 164. (see Ibid. Mosiah 15:1-5; 2 Nephi 31: 21; Alma 7:9-10)

12. Early Americans practiced the ordinance of baptism which meant being born again—pages 167, 168. (see Ibid. 3 Nephi 11:32, 33; Mosiah 27: 25; Alma 5:49)

13. Divine Providence kept land of America hidden from Europeans—page 38. (see Ibid. 2 Nephi 1:8)

We note a familiar citation in the Book of Mormon, 1 Nephi 13:39. "And after it [Book of Mormon] had come forth unto them I beheld other books, which came forth by the power of the Lamb, from the Gentiles unto them, unto the convincing of the Gentiles and the remnant of the seed of my brethren, and also the Jews who were scattered upon all the face of the earth, that the records of the prophets and of the twelve apostles of the Lamb are true."

May the reader find interest in this new translation of a very signifacant record which parallels some of the events in the Book of Mormon

Note: This note is for those readers who are not acquainted with the Book of Mormon.

The Book of Mormon is a collection of religious writings somewhat similar to the Holy Bible. It covers a period of time on the American continent from about 2000 BC to about 420 AD covering the histories of two distinct civilizations. Mormon, (C. 311 AD - 385 AD) a military general and leader of his people was the major compiler of the book.

The earliest history in the Book of Mormon (Ether) begins at the Biblical tower of Babel and the confusion of tongues. There a group of families got together and prayed to the Lord to retain their original language. This request was granted and then the Lord directed the group over land and ocean to go to a promised land which we recognize today as America. They developed into a great civilization which existed approximately 1800 years. Eventually they became involved in an extensive civil war by which their civilization as ultimately destroyed.

The Book of Mormon also tells of two other groups of people who left Jerusalem and came to America about 600 BC. (1 Nephi, Mosiah 25:2; Helaman 8:21). They eventually joined together and populated the land. Again a great civilization was developed which is generally considered to have flourished chiefly in Mexico and Central America. This civilization lasted for over 1000 years from 600 BC to 420 AD.

Climaxing the teachings of the leaders and prophets of that group was the visitation of the resurrected Lord Jesus Christ. His teachings are contained in many chapters in the section called 3 Nephi. Also related in the book are other significant events. Christ's birth in Palestine was recognized in America by the sign of day and night and day of continuous light and the appearance of a new star in the heavens. At His death was a devastating earthquake.

From early times this civilization was divided into two factions, one with a light skin and the other with a dark skin. They were enemies and fought many wars and contentions against each other. For a time they were united after the visitation of Jesus Christ but eventually the factions divided again. A final warring conflict between them brought about the end of one group, the light skinned faction, as millions of people were destroyed. Those victorious are the ancestors of the natives of North and South America today.

The Book of Mormon was written (inscribed on metal plates) by prophet leaders passed down from generation to generation. The final writing was made around 420 AD and then the collection of plates was hidden away in the earth.

The plates lay hidden until 1823 when a young man, Joseph Smith, was directed by an angel to find their location. By the gift and power of God they were translated and first published in 1830 in Palmyra, New York. Thus they stand today as the Book of Mormon. Since it relates so much detail of the visitation, doctrines and teachings of Jesus Christ, it is declared to be another testament of Jesus Christ along with the Holy Bible.

Parallel events as related in "Historia Antigua de Mexico" of Mariano Veytia and the Book of Mormon are of great interest. A few citations have been made in this Foreword to similar incidents in both books. Many more will probably be found by the careful reader.

Neither Veytia nor Joseph Smith, living in different centuries, was aware of the other as to the source, writing, historical background or final publication of their books. The Book of Mormon was published in 1830. Veytia's "Historia Antigua de Mexico", written prior to his death in, was published in Spanish in 1836.

Donald W. Hemingway

HISTORY
OF THE ORIGIN OF THE PEOPLES WHO INHABITED NORTH AMERICA CALLED THE NEW SPAIN; WITH INFORMATION ON THE FIRST PEOPLE WHO ESTABLISHED THE MONARCHY OF THE TOLTEC NATION THAT FLOURISHED IN IT AND INFORMATION GOING BACK TO THE CREATION OF THE WORLD

AUTHOR

THE HONORABLE MARIANO FERNANDEZ DE ECHEVARRIA Y VEYTIA PROFESSED KNIGHT OF THE MILITARY ORDER OF SANTIAGO

1

ABOUT THE AUTHOR
(See page 17—footnote)

In the year 1820 I set about to publish this history; but inasmuch as the spirit of the Mexicans was occupied with the great events of that era, there were few people who answered the invitation that I addressed to my compatriots to assist my undertaking. So I judged, as now, that the public would more gladly receive the work if information were given at the front of it about the author, which has been done not only in Europe by all the editors of posthumous works, but becomes more necessary in our country, where the curiosity of the readers cannot be satisfied by turning to dictionaries, biographies, encyclopedias, libraries, and other similar works, because those that we have of this nature are few and so abbreviated that they must be compared to those of the writers of the ancient world, much more advanced than ours in sciences and literature.

And so, for example, the library of Dr. Beristain, a truly valuable work, cannot be considered as anything but an outline of Mexican literary biography, in the way the Diccionario de Moreri [Moreri's Dictionary] was of the historical dictionaries that came to light and continue to come to light in France; and it is truly hoped that a master hand, familiar with the three volumes that comprise a good part of it, will rewrite it, adding the articles that are missing, and above all, filling in some that are quite lean. One of them is that of our author, about whom the following is read in volume 3, page 278:

"Veytia (D. Mariano), a native of la Puebla de los Angeles, a Knight of the Order of Santiago, Lord of the noble ancestral house of Veytia, and Alderman of his country and Advocate of the Audience of Mexico. He wrote:

"BALUARTES DE MEXICO" [BASTIONS OF MEXICO]. History of the four miraculous images of the Virgin Mary that are venerated to the four winds of Mexico City, with the description of their sanctuaries. Manuscript dedicated to the Excellent Sir Antonio Maria Bucareli, Viceroy of Mexico.

"This work, which has been seen to be very close to the source, exists in the original in the archives of the viceroyalty of Mexico; and the copy which I have has some wonderful notes by Francisco Sedano, of whom I have talked in this library. The four images that the author calls Bastions of Mexico are: on the east, that of Our Lady of the Bale [Translator: Bala could also be translated Bullet or Cannonball; without knowing the history of this appearance of the Virgin Mary, it is impossible to know for sure]; to the west, that of Our

Lady of the Remedies; to the north, that of Our Lady of Guadalupe, and to the south, that of Our Lady of Piety.

"CURIOUS PAPERS ABOUT JESUITS, translated from Latin and from French. I have seen up to seven volumes on the shelves of Dr. Agustin Pomposo Fernandez de San Salvador."

The diminutiveness of this information will leap out in the eyes of anyone who knows that Beristain was a fellow countryman of Veytia, whom he must have associated with in Puebla, where he did his literary career. It is true that this young man was transferred to Valencia with his protector, the illustrious Mr. Fuero; but it is also true that in that city was where he conceived the idea of writing his library, and that being appointed canon of Mexico and having settled in that city, he worked on that project, as he himself asserts, for more than twenty years. During this long period he must have associated with many persons who undoubtedly knew Veytia, especially his children or relatives, particularly two of his children, whom I knew, one of whom, namely the Reverend Father Antonio Maria de San Jose, a Carmelite Monk, was very well educated and obtained the first offices of his Order.

It was to this monk that I went in 1820 for him to entrust me with some information relative to the life and writings of his father, the author of this history, which he did with the greatest kindness, writing the following letter to me:

"Carmelites of Mexico Convent, November 11 of 820 [Translator: Here and elsewhere the 1 is left off the year]. —My very dear and esteemed sir, with this letter I am answering your letter of August 20 of this year, thanking you for the diligence you have taken as a good American, in honoring your country and countrymen, again presenting to the face of the Universe the laborious works that some rare minds of our countrymen have produced in all times. Such is the work of the general History of the kingdom, which was written by my father and which you are now trying to have printed, impatient to have it to sleep any longer in oblivion, and for the erosion of time, which consumes all, to put an end to all of it, as has already occurred in one part.[2]

"For that purpose you ask me to please provide you with all the information and papers conducive to that intent, in which I gladly concur, and you will have all those that with infinite work I have been able to gather after more than 38 years in which I separated myself from my family to be a monk.

"Likewise you ask me for some detailed information about the author, that will make his work more recommendable, and here I find myself in the greatest conflict: perpetuating where possible the pleasant memory and name of my Christian, virtuous, and wise father imperiously compels me to do it; but I fear on one part that I will be described as impassioned in the narration that I make, and on the other part, that having resolved to live as dead and buried in my cloister, I wouldn't want the world to again hear of me, nor hear my name.

"But as I owe it to him to honor his ashes, and he still has descendants who are following his footsteps, I am going to form the narration, being very precise in it, that by fulfilling your intent, his grandchildren and fellow countrymen may also see the model of a good citizen dedicated to the service of his country.

"The work that you want to print was written by Mariano Jose Fernandez de Echevarria y Orcolaga, Alonso de Linage (or Alfonso, which is the same, because of tracing his ancestry to a son of Alfonso the eleventh, King of Leon) Veytia, Lord of the noble ancestral house of Veytia. A professed Knight of Santiago, Advocate of the Royal Councils, etc., etc.

"He was born in the city of Puebla de los Angeles on July 16 of the year 1720. The shadows of childhood had barely started to dissipate when he discovered a great talent and dedication no less to virtue than to the sciences; and having moved to Mexico [City] (because of the employment that his father, Jose de Veytia, was a candidate for as the Senior Judge of the Royal Audience and first Superintendent of the Mint), on March 9, 1733, he received the degree of bachelor in the school of arts at the Nacional y Pontificia Universidad (National and Pontifical University), following a public act of all philosophy attended by the Royal Audience. The same University conferred the same degree in law on him on July 13, 1736, following ten lessons of various subjects for a half hour and a public act of the subjects of Hoereditate jacente; of Jure accrescendi in Hoereditate; of Legatis; of Jure accrescendi in legatis; which he generally maintained in the presence of the Royal Audience. The following year of 1737 this Audience argued for him to take the Attorney examination, and he was approved as an attorney, exempted from the time that he was lacking to fulfill the requirement set by the Lord viceroy.

"He had scarcely been licensed when his father, who had many serious personal matters in the court, conferred a very ample authority upon him to take care of them. This occurred on April 6, 1737, before Juan Antonio de la Zerna, a Royal Notary. He promptly went to Veracruz to get on the cargo ship of the Excellent Manuel Lopez Pintado, as he confirmed in the middle of July of that year, such that he turned 17 years old at sea, from the first day of his sailing starting to write a very instructive and curious work which he entitled: My trips. This consisted of two quarto volumes, and his story line was a lengthy and detailed diary of the degrees, heights, weather, distances, cities, villas, towns, and places where he went, and of anything curious he found of painting, architecture, and sculpture; but we were deprived of it by an unknown hand who on the very day of his death took it from his bookcase.

"Once he arrived in Spain, he presented himself at the Royal Council of Castille, in order to join with the attorneys of the Royal Councils, which was granted to him and he was given the accustomed certification of incorporation [membership] on February 11, 1738. He immediately started to concern himself with the dealings of his commission with so much skill and sound judgment that he won them all.

"Now having rid himself of these assignments, in 1738 he went to the town of Oña, where he was from, because of his paternal grandmother, who was still alive, and there they made him Magistrate of the Holy Brotherhood; and so in 1738 that town appointed him Magistrate of the Noble State of Gentlemen, when he was still in Mexico. He concluded his magisterial service, and in the following year of 1739 they made him a Special Attorney and Perpetual Alderman; in the year 1740, the Trustee Attorney General for the mentioned Noble State, and he served in everything satisfactorily.

"Finding himself now free of everything mentioned, he wanted to see courts; he traveled throughout all of Spain, Portugal, Naples, Italy, Rome, Jerusalem, Morocco, England, and France; but looking everywhere for monuments of antiquity: medals, coins, inscriptions, curious and rare papers, of which he made a considerable collection, so many that he formed up to 24 or 25 very thick quarto volumes, the whereabouts of which I do not know. He lived for a time on the island of Malta, under the direction of the Great Master of that Order, and as the novice that he was, with those knights he made up to three forays against the Moors; but determined to marry, he left the cross of St. John and took up the one of St. James. He conferred and consulted with the wise people of the nations on his questions about the antiquities, and until he was convinced, he wouldn't make a decision on either side, which is inferred from the massiveness with which he wrote his histories. Add to this the perfection with which he possessed the Latin, Portugese, Italian, French, Mexican, and part of the English languages.

"In all this time that he was in the courts he did not forget his country, and he came to it three times, always taking advantage on his return to the peninsula to travel through the provinces of Guadalajara, Goatemala, Oajaca, and various other provinces of this New Spain.

"His father having died here and his first wife in Madrid, he then came here to take care of the interests of his house. He established his residence in Puebla, where he remarried Josefa de Arostegui Sanchez de la Peña, and since that time he dedicated all the time left to him by the many concerns and consultations made to him, to putting in order such a multitude of items and documents he had for the history that he was considering writing; with many more that he added by virtue of royal order that Sir [King] Carlos III (may he be in holy glory) had provided to him, knowing of the work he was doing, so that he would be provided with all the manuscripts and archives of the universities, colleges, town councils, and monasteries of this kingdom.

"The esteem and appreciation that the monarch showed toward this gentleman was so extreme that he frequently wrote to him with the familiarity of one friend to another. He would consult the monarchy on very serious and interesting points, resting his conscience on their resolutions. When His Majesty resolved that the libraries of the Jesuit fathers would be awarded to the library of the Seminary of St. John, he commissioned my father for the delivery, warning him not to carry it out until he personally got to know all of them, and to remove all the books and manuscripts that seems to him inappropriate to expose to the view of the public, or which could offend the mentioned fathers, as he carried it out, and of these he formed seven thick volumes in folio, and they are undoubtedly the same ones that Dr. Augustin Pomposo saw, and which he mentions in his little work entitled: Los Jesuitas quitados y restituidos al mundo [The Jesuits removed from and restored to the world]; but since he was unaware of this matter, and of the kind of great affection that this man held for these monks, who were his first teachers, it is excusable for him to place him among those who wrote for the depraved purpose of defaming them; with this narration that is pertinent to me serving to go back for the honor of the one who gave me being and lessons in all virtue, which I did not know how to take advantage of; likewise regretting that such papers exist, which I supposed burned or rotted under the earth, for which effect my mother delivered them to a certain gentleman and with the same reserve with which my father had them.

"The king being satisfied with the talents, uprightness, good judgment, and virtue of the Gentleman Veytia, and how well he would carry out whatever business was entrusted to him, he wanted to reward him as from his royal hand. He offered him the title of Castile, with the gown of Mexico, with whatever employment he wanted, and he always urged him to ask for favors; and as he would accept nothing from his royal will, he conferred upon him the most exquisite and rare titles and privileges that any house in America enjoys, but I do not name them individually here because it does not pertain to our purpose, and to avoid any feeling that it could cause to other noble families. For if at some time his descendants would want to make use of them, they were all recorded in Puebla de los Angeles, in the office that belonged to the Notary Zambrano, and there they are kept. There is one alone that I cannot pass over in silence, because it is an unmistakable proof of the high opinion and esteem that the king held for this wise citizen, and the rare unselfishness with which this citizen rendered his services in honor of his country.

"With King Carlos III seeing that he asked for nothing, nor received anything of all that he was offered, he sent him twelve of his signatures on blank sheets, telling him in the letter that since he was asking him for no favors, he had those signatures there to use them in his behalf, or in behalf of his children or friends, filling them in for any use that seemed best to him. A very great favor3 equal to the sincerity of the favored. He kept this so secret and hidden that not until the very day when they ministered the Holy

6

Sacraments to him did he reveal it to his wife, telling her the place where he had them locked, and charging her greatly to destroy them at the time of his death.

"In view of this, no one will be surprised that once they learned of his death in Spain, the minister to Viceroy Martin de Mayorga would communicate an order from the King for the manuscripts and papers that he had left relative to the ancient history of New Spain to be gathered up from the possession of his executors or heirs. By virtue of which my mother, in the house of her dwelling, delivered to the presence of Gaspar de Portola, Colonel of the Royal Armies and Political and Military Governor of Puebla, and that of Mariano Francisco Zambrano, the Notary Public and Town Hall Notary, the following works:

"A volume of the general History of the Kingdom, with two books, first and second, and parts of another one, composed of forty-four notebooks, and four hundred seventy-six sheets, excluding the loose sheets of notes and additions.

"Another book entitled: Preliminary discourse of the foregoing history, in two notebooks.

"Another first, of the mentioned general history, with seven notebooks and eight calendars, which is the order in which they were to be placed, in seventy-one sheets, and it concluded with the Mechoacan method of counting the weeks.

"A notebook of chronological tables.

"Nine other loose notebooks.

"A quarto volume, entitled: Book of festivals of Indians and their explanation, in four notebooks with seventy-four sheets, and twenty-two illustrations of the idols with their names.

"Another one which is entitled: Bastions of Mexico and history of the four sacred images of Our Lady.

"History of the founding of Puebla, in forty-eight notebooks that consisted of four-hundred seventy-four sheets, without including the little papers of notes and additions.

"A painted chart, what Mexico City was like before, three yards long and with a cane [stick] to roll it up: this went back to August 25, 1780, with nothing more than the drafts remaining in our possession.

"All these papers were received in Spain by the King with the appreciation with which he had always looked at the productions of this wise man, and His Majesty manifested it thus by having the Minister give thanks in his royal name to the widow of such a gentleman, likewise offering her that if she wanted three crosses of Santiago [St. James] for her three children, to give notice to send the necessary items.

"Besides the mentioned works, he wrote an ecclesiastical history.

7

Another history of the Image that is venerated in the Franciscan convent of Puebla with the name of the Conqueress [feminine of Conqueror]. A half volume of sheets of Spanish poems from his own hand. Various political dissertations. But of these last works only the name has been left to us.

"With which my letter concludes, hoping that this narration is satisfactory to your wishes to place it at the beginning of the work, it being a great pleasure for me to have been able to express in this small way the sincerity of my affection, with which I reiterate as your friend and humble servant who kisses your hand. – Fr. Antonio Maria de San Jose."

I am also indebted to the illustrious Dr. Francisco Pablo Vazquez for other literary information about our author, and it consists of the paragraphs of a letter that he wrote to me on December 3 of the same year and which I copy as follows:

"I have two volumes of Veytia's ecclesiastical history. of which the first has the Frontispiece, of which I am attaching a copy.4 Both are drafts with very repeated references either to loose slips of paper or to the end of each volume, and there are even references from one to the other. There are infinite corrections and writing between the lines of poor handwriting; therefore it is not easy to form an exact idea of the work, except by taking a lot of time. But through what I have examined of it, I feel that the author varied the plan of the work, and that instead of an Ecclesiastical History, which embraces so much, he reduced it to an Evangelical History, of which I have a volume written cleanly and in good handwriting. It consists of thirty-one discourses, the first being on the conception in grace of Holy Mary; and the last, on the beheading of the Baptist, the multiplication of the loaves, a declaration that for this reason Jesus Christ did the instituting that he was going to do of the Eucharist, but not being understood by some of his disciples, they separated from his holy school.

"Besides these discourses, he has a preliminary one, which is about the Holy Gospels. The Evangelical History has merit in my opinion, for the main questions that move the expositors of the gospels are treated with discernment and soundness.

"In another manuscript volume, which was Veytia's, I find the compositions that go after the frontispiece."5

The foregoing letters reveal that Veytia spent his entire life on literary tasks, directed mostly toward illustrating the history of his nation. The decided liking that he had for the historical investigations is manifested not only in his original writings, but also in the compilations that he made of the productions of others.

Four manuscript volumes of curious papers are still preserved in the books of the deceased school master, Dr. Jose Nicolas Maniau, some simply gathered and others translated by Veytia, and which show that they had belonged to a more abundant collection, all of which deal with history. One has the title of Los Anales de Madrid [The Anals of Madrid], by Antonio Leon Pinelo, volume 1. Two others, one of Papeles Curiosos [Curious Papers], volume 3 and 6, among which there are some translated from the Portuguese by Veytia around the years of 1761, 1762, and 1765 , and they are about Jesuits; and the other, that of El Duende de Madrid [The Goblin of Madrid]. This is a collection of pasquinades or anonymous works that were sent to Jose Patino, the Clerk of the Universal Dispatch in the reign of Phillip V for the years of 1735 and 1736, with such art and astuteness that whether under the pillow, in the fold of the napkin, or at the most unexpected times the Minister would find himself with some paper from the Goblin, without ever being able to find out from what hand it came. The celebrity which this collection enjoyed must have been great at a time when newspapers were very scarce to occupy the attention of a court like Madrid, which on the other hand was so supportive of its monarchs, and looked with such respect and veneration on the persons who surrounded the throne, that it was very natural that for a long time the public was very interested in the skill with which the mysterious and talkative goblin was able to penetrate even the most hidden retreats of the Minister, and the liberty with which he was explained. And so several copies were made of it, and the curiosity of Veytia was not neglectful in providing himself with one of them, just as he obtained a copy of the Duende de Mexico [Goblin of Mexico] (which would visit the viceroyal palace from time to time twenty years later, imitating the one in Madrid), as he did with everything that piqued the interest of his enquiring and hardworking nature.

During his residence in Madrid he had a very close friendship with Boturini, of whom he was later the executor; and having had him as a guest in his own house, that was where that famous and unfortunate antiquarian wrote his Idea de una Nueva Historia de la America Septentrional [Idea of a New History of North America], and where our author, as he himself mentions in various places in his book, received his first ideas of Mexican antiquities. He must have been 25 years old at the most at that time, for Boturini printed his history at the beginning of 1746.

The verbal instructions that he received from Boturini, as a seed scattered on fertile ground, were developed in Veytia's spirit in a surprising manner after he returned to his homeland of Puebla, where his father, after having given up the magisterial gown and the Superintendency of the Mint, and embraced the ecclesiastical state, obtained the dignity of Precentor. Dedicated there with the greatest determination to the study of Mexican history, there was no author that he didn't read and compare, nor manuscripts and monuments that he didn't consult to write his history, as will be seen by simply reading it. But what undoubtedly helped him more than anything to enter with firm footing into the labyrinth of the indigenous antiquities and chronology was the rich museum of that tireless searcher, whom, as he himself tells us, he had available to him and was able to consult at his pleasure.

I do not know if Veytia achieved this precious acquisition by virtue of powers that the former conferred upon him so that as his executor he could claim it from the Government of Mexico, or by virtue of the Monarch's orders mentioned by his son Fr. Antonio to provide him with access to the archives and public libraries. I am inclined toward the second, as much because the Government's resistance to return Boturini's museum to him is well known, as because if Boturini's museum had been delivered to Veytia as his testamentary representative, it would have gone to the heirs of one or the other, and would not have gone back to the Office of the Viceroyalty, where, according to public record, it was afterwards preserved, with part of it still existing in the general archives that have been formed in the same office in which the mentioned Viceroyalty Office was. This concept is confirmed with the delivery that Veytia's widow made of the papers and documents that he had relative to the Ancient History, among which Boturini's museum, or part of it, would perhaps be found, although Fr. Antonio does not so indicate. Otherwise one cannot conceive of the grounds there could have been for that delivery to take place with the solemnities that accompanied it, nor for the original writings of Veytia to be included in it, if it weren't that Veytia wrote his work by virtue of higher orders; and that whether because of this, or because of the manuscripts that had been provided to him from the public archives, the Government would feel it had a right to collect from his estate anything related to the charge that had been entrusted to him.

The fact that the mentioned Monk assures us that the delivery was done by virtue of a royal order leads us to believe this, which indicates that the court of Madrid not only had information but also an interest in the works of Veytia; and although this interest may have been motivated, as the Monk himself supposes, by the reputation that the author had acquired, and the estimation that the King made of his talents, it is rare for governments, especially over such a great distance as that which separated us from the government of Madrid, to pay this type of consideration to men of literature. It is true that our author, in his long residence in Spain, had to enter into relationships with the most distinguished persons of the court, especially with his ancestry being so illustrious. And here I am not only referring to the nobility of blood, which at that time was sufficient to be distinguished, but to that nobility that really makes us worthy to occupy a high rank in society, namely, that which consists of the happy union of virtue and talents, and that which in an enlightened government leads men to first-rank positions. Veytia could boast as much as any other of this type of nobility; for not only was he highly recommendable in himself for one chapter or another, as proven by the useful and wise tasks that always occupied him, the posts that he obtained and those that he rejected, not only had he been born of a father who achieved the highest ranks in the civil order and in the ecclesiastical, as has already been seen, but among his ancestors he had a great uncle (Juan Veytia Linage, Knight of the Order of Santiago) who had been an Indies Counselor, and another who was the Cleric of the Universal Dispatch of the Indies, namely, Jose Veytia Linage, a Knight of the same Order, and author of the famous work entitled Norte de la Contratacion de Indies [North of the Indies Trading]. All this, I say, must have come together so that the name of our author was distinguished in the court, and makes the account of his son Fr. Antonio somewhat probable.

There may be no shortage of my readers who claim to confirm it with what the father himself adds, namely, that all the papers he deals with were received by the king with the appreciation with which he had always viewed Veytia's productions. And it will be claimed even more strongly when it is learned that there are great apparent reasons to believe that the originals were in fact sent back to Spain. I at least conjecture it to be so, and in addition to the testimony of Veytia's son, I base my thinking on the following reasons:

1st. The manuscript that I possess, although very authentic, is not original. It was given by the Brigadier Antonio Bonilla, the Clerk of the Viceroyalty, to Joaquin Perez Gabilan, the Indies Solicitor Agent, who delivered it to me. Its title page indicates that it was a copy that was made in the year 1782 from the dossier formed on the general history of this America.

2nd. Nor does the one existing in the Museum seem to be the original, because in addition to missing the tables of the century and of the months of the Indies at the end of chapter 8, which are found in mine, in comparing the reading of one with the other, the one that I possess is perceived to be the more genuine. Also, a cleanness of writing is noticed in both which is very rare in originals, and although in the one from the Museum there are some corrections, the freshness and the blackness of the ink manifests that they are of a very recent hand. This manuscript belonged to Colonel Diego Garcia Panes, and afterwards to Jose Ignacio Esteva, who gave it to the first congress, being a deputy, from whose office it went to the Museum.

3rd. The mentioned original does not exist in the general archive, nor through diligent efforts that I have made for the space of several years have I been able to verify that it existed in any other period. All this persuades me that it was in fact sent to Spain and that here only copies remained; and the statement of Fr. Antonio and the supposition that the appreciation that the king had for the works of his father was the reason for this remission is corroborated. But without openly denying this I assert, couldn't it also be attributed to the interest that the court of Spain must have had in their not being lost, or in some works being examined in which they had some part, in the supposition of having ordered and protected them? Is it not more natural to believe this in view of the circumstances with which they were gathered from Veytia's heirs? Where has it been seen that the appreciation and esteem held for a person is sufficient title to deprive his heirs of the fruit of his work? Therefore, it is more probable that the Government, in gathering Veytia's papers, worked not so much as an appreciator of his talents, as much as the interested party in his historical endeavors.

But however all this may be, what does not leave room for doubt is that the Government put importance on these endeavors and that the fame of our author was not limited to the place of his birth, but rather that in crossing the seas he was able to focus the attention of the throne on him and be looked upon as a writer endowed with sufficient capacity to exploit the rich but hidden mine of Mexican antiquities.

But Veytia's name not only made itself heard in Spain, but it also penetrated into Italy. This is manifested by a letter that was sent to him from Bolonia by the wisest and most sensible Mexican historian that we can boast of, the famous former Jesuit, Francisco Javier Clavijero. And as in the prospectus I offered to publish this curious document, which I also owe to the favor of the illustrious Mr. Vazquez, who sent it to me in the mentioned year of 1820, I am hereby fulfilling my offer. It says this:

"Bolonia, March 25, 1778.

"My dear sir: even though I have not had the good fortune of meeting you except through the information that they have given me of your birth, of your talents and of your literary difficulties, I am motivated over such a large distance to write to you by the common zeal for the homeland that encourages me, and the uniformity of the subject matter in which we both work. One thing and another we understand in the History of that Kingdom: You, as they have informed me, in the General History of New Spain, and I in the Ancient History of Mexico, which will necessarily be included in your history. I undertook this work to serve my country in whatever way I could, and to honestly divert the disagreeable idleness of my exile: the work has been imponderable, because first it was indispensable to request the necessary books here, in Ferrara, in Venice, in Genoa, in Rome, in France, and in Spain, and deduct from my food what I was to spend in acquiring them; but my diligence has been such that scarcely has a book been published concerning the antiquities of Mexico, either by our Nationals or by Foreigners, which I have not studied. In addition to printed works, I have benefitted from information acquired in the manuscript histories of our Indians, which were preserved in the library of the Colegio Maximo de Mexico [Maximum College of Mexico], and from their paintings themselves, a part of which is seen in that Kingdom and a part here. With the detailed study that I have done of those appreciable monuments of Mexican antiquity, I have acquired competent instruction in the method that they had in representing the objectives and in preserving the remembrance of events, and I am proud to have progressed more in this point than the historians who have preceded me. The work of collecting the materials was followed by the work of digesting them, combining the frequently indigestible narrations, found many times by our Authors, and seeking to draw the truth from the well of Democritus. You must know by your own experience better than any other the difficulty there is in this part because of the negligence or unfaithfulness of our historians. I have not spared any efforts for the perfection of my works: I have strived for the greatest purity and propriety in the language, the greatest exactness in spelling, and the greatest conciseness, the greatest clarity, the best order, and above all, the greatest impartiality and faithfulness in the narration. If I have incurred any defects, as I don't doubt, it has not been because of lack of diligence or malice; but rather because of a scarcity of enlightenment in such obscure and such difficult subject matter. It has been of great importance to me to know the Mexican language, to have traveled through a good part of the Kingdom, and to have dealt closely with the Indians. I have now totally completed the work, and a good part of it would be printed now, if my abilities were in proportion to my desires; but the printing with the sheets that I will talk about will cost more than 500 strong pesos, and I barely have sufficient for a miserable life. It does not weigh upon me that it has not been printed, because having learned, through what was told to me by the Marquis of Moncada when he was passing through here, that you had already completed a folio volume of your history, it does not seem appropriate for me to take a step forward in the printing of mine, without knowing first if your concern is perfectly included.

"To the three volumes of History will be added another one of interesting dissertations, and agreeing for the most part with the History itself. These dissertations, which I have completed, are eight. The first, about the big problem of the population of America. Second, about the chronology of the ancient History, one of the points most entangled by our historians. Third, about the land and climate of Mexico. Fourth, about the Animals of Mexico. Fifth, about the physical and moral constitution of the Mexicans. Sixth, about the number of settlements and inhabitants of the Mexican Empire. Seventh, about the Politics of the Mexicans. Eighth, about the religion of the Mexicans compared to that of the most educated nations of Europe. These are especially directed toward refuting the errors of Mr. Buffon, of Mr. Paw, of Mr. Raynal, and of other celebrated authors who promote degeneration in the plants, animals, and men of the New World. Even if my History is not printed, I believe that the publication of these Dissertations will be very beneficial.

"I hope that you do not poorly receive this letter, even though it is so long and poorly written, and that you will be pleased to see a fellow countryman so well employed in service to the country in the midst of the greatest tribulations. I plead with you to answer me and let me know, if my work seems useful to you, of the enlightenment necessary to perfect it. I am preparing to work on other works that will be even more useful in the benefit of the same country, and in the meantime I ask the Lord to keep you for many years, and to give me life to enjoy your precious efforts. – Sincerely yours, Your affectionate servant and chaplain. – Francisco Javier Clavijero.

Undoubtedly either Veytia did not receive this letter because he had already died, or if he was still alive and answered it, the reply got lost, because Clavijero, who at the beginning of his History gave us such a detailed catalog of the Mexican historians, does not make any mention of our author. This shows that he did not come to have any more than the confused idea of his works that the Marquis of Moncada gave him in passing through Bolonia, which was not certainly sufficient to insert it into the catalog, and if he had done so, he would have made the same mistake that he makes in the letter, supposing that Veytia was writing the General History of Mexico, and not the ancient history, which was the one that both men set about to write. How much the History of Mexico would have gained if these two literary men had met before, and had communicated with each other on the investigations that they were doing separately! The reader who carefully reads and compares the two will notice their agreement on very important points, and will come to a knowledge of how many other points, no less important, would have been clarified with the combination of the enlightenment of these two historians. But they met each other too late, or rather, they never got to know each other, because, as I have indicated, undoubtedly Veytia had already died, or was about to die, when Clavijero wrote to him.

This opinion is supported by the letter from Fr. Antonio when he says that on August 25, 1780, his mother delivered the writings of her deceased husband to the notary Zambrano, and as this delivery was done by virtue of the royal Order, which could not be carried out or obeyed until some time after the death of Veytia, it is very likely that this occurred around 1778, the year in which Clavijero wrote to him, or perhaps before. And it is confirmed by the fact that a daughter of our author, the celebrated Sister Mariana de San Juan Nepomuceno, the founder of the Convent of Capuchins of Guadalupe (of whom I will later speak), after she obtained license from the Archbishop to negotiate for the construction of that monastery, which she had requested for some years, wrote directly to the king for this purpose on May 16, 1778,6 which she probably wouldn't have done if her father were still alive. The matter of the founding had been presented to her full of difficulties, and to resolve them there was no better means than to take advantage of the influence of a person so connected at the Court as Veytia must have been. And although there is room to believe that she would take advantage of the support of her father and at the same time pull the strings of the pious heart of Carlos III herself, knowing how much interest is created by a woman who, going out of the common sphere of her sex, undertakes manly enterprises, to me the more likely conjecture is that because of the death of her father she took on the business on her own account.

Our author had four children, three boys and one girl, two of whom embraced the religious state, namely, Father Antonio Maria de San Jose, who wrote the biographical letter that our readers have already seen, and Sister Mariana de San Juan Nepomuceno. I frequently had dealings with Fr. Antonio in this city. He had a kind presence, an affable and instructive conversation, a very innocent soul, very polite manners; on his face he never showed the frown that is frequently worn by those of his austere profession; rather, and particularly when he was devoting himself to the confidences of friendship, he would customarily enliven his conversations with festive sayings and funny anecdotes, manifesting in everything that his heart was at peace, and that in him resided a solid virtue and an education not at all common. He died in Puebla on December 25, 1827.

Sister Mariana became famous in this capital because of the difficulties that she faced and overcame to carry out the founding of the Convent of Capuchins of Guadalupe. She was a nun in the convent of this capital since the year 1771, and from 1773 until 1780 she fought against all types of opposition; but in the end she got the king to issue the construction certificate. She mentions that the Archbishop, before granting her the license to take the steps necessary to accomplish her project, repeatedly pointed out to her the obstacles that were in the way; and that on one occasion Sister Mariana, firm in her purpose, told him: "Here I have two reales which are to serve as a beginning to the founding;" and delivering them to the two clerics who accompanied the prelate, she succeeded in moving him with this gesture of perseverance; and once the license was granted to her, she immediately went to the king, and to all the powerful corporations and individuals from whom she expected cooperation. Her diligent efforts were so effective that in a little over six years the construction of the new convent was completed, costing close to 3,000 pesos, and she the satisfaction of having it opened on October 15, 1787, with all the solemnities that are exercised in such acts, and which the previously mentioned gazette tells about in great detail, she being its first Abbess.

Regarding the other two, both laymen, Juan and Manuel, there is no one who has anything but vague memories of the first, because he died during the last century. But the case of the second is very much to the contrary. By birth, by education, and by character he was, as was said in olden times, a total gentleman, and therefore he was generally highly esteemed. If he had

15

been ambitious, he would have occupied distinguished positions, of which he was worthy because of the merits of his ancestors, because of his clear enlightenment, and because of his other personal qualities; but his generosity caused him to be content with the Inspectorship of San Andres Chalchicomula, which income and that from a labor farm provided him a decent although average subsistence. All his friends foresaw the tragic end he came to when, now a sexagenarian, but animated by the holy fire of patriotism, they saw him in a not-very-cautious correspondence with our bold liberators, to whom he provided information, weapons, munitions, and whatever he was allowed to by the modest state of his fortune. He was given some healthy advice to be more cautious in his patriotic efforts; but his noble and simple soul, not knowing the ground he was treading, as well as the artifices of treachery and the blunders of inexperience, for it seems that an impetuous young man had a part in his misfortune, did not understand all the danger that was threatening him. As a result of a denunciation, he was caught with arms and munitions that he was taking to the patriots of Tecamachalco, and on July 16, 1816, he was shot in Puebla de los Angeles, his homeland. That was a day of mourning for the entire city: His friends wept for him for a long time; and I, who was also his friend, would have wanted to avoid this painful memory if I didn't feel that the honor of his country was interested in having the memory preserved of the worthy and illustrious sons who have sacrificed for it.

This is the information that I have been able to obtain about the distinguished historian who, thanks to the goodness of the peoples who have favored me with their subscriptions, is going to come to public light for the first time. If any of his descendants, whose whereabouts I do not know, or any other person who is better informed than I, notices any mistakes in my narration, I plead with that person to make them known to me, to correct them at the end of the book.

I wish its author had lived long enough to finish it and perfect it, and so that the task of its publication had not fallen upon an individual so lacking in knowledge as I am in the antiquities of the country. For this reason I have abstained from making a critical and extensive judgment of it, as foreign writers and editors were accustomed to doing, being content to faithfully give Veytia's entire text, the merit of which will be determined by the intelligent. But as I am persuaded that although the work may be full of defects, which doesn't likely to me, at least with regard to the style, which in my small understanding is clear, easy, and natural, although sometimes very protracted, I was doing a service to my country with its publication, I have not hesitated in doing so. There are still incredulous people who describe what is mentioned in the history of our ancient indigenous peoples as tall tales or illusions, but these people will be convinced of their error when reading our author and comparing his narration with that of Clavijero, who was writing beyond the sea and at the same time as him, although without communicating with each other; they notice the remarkable agreement of the two in the fundamental facts of the ancient Mexican annals; and if they are lovers of the truth, they as well as others who do not need these irrefutable proofs that confirm them should appreciate the fact that without the luster that the polishing of its author would have given it, these new materials are now presented for our great historical building, the construction of which we should all cooperate with, and the majesty of which has caught the attention even of foreign groups, when they have examined it closely, stripped of unjust preoccupations.

Before concluding I must state that the faithfulness with which I have sought to transmit Veytia's text to the public has not been so trivially scrupulous that it has allowed some mistakes or repetitions to continue, which of course are known not to be his, but rather those of the copiers. I have corrected them or deleted them, as the author undoubtedly would have done if he were alive. I have also taken the liberty to put in some light notes, in consideration of less instructed readers, and in order to distinguish them from those of the author they are indicated with an E. (C. F. Ortega)

P.S. – Mr. Isidro Rafael Gondra, one of those in charge of the National Museum, has assured me that the few remnants that existed from Boturini's Museum in the General Archive were transmitted to him.

Footnotes, "About the Author"

(1) This information about the author appears as the preface in the 1836 edition, which was published by C.F. Ortega, with various notes and an appendix. The present edition was published in Mexico, D.F., 1944, in accordance with the 1836 edition. Notes written by C.F. Ortega have a capital E at the end.

(2) He is alluding to the chronological tables and to the illustrations that the author mentions in his History, and which are missing in the manuscript; but I have hopes of replacing them and having them printed, distributing them to subscribers for a moderate price at the end of the work.

(3) And so great that if it is true, it is perhaps unique of its type. But perhaps Fr. Antonio, raised in the simplicity of the cloister, although on the other hand he was not a common man, heard it told to someone in his family, and the candor belonging to his profession, as well as filial love, caused him to adopt it without examination. It is true that Carlos III loved literary men, and it is not strange for him to have taken a particular liking toward Veytia when he resided in Madrid, where it is not unlikely that such an educated and hardworking Mexican would attract his attention; but besides the fact that

kings do not give this kind of favor, everyone knows that they have ministers and that these ministers are the ones who, with their signature, authorize the favors that they dispense.

(4) This copy is the following: "Academic Discourses on Ecclesiastical History." Favorites at the Academy of the Curious for Mariano Fernandez de Echeverria y Veytia, Lord of the Noble Ancestral House of Veytia and Knight of the Order of Santiago. Volume 1, in Madrid, year of 1749.

(5) They are the following: "Harangue that Mariano Fernandez de Echeverria y Veytia spoke for the opening of the Academy of the Curious in Madrid, on September 7, 1747.

"Dedicatory prayer at the solemn dedication of the same Academy under the protection of Holy Mary of Guadalupe of Mexico, pronounced by Mariano Jose Fernandez de Echeverria y Veytia on December 14, 1747.

"Panegyrical prayer pronounced by him at the same Academy to the Resurrection of Our Lord Jesus Christ.

"Dissertation on the greatest benefit between jurisprudence and medicine.

"Another dissertation on what is more powerful to destroy friendship, honors or riches.

(6) See the gazette of Mexico of Tuesday, October 23, 1787.

PRELIMINARY DISCOURSE

It has always been a difficult undertaking to write for the press, bringing to light news of antiquity solidly founded on sure monuments that support the information and satisfy the learned, especially in those matters in which many serious authors who consider themselves well versed have worked and written, and much more so in the era in which we are living, in which criticism has been exalted to its highest point, and so modern critics do not give way to novelties so easily as did the uneducated simplicity of the ancients. Therefore, how much greater this difficulty is in the subject in which the main purpose of those who have set their pen to it has been to gain attention and delight the minds of readers by mentioning information that is entirely new, rare, and unique, already described by them, or already acquired from good sources? Such is the history of the New Spain which I undertake to write, of which, since the Spanish nation accomplished its happy conquest, the pens are innumerable, national as well as foreign, who have dedicated themselves to satisfying the curiosity and the good taste of educated people, since with discourses and combinations of the times and customs to find out the origin of a large number of nations who inhabited this continent, where they came from and what they went through, their monarchies, government, and religion, or finally of other rare and prodigious events of which they have had knowledge, which have happened to these regions prior to this time, and the missionaries who, by reason of their ministry, have gotten closer to the Indians, and by this means were able to acquire some knowledge of their antiquity. Being that so much has been written about this matter, my attempt to write a new history of this kingdom seems presumptuous, bringing to light new and singular information unknown until now. However, in its discourse my reader will find a prodigious collection of extraordinary knowledge, which either has not so far been brought to public light, or which has come forth totally distorted from its true nature. The monuments from which I have taken them have all the authority, validity, and recommendation possible in the matter, and they are the same ones on which our authors and foreign authors have based their writings in the news that they have published in a distorted and twisted form because of lack of explanation or caution of those nationals from whom they were acquired.

It was very public from the beginning of the conquest that the natives of this kingdom knew and exercised the art of painting, and they used it to record events, and in this way the authors speak, those who wrote that famous canvas on which Teotlili, the governor of Cempohualan, had a painting made of the ships in which Cortez and his companions came, and of the suits and armors, the horses, the firearms and everything else that seemed necessary to him to give an account to Lord Montezuma with the greatest exactness and detail. But the Spanish of that time did not come to understand with all clarity that these paintings were what kept the information of their history, the codes of their laws, the decrees of their nobility, the titles of their possessions, the rules of their religion, the guidelines of their festivals, the calendars of their astronomical calculations; and finally, that the figures on these paintings served them as letters and characters just as the ones we use serve us, and that knowing how to form and understand these charts is an ability that was taught among them and learned just as reading and writing are taught and learned among us. These paintings were made up of not only all the visible and physical objects, but also of many invisible and incorporeal objects that they depicted with various characters to explain events. They showed the sun, the moon, and the stars; the earth with its mountains, valleys, rivers, and lagoons; all kinds of birds and animals, without leaving out the most insignificant insects; many human figures of both sexes, some dressed, others naked, some white, others black, others of various color blends; most had their heads adorned with an infinite variety of insignias, some seemed like tiaras, others miters, others crowns, others plumes, tassels, or fringe, many of them with ears of various animals, heads of birds and wild beasts, and still others with even more extravagant adornments, such as a man's leg or hand, a skull, an arrow and other such things, all of which are symbols or hieroglyphics that explained the name or the rank of the person on whose head they are placed. For example, the image of the emperor Xolotl which has an eye over the head, that of Nezahualcoyotl, which has some wolf ears, that of Acamapichtla, a hand grasping some stalks; that of Tizotzin, a leg pierced by a dart, which are the explanation of the names of these personages. The black ones were the priests, and over the supreme rulers or principal chiefs they would put a figure like a tiara that showed his rank. The red tassels or ribbons denoted the Tecuhtña [translator: this word is not totally legible] knights. The people painted in colors were the prisoners of war, or those miserable people destined to be the sacrifices, and thus all the other things that could be seen in them had their own meaning.

Locutions, complaints, entreaties, and other incorporeal things appeared in the way we represent angels and the wind. They would show the years, the months, and the days, and they had their own characters for all this, which they would place in their paintings with order and method according to their art, in such a way that this whole combination of figures was meaningful and intelligible. And so, through these pictures, they kept the information of their history, of the foundations of their monarchies and cities, the property titles of their possessions. In this way they had a written record of their laws and the ordinances of their policies and government, the regulations for exacting taxes according to what each town had to pay and what they would actually pay at different times, and also the order and governance in the distribution of the royal treasury, everything concerning their religion, festivals and sacrifices; and finally, everything necessary for them for their governance, so that these charts, or paintings, were their books and guidelines. Not everyone knew how to make them, nor understand them, and many of them ended up in the possession of persons who did not understand them, even though they had inherited them from their elders, just like among us there are many who do not know how to read or write, and they find themselves in possession of the property titles of their possessions, or papers of nobility, or of other businesses and trades of their ancestors, from whom they inherited them; but they do not know how to read, nor do they understand them.

Nor was there just one method and order that they observed in the formation of these charts, or paintings, because the historical records were formed in one way, titles of possession were done another way, those of nobility another, those of taxes another, and in the end, each one had its particular form, so that intelligent people knew the subject that a chart dealt with on first sight. What was missing by way of explanation of the paintings was supplied by the living voice of the master, instructing the disciples in the traditions that, together with the charts, formed a complete history, or gave a whole and perfect knowledge of the matter. To preserve these traditions they invented the poems that were told at all the solemn festivals and at the public dances, through which a great deal of instruction was given in the events of history, and in the most notable events of the common people who did not understand the meaning of the paintings.

The first Spanish who went to those parts, and mainly the gospel ministers full of fervor for religion, and for the conversion of these gentiles, firm in the concept that these peoples were great idolaters (seeing the forms of their idols in the temples, and comparing them with these paintings, in which copies of many of them were actually found, especially in the paintings about their rights and festivals), believed that all that multitude of figures were so many more false gods that they were worshiping, the images of which they had in their houses to idolize; and without further investigation they condemned these charts to the flames, dedicating themselves with the greatest zeal to gathering up as many as they could to carry out the ultimate torture on them, the first to suffer burning being the most precious, those that were kept in the public archives of the main cities, such as those of the cities of Mexico and Texcoco. The Indians regretted this destruction very much; but frightened on one part out of fear of the weapons, and on the other part by the exhortations of the missionaries who, convinced that they were idolaters and superstitious figures, incompatible with the true religion that they were teaching, forbade them from using and keeping them; they did not dare to defend them, and even though some tried, they were not listened to or believed, of which we have undeniable proof in the work of the Reverend Father Juan de Torquemada, who, with the title of Indian Monarch, wrote almost a century after the conquest, when the Spanish were already familiar with the Indians, that they had acquired much information of their antiquity, and that the manner they had of keeping their history were these charts and paintings, and nevertheless, Father Torquemada confesses that when he started to write this work, it didn't seem possible that so much information from more than a thousand of years of antiquity could be contained in these paintings, and with such order and method, from which we can rightly infer how far those first missionaries would have been from believing it, who, with little instruction in the language, and not being able to understand more than the most essential elements to instruct them in the mysteries of the religion, lacked all the information that the Spanish had acquired after a century, and much less perceptible to them would be the fact that these figures were the titles of their possessions, the decrees of their nobility, the volume of their laws, their account books, their calendars, and other things that they contained.

Notwithstanding this simple confession that Father Torquemada makes in the place mentioned, and going on in the next chapter to discuss the divinatory art that these natives used, he talks about the count that they followed in ordering the periods of thirteen days that they had in place of our weeks and which appeared on their charts and chronological wheels with the hieroglyphs and characters that he says, and because he didn't come to fully understand the skill with which they used it, he describes it as divinatory and superstitious; and although he states that some said that this count of 13 days were weeks, he says that it should not be believed, and he asserts in his report that it is illicit, very harmful, very superstitious and full of idolatry, for no reason other than the fact of not having understood it, as will become obvious later on. Many other passages similar to these could be produced, in this author as well as in others who have written about things pertaining to the Indians many years after their conquest, giving us various information that they claim is taken from their paintings; nevertheless, they deny other knowledge which they were unable to penetrate, and in general they do not give up the idea that these charts were superstitious and idolatrous. I do not deny by this that the Indians used a combination of these hieroglyphics and figures to make their predictions and divinations, just as in the old world wheels, lines, letters, and numbers, and even the very words and text of the Holy Scriptures, have been used for it; but just as these have not contracted any infection thereby to degrade them in their sacred nature and holy intelligence, nor would the numbers, letters, and wheels of that wholesome and lawful use for which they were formed cause the purely astronomical charts of the Indians to incur anything superstitious or idolatrous because the diviners or priests used them in forming the combinations of their figures and hieroglyphs for their divinations, predications, and oracles, much less the historical charts, those of their laws, nobility, taxes, and others which the priests and diviners did not use for their calculations and superstitions.

When the Indians saw the reckless torment that their writings were subjected to, and the efficacy and activity with which the ministers who weren't very well informed sought these paintings to burn them, they tried to hide some of them, especially those that contained distributions of lands, that served as titles of their possessions, and those they found of taxes, and they were like lists of the taxpayers of the provinces and towns, and for this reason most of those that were found that have survived to our days are of this type. They were so diligent in hiding them that many were not content to enclose them in coffers and larders, but they buried them under the ground and in the hollows of the walls, leaving to their descendants, with great secrecy, the information of the place where they were, and in this way the Gentleman Boturini found many of those that he gathered, and he assured me that he had taken a box of them from the concealed hollow of a thick old wall in the town of Huamantla which he found out about from one of the descendants of the one who had hid them there; and in the year seventeen fifty-eight, when I was in that town, some people certified to me that they were witnesses of this find, and they showed me the old wall from where he took them. The discovery of these and the other ancient instruments that he gathered was at the cost of much diligence, getting very close and familiar with these natives until they would confide in him and reveal to him the great treasure of antiquities that he gathered over the nine continuous years that he spent in that difficult and tiresome undertaking, traveling from town to town with incalculable work and discomfort, because even after the many years that have passed since the conquest, the charge has been perpetuated from fathers to sons to hide these charts and paintings with the greatest care and secrecy so that they don't fall into the hands of the Spanish, notwithstanding the fact that today there is no longer anyone among them who understands them or can explain them, and from one and another I have sufficient experience in the tasks that I have exercised to decipher those that could be useful to me for this history.

Not only have they hidden these paintings with greatest diligence, but also many manuscripts in our characters, in their language as well as in ours. Because some of those first converts who in the early times of the conquest learned to write in them, and others in later times, formed various narrations of that information that they acquired either by tradition from their elders or through the historical songs that they would compose and sing in their festivals that were being preserved and passed on from parents to children, and it was one of the ways that these peoples had of keeping a history, then finally by the very charts that they were hiding, that they knew how to understand and interpret and by deciphering their intelligence by means of our letters with their language or in our language; but this was precisely to provide their children with private instruction with the same charge of hiding them from the Spanish, and keeping the greatest secrecy in their content. From there, some errors and distorted or twisted information have arisen that are found in the authors who have written of the ancient history of this kingdom, because in times following the conquest, the Spanish now being enlightened to the fact that these peoples, as gentiles, had regulations and government, powerful kings and monarchs, scientific learning, military expertise, and various arts. Some curious individuals at various times have attempted to find out this information from the Indians; but some turned to subjects who, either because of malice or ignorance or passion or lack of understanding, filled them with fables or information that was distorted from its true meaning, or dislocated from their times and circumstances. Others, although they went to persons capable of instructing them, either because of their age or because of the paintings and manuscripts they were keeping, refused to do so, or did so very superficially and in passing.

This is attested to constantly by Fernando de Alba Yxtlilxochitl in his Relaciones Históricas [Historical Narrations] which I have in my hands for the formation of this work. This individual was a descendant of the emperors of Texcoco and worked as an interpreter of the vice royalty around the end of the sixteenth century in which he wrote these narrations, and even though he had the charts and ancient paintings which he knew how to interpret, and even though he was very well versed in the information of his antiquity, through the poems that he had learned since he was a child, as well as through other traditions of his elders, he says that to write his narrations he conferred with many old and well-versed individuals eighty, ninety, and one hundred and more years of age, whom he mentions with all individuality by their names and circumstances in the Relacion Quinta [Fifth Narration], who he says had acquired good and well-founded information; but as proof of my point, he concludes this Narration with the following paragraph which I copy to the exactly.

"I have read many histories of Spaniards who have written things of this land, all of which are so far away from what is in the original history, and the histories of all these Spaniards, and among the false ones, the one that conforms in something is that of Francisco Gomara, a cleric, a historian of the Emperor Don Carlos, N.S. [Our Lord], may God keep him in his glory; and it doesn't surprise me that inasmuch as they are accounts of the past, some say cestas [baskets] and others ballestas [springs], as it is commonly said; to say one thing they say another, some talking of passion, others of fondness, and others tell fables made up of certain recurring words, and others, not understanding the language well or what the old people tell them, as has happened to me many times with the natives, being born and raised among them, and being so well known by all the main chiefs of New Spain, such as those of the Aculhuas, Chichimecs, as well as Mexicans, plus Tlascaltecs, Tecpanecs, and Toltecs, and other nations; and as I have said, some talk about fondness and others of passion. What I will now tell happened to me, without telling of other times when almost the same thing happened to me, but this was the most remarkable. Going to the town of Cohuatepec, two leagues from the city of Texcoco toward the south with respect to the city, to see a certain friend and gentlemen named Lope Zeron, who has a very good work in this town, after having arrived, relaxing in his house all that afternoon, the next day asking Sir Lope about the main people of the town, and about some old people, he gave me some explanation like this, telling me that there were none, but that there was a young man who at the time was governor, and an old man whom they always made governor thirty or forty years ago, because of being raised with the monks and being very ladino, although he was a lowly [Indian] peasant by nation. Taking this information, I bade farewell to this gentleman, and went to his house to ask him certain things about his town, especially about something that is in the original history, that this town was the head of a province, and where certain men from certain parts of this land descended from, as I relate further on; and having arrived, I asked him, and he told me as many foolish things as our Spaniards have written, telling me that the town was always the court and head of a kingdom, and Azcaputzalco and Chalco, and the other parts, were little towns subject to Cohuatepec, and that the first lord named Toxamilhuatzin, who came from the Chichimecs with other vassals of his, being so much the opposite; because this man was the great-great-grandson of Cuachuatlapal, one of the six vassals of the great Chichimecatl Xoltotl, and he brought them with him, and that he was now the fourth lord of this town; and he also told me that Acamapichtli, the lord of Mexico, was the son of Yllancueytl, a transported slave woman, about whom the historians write, and that Nezahualcoyotl, if it weren't for those of Cohuatepec who helped him, would never free his city and the lords of Mexico, his uncles, from the power of the great tyrant Maxtli. These and other fables, like those that the historians have written, and contradicting the old songs and stories that I showed and told him, and bringing other things to memory, there was nothing he could do but concede in what I was telling him, and showing him the original didn't help either, but rather he was very stiff, finally like a lowly [Indian] peasant; and he, knowing who I am and that I am not unaware of anything of what this is, he still contradicted me; of which

25

everything, as I have said, were words of fondness and of passion said by a peasant, who, if he were a nobleman, later, with the information, would admit his mistake. These and many other things have happened to me, and also many principals refused to tell the facts of the truth, seeing that each day they would ask them, and they never see anything that comes to light as happened to a certain gentlemen, a descendant of the house of Texcoco, who, asking an old principal of a history of Tepetlaoztoc, about who were the parents and grandparents of Ixtlixochitl, the father of King Nezahualcoyotl, he answered telling him, Ixtlixochitl did not have a father or a mother, but rather a very large eagle came and made a nest in a large tree that was in the city and made a very large egg, and at a certain time there the eagle broke the egg and took out a child and lowered him from the nest, putting him in the middle of the plaza of the city, and seeing this the Aculhuas raised him and, as they did not have a king, they lifted him up as king and gave him the name, calling him Ixtlixochitl. This gentleman, hearing the foolishness, gave him an enormous smile, telling the old man that it was foolishness to speak such words, and the old man answered him that to him and to all those who would ask him about this, they had to answer with this and other things such as these, especially to the Spanish, and as I have said, the historians are not to blame, that because of having given them false accounts they have written what I have declared, and certain that with having these stories in my possession and knowing the language like the natives themselves, because I grew up with them, and knowing all the old people and principles of this land, to go about clearing this up has cost me a great deal of study and work, always seeking the truth of each of these things that I have written and will write in the history of the Chichimecs."

If an individual whom [as he says] they all knew and knew his lineage, and who was well versed in the knowledge of his antiquity, was mocked by his own fellow countrymen just because they considered him to be a supporter of the Spanish, wouldn't there be those with the Spanish who have always looked and even today look on the average Indian with distrust? This is the reason so many errors have proliferated in the writings of the authors. The main topic in the work of Francisco Lope de Gomara is the conquest of this kingdom, and he just incidentally discusses the customs, laws, and rites that the Indians observed at the time of the arrival of the Spanish, and Alba's expression should be understood from this viewpoint, because with respect to his ancient history he writes very succinctly and superficially, but with much judgment, as can be seen in that work from chapter 190 up to chapter 224. It is not lacking in errors, for there is rarely a history without errors, except in sacred history. Father Torquemada, a learned and curious individual, strove greatly to discover information on the ancient history of this kingdom, and with the breach being opened up by his apostolic ministry he succeeded in gathering much more than anyone else of those who have written up to now. In fact, it is he who most closely approaches the truth of history, however, much information is lacking and other information is mixed with fables, and not a few contradictions and anachronisms are noticed. Some I point out in the course of this work, and others can be seen by the curious in his work by comparing it to this one. Nevertheless, he is the only one who has so far undertaken the task of writing the history of this kingdom, because all the other authors who write about it do so superficially in fragments and mostly incidentally, each person publishing whatever information he acquired, and copying one another, and with everything, what the mentioned Father Torquemada wrote about the founding and establishment of the Toltec kingdom, its advances and destruction, is very succinct, with everything comprised in one short chapter, which is chapter 14 of book 1, missing the true events with others that are fables and improbabilities, as we shall see.

The same Fernando de Alba who regrets that this knowledge of the ancient history of this kingdom has not come to light wrote different works at different times, all of which I have in my hands, one in the form of a letter to Viceroy Luis de Velasco. The second is quite vague and well ordered, and another one that he entitled Compendio de la Historia General de la Nueva España [Compendium of the General History of New Spain] is also well coordinated and authenticated at the end by the governor and mayors of the city of Otompan or Otumba, and of the towns of Ahuatepec, Tizayucan, Amaquemecan, and others, all distinguished persons in their nation, old and learned in their history and experts in the interpretation of their paintings, who testify that everything contained in the compendium is taken from the mentioned paintings, which are well and faithfully translated and interpreted, and with everything, he brought none of these works to public light, but instead, following the example of his countrymen, he left them buried in the hands of his descendants, from where the celebrated mathematician Carlos de Sigüenza y Góngora managed to get them after nearly a century.

This mathematician prospered in Mexico at the end of the past 17th century, and left a great reputation for erudition in all areas of good letters, but more particularly in the learning of the ancient history of this kingdom, through the many ancient monuments that he succeeded in collecting, and having worked on them diligently, it is known that he wrote some works, but none came to public light, with the exception of his annual calendars and predictions, in some of which he inserts a tidbit of antiquity here and there. At his death it appears that a cry went out about his papers, and each one took possession of whatever he could, some of which have ended up in the libraries of various religious communities, and in the possession of private persons, from where the curious investigation of the Gentleman Boturini acquired them; but I am persuaded that many of those that he gathered have perished, and certainly many of those that he wrote are missing, that only a few fragments of some of them have been found, and of others, nothing more than their titles and the notice of his having written them have been found, in spite of the exquisite diligence that the mentioned Boturini exercised, and I myself subsequently because of having two in my hands that he is especially known to have written, one with the title of Fenix del Occidente [Phoenix of the West], proving the coming and preaching of the apostle Saint Thomas in these regions, and the other Esplicacion del Calendario Tulteca [Explanation of the Toltec calendar]. Neither of the two reached the press, I don't know why not, but I have known two individuals who knew Sigüenza and associated with him, and they affirmed to me that they had seen and read them.

In the year seventeen thirty-five, after having toured a large part of the kingdoms of Europe, the Gentleman Lorenzo Boturini Benaducci came to these kingdoms, he being the lord of la Torre and of Hono, a native of the city of Milan, whose great literature, profound erudition, and high talent is a sure indication of the work that he printed in Madrid in the year seventeen forty-six, with the title of Idea de una Nueva Historia General de la América Septentrional [Idea of a New General History of North America], which meditated writing about the copious material of ancient monuments that he gathered over the nine years that he spent in this difficult undertaking, making many laborious trips through various parts of this kingdom. He was not drawn so much by the desire to acquire wealth, which has been and is the common stimulus of some who have gone there, as by his curious temperament, desirous of seeing and of knowing, and having arrived at the famous Sanctuary of Our Lady of Guadalupe, a league away from the imperial city of Mexico, having learned of the event of her miraculous appearance, he of course developed a very tender devotion to holy Mary in this her Sovereign Image. He found out at the same time that no authentic instruments to confirm the impressive wonder of her appearance had been left, although with more than ample basis, and through reports that have been made subsequently by law and with the greatest diligence it is believed that there were some such instruments in existence in those first times immediately following the event, but through a high provision of inscrutable Providence their whereabouts are absolutely unknown today. This intensified his devotion and made him resolve to take upon himself the task of writing a new history of this miraculous appearance, which would establish the truth of this wonder on a solid foundation. For this he dedicated himself with the greatest diligence to requesting and describing ancient papers and old books contemporary to or immediately following the event, which could provide him with evidence of its public notoriety in those early times, and of its constant and continued tradition up to our times, without the least variation or conflict, not only in the substance of the miraculous appearance, but also in all the other circumstances of the day, month, year, names and qualities of the persons, and even of the smallest accessories, and of the successive and permanent idolizing of the Holy Image; and, in effect, in the elegant defensive prologue that he started in the Latin language, which is found among his papers, he establishes thirty-one foundations on which he was pondering establishing the truth of this wonder.

His request for these documents put some charts and manuscripts from ancient history into his hands, which motivated him to more effectively and diligently investigate anything that could enlighten him and instruct him on this subject, not sparing any work, inconvenience, or expense to acquire the copious accumulation of ancient monuments that he gathered, which are now in his archive. He associated and conversed with anyone, Spanish as well as Indians, whom he believed could give him some information or enlightenment to find them. He undertook journeys of twenty, thirty, and more leagues along lost roads, just to talk to someone whom he believed could give him some information, or in the hope of finding a chart or a manuscript, with such discomfort because of the roughness of the road, because of natural conditions, especially the heat and abundance of mosquitoes and other bothersome insects, and because of the lack of supplies, which caused him to live for eight straight days on cherimoyas [translator: a wild fruit], on other occasions he lived on hard corn tortillas, and at other times just on toasted corn, taking shelter in the miserable huts and hovels of the Indians, and not a few times with fear and danger to his life, because they were distrustful of his intentions and suspected that he was going to rob them or do them other harm.

Having already gathered a large part of this treasure, he withdrew to Guadalupe, and with the consent of the chaplains of the Sanctuary, which had not yet been erected in a collegiate church, he went to live in a small chapel on top of the hill, in the same place where the one existing today was later built. He stayed in that solitude for three years, completely employed in studying these charts, which, as he told me, he would spread out on the floor and lie on them to examine them, having in hand the manuscripts of the Indians interpreting them and the notes that he had made of the verbal information that he acquired. He spent many hours a day in his mediation and study, particularly on those charts that dealt with their astronomical and chronological calculations to understand their systems; but inasmuch as his principal object, and the point of view to which all the lines of his desires were directed, was the history of the appearance of Our Lady of Guadalupe, he spent most of his time in mediating on it and in finding solid documents to support it.

But by one of those supreme judgments of inscrutable Providence, which men see and do not understand, it was assured that the same fervent devotion and affection he felt toward the Holy Virgin, and the high concept that he formed of the marvelous wonder wrought by Omnipotence in the Sovereign Image of Guadalupe, would give rise to all his works and afflictions. His fervor desired to further promote the idolizing and devotion of this miraculous Image, making it more famous and valid, and for this he believed that it was appropriate to crown it with the golden crown that was usually granted by the Illustrious Council of the Sacrosanct Vatican Basilica to miracle-working images, through the legacy and provision of Count Alejandro Sforcia Palavicino with certain ceremonies and solemnities. In order to obtain this grace for the sacred replica of Guadalupe, he made a report to the mentioned illustrious council in which he used his literacy and erudition, not at all of the common people, to prove with valid arguments the certainty of the miracle, the constancy of the tradition, the uninterrupted continuation of their worship, and the multitude of miracles that the Holy Virgin Mary has worked through it. The report had the effect that he wanted, because afterwards the grace was granted by the illustrious council and the decree was issued with the date of the eleventh of July of seventeen forty, addressed to the Archbishop of Mexico, with instruction of the order and method with which this function should be carried out. After it reached the hands of the Gentleman Boturini, he presented it to the royal audience requesting his pass, which was in fact given to him on the first of March of seventeen forty-two.

Joyful with the happy success of his project, he dedicated himself to preparing everything necessary for the solemn function that he was planing on carrying out, but lacking the resources to cover its costs, he determined to ask for contributions, not just within the city, but throughout the kingdom through circular letters. This was his mistake, because he proceeded to carry out his thought without gaining the approval of his superiors; and as no one lives without rivals, the superiors of Boturini found occasion to incriminate the action, painting it with an insidious aspect, when down deep there was no malice in it, but just lack of instruction, along with the fact of having gone to these kingdoms without licenses, being a stranger. He was ordered to exhibit what he had gathered from contributions, which up to then was just a little gold and some emeralds for the crown that he was going to craft; his property was ordered impounded, which amounted to his museum, his person was arrested in the town hall, and after some prison time, he was ordered to return to Spain.

It was the year seventeen forty-four, and because of the war we were having with England, the seas were infested with pirates. He boarded a merchant register named the Concordia, which put up some resistance when attacked by two well-armed English frigates at the height of the Cape of St. Vincent, but it finally had to yield to the greater strength and they seized it. They took it to Gibralter, and there they left the passengers and crew on the land, stripped not only of the baggage and resources that they were carrying, but also of the clothing that they were wearing. Boturini lost some curious charts that he was carrying on animal skins, some special manuscripts that he had been able to keep from being sequestered because at the time he had them out of his home, loaned to various friends, and some notes that he had made of the verbal information he acquired on the trips he made, and curious observations on them, and in exchange for the decent clothing he was wearing they gave him a shirt and sailor pants of canvas.

Nothing else was able to escape this storm other than a gold shield worth two pesos and a letter that he was carrying from my father to me, in which, telling me all about his appreciable talents, and the reason for his disgrace, he was directing me to take care of him in whatever he might need. With this baggage he took the road to Madrid, on foot with the labors and discomforts that can easily be understood. I welcomed him and had him stay at my house, where he remained for nearly two years, during which time, with the ultimate familiar communication, we developed a close and true friendship that lasted until his death, even though for his own reasons he had to separate from my company. We were together during that time for most of the day, and the conversation regularly centered around the matters of this history, with which I was able to benefit from how much he had worked on it, because his friendship kept nothing from me, but on the contrary, he regretted not having his documents at hand to instruct me with all precision in some matters in which memory was failing him, and to aid my memory he wrote various notes in his own hand, which I still have in my possession, which were afterwards useful to him to form the book that he printed in Madrid in the year seventeen forty-six, with the title of Idea de una nueva Historia General de la América Septentrional [Idea of a New General History of North America].

Things were not provided according to his desires to be able to return to this kingdom as he was permitted to write the history, he was unable to obtain the order to have his archive taken to him in Spain, and Providence having arranged for me to need to be restored to this kingdom, in the year seventeen fifty he gave me the charge to request with greatest diligence to get him copies of some instruments contained in his archive, of which he gave me a list in his handwriting, and a list of others that he knew about and hadn't been able to have in hand, to see if I could obtain them, with which he would be happy to be able to write the history from there. After I arrived in Mexico and was given some breaks from the occupations of the serious business that was the reason for my trip, I sought to satisfy his charge, and enjoying the favor of Mr. Jose Gorraez, a government secretary, in whose charge the sequestered museum is found, and following the order and license from the Excellent Sir Viceroy, Count of Revilla-Gigedo, I succeeded in seeing him and getting to know him to my entire satisfaction, and getting from him the copies that Boturini was asking me for; but as this was within the same office where I could not have multiple scribes, and the instruments were full of information and somewhat confused, the operation lasted a long time. I did not fail to request the other documents that he had not been able to acquire, some of which I obtained, but before completing the copies and being able to send them, I got the sad news that he had died.

And so this frustrated my hope of seeing this history come from his pen, with all the adornment and erudition that he promised in his Idea, and which his great talent would have fulfilled to great advantage. Finding myself with that accumulation of documents that I had copied and gathered, and what's more, having been instructed in his doctrines and rules that I learned from his living voice, I was seized by the first impulses to take on the task of writing it. I was not carried away by my own love of being able to fill Boturini's void, but on the contrary, I remembered the arduousness of the undertaking, which was very much beyond my strength, but it was very sad for me to think that this information, which I came to acquire at the expense of so much fatigue and suffering, and in which I found myself somewhat instructed, should once again end up buried in oblivion. And so battling between these emotions, the second one was victorious, and I finally resolved to work in this matter. He had proposed the idea of dividing the Indian history into three ages: the first, that of the Gods; the second, that of the heroes; and the third, that of men, following the famous division of times of the Egyptians into the obscure, the fabulous, and the historic, as Varron calls them, the first period comprising from the creation of the world until the flood, which they called "adelon" because it was unknown; the second period comprising from the flood to the first olympiad, which they called mythical because of the fabulous; and the third period, from the first olympiad until us, which is the one that truly comprises the events of men, and for this reason they called it historic. But I, very unlike Boturini in talent and erudition, did not propose any other plan for myself than that of a simple historical narration, faithfully taken from the ancient documents that I have gathered, subjecting it as far as possible to the laws and precepts that a sincere and impartial historian must observe; using the rules and warnings that I learned from him in order to discern the fabulous from the real, and the true information from the untrue; because the ancient national historians who wrote in their hieroglyphs as well as the modern ones who interpreted them were men, and from various nations, among whom there were rivals and animosities, each one respectively seeking glory for his own history, and thus they sought to distort the events that are not advantageous to them, and paint those that favor them with more relevant colors.

One of the subjects that he considered to be most difficult, and in which he told me he had a lot of work to do, was that of the astronomical and chronological systems for the perfect understanding and explanation of the wheels and calendars of these natives; and in truth he was right and was speaking from experience, as someone who had taken the pulse of the difficulty, for even though I centered on the enlightenment and knowledge that he acquired, the work and the time is imponderable that I have expended in the study, comparison, and combination of many of their chronological and astronomical wheels of centuries, years, and months, with the succinct and confusing explanations of their interpreters, and of the most certain eras and dates of all history, to come to understand these matters in the way that he explained them, which seems the most reasonable to me, following the same principles and rules that are learned from Boturini, and even though I find myself required to contradict some of his observations for the reasons that I explain sincerely for the judgment of the readers, I do not do so with presumptions of being a master, of whom I consider myself to be a disciple, but rather on one hand I complain with ingenuousness that I cannot attain anything else, and it would be great foolishness to undertake to explain what I do not understand; and on the other hand, it is perfectly clear to me that he was persuaded that he had not yet come to understand this and other points of this history in all their perfection; and so he frequently repeated to me that he still had a lot of work on them. To this I should add that the work that he brought forth in Madrid, which I mentioned in the objections I raise, I saw him write in my own home, without his being able to see any of the documents that he gathered to use them as a guide, but rather through a restoration that he was making from memory of the items that had been deposited in it, in which it is as easy to be mistaken as to be strictly correct. But this does not mean that I am so well rewarded with my report or so satisfied with my work, that being flattered by its correctness, I am convinced that there was no other wit that could go forward much in this subject; but I still believe that my work will not be lacking in benefits.

I have also spent not a small amount of time in ordering the chronology, such an essential ornament of history that without it the narration of the events largely fades and lacks a certain harmony that gives it its most polished complement. These natives were very precise in indicating on their charts and paintings the hieroglyphs and characters of the years in which the most famous events occurred, and on many of them, those of the months and days, and even of the seasons of the day, which take the place of the division and distribution of the hours, which they did not achieve. For this reason the writers who interpreted these charts generally agree in the assignment of these characters, but they vary infinitely in the correspondence of their years, which are those of our calculations, because inasmuch as a century has no more than fifty-two years, indicated with the same hieroglyphs, of thirteen on thirteen, as I explain in the respective place, it was necessary for the character of the year that they indicate in the narration of an event to be identical in each century. Knowing, then, what century it corresponds to, and consequently which of our years it corresponds to, this is the difficulty in which the interpreters have gotten entangled, with their calculations varying by two, three, or more centuries of fifty-two years each, which means two hundred or three hundred with respect to our count. So to verify the truth, and to proceed on this point with the greatest exactness, Boturini had resolved to form general tables on the chronological system of these natives, comprehensive from the creation of the world to the conquest, which he in fact started and they are in draft form among his archived papers. I used his doctrine, and having copied what he had worked on, I continued them until the year fifteen thirty-one, and they are placed at the end of this volume to satisfy the good taste of the curious who can come to know my calculations for themselves, and perhaps correct them and advance the thoughts, advising that the rule that I have followed for those that I have created has been to take advantage of the sure eras to count those periods that the Indians affirm to have transpired from particular events to other events, always attentive to the character of the year in which they indicate the event in question, omitting the partial ones that result when they count by centuries until finding the year that they note. Not only have I followed this calculation, going from the creation to our times, for those set periods and eras that they establish, but also in the reverse, counting from the year in which Hernando Cortez arrived in these lands, which was the year fifteen nineteen, which all unanimously agree was indicated in the Xiumolpia or Calendar of these natives with the hieroglyph of the reed, in the number one, and therefore it is a very fixed era from which to calculate backwards.

But inasmuch as in many notable events the Indians indicate not only the years, but also the month and days, these tables were not sufficient to verify it, and so it was necessary for me to create three more: the first, of the order in which they placed the hieroglyphs of the twenty days of each month, according to the character of the year; the second, of the days of our months on which each year of theirs started, following the opinion that has seemed the most certain to me among the great variety found among authors in assigning the first months of their year, and which of our years it corresponded to; and the third, of the centuries with which they started and ended, counting the days of all the fifty-two years of each century, including the intercalary and leap years, with respect to the period of thirteen days that they had in place of our weeks, the numbering of which they would join to the symbols of the days. I have placed these in chapter 8, because for their understanding and use it is necessary to be instructed in their entire chronological system, not just of the rotation of the years in the century by the repetition of the four initial characters, but of the rotation of the months, weeks, and days, the explanation of which is found in that and the foregoing chapters.

I have sought to examine the historical events mentioned to us in the light of a judicious review, to affirm some as true and others as false, or fables, working to search out the origin that these fictions may have had through the combination and comparison of some writings with others, and of some events with others, exposing all of it with sincerity as I perceive it and without vanity of accuracy. Many things will seem strange and not very realistic, especially to those persons who do not know these countries and their circumstances, who are ignorant of the nature of their natives, or who still live enthralled with the idea that they were absolutely barbaric; nevertheless, they are confirmed by the national writers of those times immediately following the conquest, supported in large part by the narration of those first Spaniards who went to those parts, such as Hernando Cortez in his letters to the Emperor, Bernal Diaz, Francisco Lopez de Gomara, and others who saw their government, learned their laws and customs, their religion and rites, their artifacts and handiwork, and even though they talk about all these things in passing, superficially and with some mistakes, and many errors because of lack of instruction, what they say is very ample to authenticate the stories of the nationals who understood to translate their paintings, and preserve in our characters the knowledge of their antiquity, with respect to the events as well as with regard to their scientific knowledge, exercise of the arts, and pattern of their government; and finally, the ancient monuments themselves are irrefutable witnesses that not only powerfully corroborate the historical narrations, but also accuse them of being diminutive, causing us to believe that in some matters they omitted many things worth knowing, the information on which, enlightening us more fully, would more vividly inspire admiration.

The speeches and arguments that I put into the mouth of the heroes and personages are substantially the same ones that I find in the writers, and some are literally copied; in others I have just corrected the style of a rough and misused Spanish, which, because of being from those natives who did not speak with perfection, are poorly put together and full of repetitions, but these same ones, in the authors who write in their own language, are very eloquent in the opinion of individuals expert on the subject, whom I have benefitted from because my instruction in Mexican is very limited, even though, with the help of arts and vocabularies, I have worked in the translation of many names and phrases for the understanding and verification of the truth in some passages of the history, as will be seen in it, afterwards subjecting my productions to the examination of those who understand, without whose approval I wouldn't have dared to assert them in this work.

I don't apologize for bringing many words from the Nahuatl or Mexican language into it, because it has seemed appropriate to me to do so for the best and clearest explanation, but I have translated everything into our language and many times I repeat the translation so that the reader does not have to go look for the meaning elsewhere. For many words I give the etymology, especially in compound words, which are very abundant in this language, particularly in the nomenclature of persons and places, all of which are significant, and therefore I have used many of them to verify some points of the history, and I cannot deny that this was one of the rules that I learned from the Gentleman Boturini, who had planned to follow this maxim in his book. Some of these traditions are neither mine nor of the intelligent individuals whom I have benefitted from, but of the national writers themselves, and thus I put them in, even though the experts of the language with whom I have shared them do not understand them, and they all argue that the Nahuatl language has changed a lot from what it was at the time of the gentilism, but they disagree on the reason, because some believe that this difference comes from corruption of the language, and others disagree, saying that the difference arises from the languages having been polished and perfected. What is certain is that, concerning the songs of the Emperor Nezahualcoyotl that I am including in his language, I haven't found anyone to translate them perfectly, because there are many words whose meaning is absolutely unknown today, even though I have used the vocabulary of Father Alonso de Molina, of the order of Our Seraphic Father Saint Francisco, which I consider to be the oldest and which was printed in Mexico in the year fifteen seventy-one, which includes many verbs, nouns, and phrases that are not in use today, nor is there anyone among the natives who understands them.

FIRST BOOK

ORIGIN OF THE PEOPLES WHO INHABITED AMERICA. INFORMATION ON THE FIRST PEOPLES WHO SETTLED IN THE NEW SPAIN, AND OF THE FIRST MONARCHY THAT FLOURISHED IN IT OF THE TOLTEC NATION.

CHAPTER I

*Location of the New Spain, the arrival of its first inhabitants and informa-
tion that went back to the creation of the world.*

The rich and fertile kingdom of New Spain, the ancient history of which
I am undertaking to write, was called by its ancient inhabitants Anahuac, that
is, land which is among the waters, because of its being situated between the
two seas, called today the seas of the North and of the South.(1) This land,
then, is a considerable portion of America, and is one of the four parts into
which geographers divide the world globe(2), giving the name of America to
the entire vast continent that is described in the middle of the globe, taken
from Americo Vespucci, of Florence, who described its northern coast in the
year fourteen ninety-seven, and even though Christopher Columbus had
discovered the Southern lands four years earlier, Americo took the glory upon
himself of giving his name to the entire continent, which is called the Indies
in common speech; and in that division they would make of the globe into
four parts, they indicated it as one of them, even though, including its islands,
in size it almost equals the other three put together, Asia, Africa, and Europe,
which some call the old world, and America, the new world, because of Divine
Providence having kept it hidden from the knowledge of the Europeans until
these last centuries.

Whether the names of America and the Indies are proper or improper,
imposed for just reason or without, is a matter which some writers address. I
am entirely disregarding the question as not at all conducive to my concern,
and adapting to common usage of speech and understanding, when the occasion arises I will use the names of America or the Indies, and its ancient
natives and their descendants I will call Indians, as opposed to the children
and descendants of the Europeans who have been born in these countries
since its discovery and conquest, whom I will call Indianos [translator:
Spanish emigrants returning to Spain] or Criollos [Creoles], also following the
common usage of speech.

This very extensive country of America extends south to the Straight of
Magellan, at 52_ degrees above the Antarctic pole, and on the North its end
is not yet known for sure. Modern maps show us the latest discoveries, up to
70 or 75 degrees from the Arctic, and so its length from North to South is

supposed to be about 2200 leagues. Its most extensive width is 1277 from East to West, which is from Newfoundland to the Cape of Mendocino, and at its narrowest it is 18 leagues, which is from Panama to Nombre de Dios. They divide this whole land into two parts or large peninsulas, which close to Panama come together in one isthmus of land which is the thinnest and narrowest of the land between the two seas. The part that runs from there to the Strait of Magellan they call South America, because the largest part of its lands are situated from the equator to the Antarctic, and they include the kingdoms of Peru, Brazil, and Chile.

From Panama to the North is the other part or peninsula which they call North America, because all its lands are situated from the equator to the North, and this is the one that embraces the extensive provinces that are now known as New Spain; although some want the kingdom of Peru to extend to Quautemalan. But there is no argument that Hernando Cortez, conqueror of the New Spain, penetrated as far as Honduras, and from there he extended his discovery and government, much less that he reached the country that the Indians called Anahuac, because of being situated between the two seas, and the information about these lands that they gave to Cortez in Mexico was what motivated him to undertake his discovery; and it being evident in the history that I am going to write that Quautemalan and all its extensive province were feudal lands of the emperors of Texcoco, supreme monarchs of this country, and under the name of New Spain I must include all the land delineated from the isthmus of Panama northward.

Whether or not all of America was inhabited before the flood is another very controversial question among authors who have written either of the entire continent or about some of its parts. I am not taking part in this argument either, I find no reason to convince me in favor of one opinion or the other, and even though the defenders of the affirmative base themselves on the sacred texts "Crescite et multiplicamini, et replete terram" [multiply, and replenish the earth, Gen. 1:28], "Repleta est terra iniquitate a facie eorum [Genesis 6]," and other similar ones that they use for their purpose, it seems to me that for its true and perfect understanding it is not necessary for the entire earth to be materially inhabited and full of people, nor to infer from the fact that the flood that covered it was universal that the whole land was populated, for even in just that part that through sacred text we know was inhabited, there were many mountains and very extensive deserts entirely uninhabited, as there are today.

Nor on the other hand do I have any difficulty in the idea that just as those who populated them after the flood found their way to these lands, other men before the flood would have found their way, and heavily populated these regions; but no convincing solid foundation or reason is presented either on one side or on the other. Not even in the ancient monuments of the

Indians, which I will use in the course of this history, is any information found on this matter, and anyway, my purpose is none other than to publish those that I have been able to gather and find of their ancient history and the multitude of nations that populated these regions and great monarchies that flourished in the area of New Spain, which, with so much care, diligence, and excellence they sought to preserve in their paintings and historical charts, putting them in with the greatest clarity and purity possible for me, to correct the errors, implications, and confusions incurred by the authors, in the little bit that they have so far written on this subject, but it is of little importance to me whether or not America was populated before the flood.

The great difficulty among the authors has been to verify what the origin was of so many and such diverse nations as were found populating these regions, where they came from and how they traveled, whether by sea or by land, whether with certain or uncertain destiny. Some make them Jews of the ten tribes, scattered in the time of Shalmaneser, King of Assyria, who took them out of Samaria to populate it with Babylonians. Others make them Spaniards who came to these lands from the Windward Islands, and they say they were populated by Spaniards in the time of King Hespero, who possessed them. Others say that the first inhabitants came from Ireland; others, that they were Tartars, and in short, each one ponders in his own way and produces the proofs and conjectures that support his opinion, which the curious can see in nearly all the authors who have written of the Indies, and with greater ease he will find it compiled in the scholarly book written by Father Gregorio Garcia Dominicano, with the title of Origen de los Indios [Origin of the Indians], where he will see everything that has been said on this matter, the bases of each opinion, and the difficulties and objections against each. Meanwhile I am not taking part in any of them, by speculations and discourses, but rather, following the ancient monuments and manuscripts that I have gathered in interpretation of the historical charts of the Toltecs (who were the wisest among all these nations), I say that the origin and first parents of all of them were seven families who, in the scattering of peoples because of the confusion of tongues at the Tower of Babel, joined together because of finding themselves of one language that they called Nahuatl, which is known as the Mexican language, and they traveled to these parts, where they established themselves and multiplied, and went on dividing into towns and nations.

The Toltec nation, among all those that populated these countries, was the best educated and the one that was best able to retain the memories of their origin and antiquity, their talent finding the way to preserve and pass on to their successors the knowledge of their history by inventing hieroglyphs and characters, which, ordered with method and rule, they put on their charts, that they made on animal skins, on maguey or palm paper in different ways, or with knots on strings of different colors, to which they gave the name of Nepohualtzitzin, which means count of the events; and finally with poems, some simple and others allegorical, and by passing down the art of story telling, understanding and interpreting these charts, knots, and poems, their knowledge has reached us, because among them this was a skill that was taught to the children of noble status, as reading and writing are taught among us.

These, then, clearly went back to the true origin and beginning of the whole universe, because they assert that the heaven and the earth and every-thing found in them is the work of the powerful hand of a supreme and only god, to whom they gave the name of Tloque Nahuaque, which means creator of all things. They also called him Ipalnemo-hualoni, which means, by whom we live and are, and he was the only deity that they worshiped in those prim-itive times, and even after idolatry and false worship were introduced, they always believed him to be superior to all their gods, and they invoked him by lifting their eyes to heaven.

Not just the Mexicans, but also those of Michoacan remained constant in this belief until the arrival of the Spanish, as Herrera affirms, and what is more, the same information was found throughout the kingdom of Peru, even though the Inca Garcilaso de la Vega denies that this was Veracocha and attributes this and other errors of the Spanish writers regarding the multi-plicity of gods, their worship, and idolatries, to a lack of information and little understanding of the language, which is very likely because the same thing happened to them in much of what they write about New Spain; and he says that the true name that they gave to the Creator God was Pachacamac, which means the Maker and sustainer of the Universe; from which it is surmised that the origin of all the inhabitants of both kingdoms was the same, as the Toltecs affirm, and in that first age they worshiped and revered no one except Tloque Nahuaque, because the idolatry and multiplicity of gods arose much later among these people, as will be seen later on.(3)

They likewise assert that this supreme Entity created a man and a woman in a pleasant garden, and that from these two single individuals the entire human race was propagated, and they paint them on their charts almost the same way we do; but with regard to the sin that they committed and for which they were exiled from that delightful place, no mention is found in any of the writings that I have in interpretation of these historical charts. But this does not convince me that the ancient Toltecs were unaware of it, but rather I have positive grounds to believe that they preserved that knowledge and that it was one of those things that they attempted with greatest care to pass down to their posterity through painting, because among the charts that I have seen there is one that appears to be very old, made on very coarse maguey paper, showing a garden, and in it a single tree, from the foot of which a snake is twisting around, and in the middle of the crown of the tree it shows the head with a woman's face, and this same figure is found on other charts, and those who explain its significance say that it is one of the gods that they worshiped afterwards in the time of their idolatry, to whom they gave the name of Cihuacohuatl, which means the snake woman.

Torquemada affirms this information as well known, and agrees with the stories of the Indians that say that this was the first woman to give birth in the world, and from whom all men are descended, and so they gave her the name of Oxomozco, written by others as Otzmozco, and they translate it as the pregnant attractive woman, making a compound of the word Otctli, which means pregnant, and Moxipehuanoy, attractive. They also gave her the names of Tititl, which means our mother, or the womb which we come out of; and Teoyaominqui, which means the goddess who gathers the souls of the deceased.

They dedicated one of the months of the year in her honor, a month in which they celebrated a festival in commemoration of their dead, and famous temples were erected, as we will see later on. All this makes me believe that the ancient Toltecs had perfect knowledge of the sin of the first man, committed at the suggestion of the woman deceived by the serpent, which provided her with the fruit of the forbidden tree, which was the origin of all our evils, through which death entered into the human race, and this was what they intended to explain in these symbolic paintings, so that through them this knowledge could be passed on to their descendants; but later on it was distorted by ignorance, which introduced fables and errors with which it confused the truth and distorted the true worship.

And perhaps the confusion and horror with which those early people looked at these symbolic figures, which brought to mind the guilt of the first man, the cause of the greatest misfortune of the human race, the root of all the evils he suffers, and the origin of death, gave ignorance a reason to feign this deity who gathered the souls of the dead, with the just horror of this misfortune degenerating into idolatry. I also find another congruity in the name that they have given to the serpent from ancient times until today, which is Cohuatlahailíloc, which means Devil snake, and this is the most general name that they give to the serpent in the Mexican language.

They say that in those beginnings of the world men lived only on fruits and vegetables, until one whom they call Tlaominqui, which means he who killed with an arrow, discovered the bow and arrow, and that since then they started to hunt and to live on the flesh of the animals that they would kill in the hunt, and so all the inhabitants of this vast continent became accustomed to it, until the coming of the Spanish; so that even though afterwards they dedicated themselves to the cultivation of various seeds, and to raising some animals and birds for their food, that did not mean that they didn't go hunting as well, and in all the towns they had days indicated on which to do their general hunting to provide themselves with this maintenance, using the bow and arrow for it, for even though later on they invented other offensive and defensive weapons for their wars, for hunting they never used any weapon other than the bow and arrow.

Footnotes, Chapter I

(1) Others say that Anahuac means next to the water, because the Mexican empire was established in the lands immediate to the lagoons of Texcoco and Chalco.

(2) Today the globe is divided into five parts; but when Veytia lived, the fifth part was unknown; it was later given the name of Australia. -E.

(3) See Herrera Dec. 3, book 2, chapter 15, page 85, col. 2. Item Dec. 3, book 3, page 119, col. 1. Item Dec. 5, book 4, chapter 4, page 114, col. 1, and the Inca Garcilaso book 6, chapter 30; and book 7, chapter 4.

CHAPTER II

Of the knowledge that they had of the flood, of the tower of Babel, and the confusion of tongues, and of the seven families of the Nahuatl language who came to inhabit these regions.

So with the belief established that the world was created by Tloque Nahuaque, they started to number their eras since the year of its creation. They indicated this year with the hieroglyph of a flint in their chronological system, which I will tell about further on, and from it they started the count of the times and numbering of the years, and they say that thirty-three of their centuries (which were fifty-two years long) after the creation of the world, which is one thousand seven hundred sixteen years [after the creation], in another year that was also indicated with the same hieroglyph of a flint, mankind suffered a horrible calamity of heavy downpours with lightning and thunder, which flooded all the earth, with the highest mountains, the Caxtolmolictli, which means fifteen cubits, being submerged in the waters, and that only eight persons escaped this general calamity in a Tlaptlipetlacalli, which means house like a closed ark, and on their charts they show it like a log ship with a canopy, on top of which eight heads appear, and so the human race was propagated again from these eight persons.

According to the chronological tables that the Gentlemen Boturini started, which I have continued up to the year 1843 of Christ, and they are at the end of this volume, about the system that these natives followed, counting the centuries of fifty-two years, the flood should be set at the year 1717 of the creation of the world, which is the first year indicated with the hieroglyph of a flint, thirty-three centuries (as they assert) having gone by since the creation.

I well know that the common feeling of exhibitors places this event in the year 1656 of the world, claiming to deduce this count from the sacred text itself through the ages of the antediluvian patriarchs, in which a difference of just 60 years is noted from one calculation to another, which is not highly significant, and it does not seem very difficult to me to reconcile one with the other. But inasmuch as it is not my purpose in this book to become involved in these arguments, much less to attempt to reconcile their chronology with ours, as it seems that the Gentleman Boturini was trying to do, I will only

44

mention with purity and fidelity what I find written in his histories, placing the events in the years that correspond in the mentioned table according to the eras that they assign and the number of years that they count from some events to others, with constant attention to the character or hieroglyph with which they indicate the years. Because inasmuch as they were very exact in this, there can be no variation in it, and it is necessary to place the events in the years that correspond to the indicated character.

I must advise here about what I am going to discuss in the following paragraphs, that in the mentioned tables, that as I already said were started by the Gentleman Boturini in his own hand, he notes the flood at the margin of the same year of 1717 of the world, undoubtedly because in all the manuscripts that he gathered he found this information to be uniform and supported, as has happened to me, even though in many of the subsequent eras there is a significant variation in the chronology, not only from some monuments to others and from some authors to others, but even in a single author, who is Fernando de Alba Ixtlixochitl, one of the most well educated and most authoritative authors in the various narrations that he wrote at various times, in which, mentioning the same events in all of them, without the slightest alteration in the facts and in the characters or hieroglyphs with which the Toltecs indicated the years in which they occurred, the variation that occurs in the comparison with our calculations is notable, undoubtedly arising from not having made tables; nevertheless he places the flood in the same year of 1717 in all of them, and the other authors that I have seen do the same thing.

From the celebrated mathematician Carlos de Sigüenza y Góngora, an individual who was very well versed in the antiquities of the Indians, and in their calendars, I have an almanac or calendar that he printed for the year 1681, in which he puts a chronological note that begins like this: This present year is the year 5641 of the creation of the world; 3985 years since the flood; and of the discovery of the West Indies by Columbus, 189; from the establishment of this city of Mexico by the Aztecs Mexitzin 354; this year being on their Xiuhmolpia or calendar the year Chicuazen Tecpatl, or sixth of the second indiction or Triadecatérida, de Acatl, etc. According to this note, Sigüenza could not place the flood in the year 1717 of the world, because from this year to the year 5641 of the creation, which he asserts to coincide with the year 1681 of Christ, there are just 3924 years, and it is a difference of 61 years, which, having to subtract them from the 1717 to complete the 3985 years that he affirms to have transpired since the flood, he has to place the flood in the year 1656 of the world, which is the common opinion of the exhibitors, but this year, in the chronological tables followed on the system of these Indians, was indicated with the hieroglyph of the reed on the number 5; and so I cannot understand how this calculation correlated with the characters of the calendar of the Indians, who assert that the character of the year in which the flood occurred was Ce Tecpatl, a flint.

He also declares in that note that he was making the world younger than the age that I assign to it in my tables when the Divine Word became incarnate, because according to these, the year 5641 coincided with the year 1608 of the Christian era, and from this year to the year 1681, with which he asserts having coincided, there are 73 years of difference. The world should be that much younger according to his calculation, and consequently it should place the birth of Christ in the year 3961, which according to the tables was indicated by the Indians with a hieroglyph of the flint at the number nine; and in spite of this great difference, he says in the same note that the mentioned year of 1681 was indicated in the Xiuhmolpia or Indian calendar with the symbol Chicuazen Tecpatl, six flints, in which, with respect to the character of above-mentioned year, there is only one year of difference from his calculations to mine, according to which the mentioned year of 1681 was Chicome Calli, seven houses, which is the year that immediately follows the year Chicuazen Tecpatl, as can be seen in the tables.

But in this same year I find another serious difficulty, because with the birth of Christ placed in the year 3961 of the world, and counting from the year 1681 of the Christian era, these end in the year Matlatliomome Tecpatl, that is, twelve flints, which coincided with the year 5641 of the world, as the tables show, and from it to the first year indicated with the character of Chicuazen Tecpatl or six flints, which is that of 5661, there is a difference of 20 years.

I again say that no matter how much I have worked, I have not been able to understand this count, nor the way in which he made these calculations, but having been such a learned and well-educated individual, whose fame endures and will endure in this New Spain, I have no desire to correct him, and the error may be in me because of the limitation of my talent, and another more elevated person may decide. But I advise that most of the eras that I will be indicating in the events of history, adjusted to my calculations, are in agreement with those of Sigüenza, and this makes me suspect that he may have made some mistake in this.

Returning to pick up the thread of our history, I say that the human race had multiplied considerably, and they say that men, fearful of another flood, and wanting to make their name famous, undertook the construction of a very tall tower to which they gave the name of Zacuali, and that four ages (which are eight centuries of theirs of fifty-two years each) having past since the flood, in a year that they also indicate with the hieroglyph of a flint, when they were the most involved in the construction of their tower, suddenly their languages were confused so that they did not understand each other, and so the construction ceased and everyone divided up, spreading out over the whole face of the earth. This information noted in so much detail by the Toltec nation, from whose historical charts it was obtained by the authors who wrote in these monarchies of Mexico and Texcoco, was found to be in agreement and without variation among the Indians of Chiapa, as affirmed by Francisco Núñez de la Vega, the bishop of that diocese, in the prologue of his Constituciones diocesanas (diocese constitutions), who asserts that in his archives he keeps an old manuscript of the first natives from there, who learned how to write in our characters, in which it is on record that they always kept the memory that the first progenitor and father of their nation was named Tepanahuaste, which means the Lord of the Hollow Pole, and that Tepanahuaste was at the construction of the great wall, as they called the tower of Babel, and with his own eyes he saw the confusion of tongues, after which the Creator God commanded him to come to these extensive lands to distribute them among men.

This event, according to their calculations and a comparison of the tables, must be placed in the year 2133 of the world, and 416 after the flood, because counting the eight centuries of 52 years each from the year 1717, the year that they assert the flood occurred, the first year that is indicated by the hieroglyphs of the flint at the number one is that of 2133, as can be seen in those tables. At this era they vary somewhat more from our calculations, because the common opinion of the exhibitors does not establish this confusion of tongues of Babel at so many years after the flood, but all are founded on mere conjecture.

The Gentleman Boturini, in the work that he brought to light in Madrid in the year 1746 with the title of Idea de una nueva Historia de la America Septentrional [Idea of a new History of North America] that pondered writing about the monuments that he gathered and that I have used for this work, touches on this point in book 16, folio 124, and it seems to me that he was inclined to follow the opinion of the Seventy who set the flood in the year 2242 of the world, and counting the four ages that they call cycles in the way he counts and explains them in the foregoing pages, he establishes as the one he likes most the opinion of this confusion of tongues having been in the year 2497 of the world.

I have instructed myself in and had in my hands all the old monuments that he gathered, and I have not been able to find the explanation that he makes at folio 122 either in them or in those that I have gathered up since, nor have I been able to understand it or accommodate it to the eras of the events of history. He says that when the Indians count on their calendars by this number of Ce, one, that is, Ce Tecpatl, one flint, it is understood to be one time every four cycles ["centuries" in book], because then they talk about the initial characters of each cycle, and thus according to the artifice of their painted wheels Ce Tecpatl comes in only once at the beginnings of the four cycles; therefore, with any character of these initial characters being placed in the history, it is necessary for four Indian cycles ["centuries" in book] of 52 years each to go by, which makes 208 years, before it can be found again further on; because in this way one doesn't count by the characters that are in the body of the four cycles ["centuries" in book]; and even though the same characters are found in them, they are not taken into account.

On none of the ancient monuments that he gathered, and which I have become familiar with, have I found such an explanation, nor is their system perceptible to me, nor do any of the Indian historians use this calculation to indicate the eras of the events of history, no matter how celebrated they may be, but rather they use the one that I will explain hereafter, upon which I have formed my own for the comparison of their years with ours, as will be seen in the course of this work.

And because afterwards I must again touch upon this point when I explain their calendars, what is said is sufficient for now to establish that according to the calculations of these natives, the flood occurred in the year 1717 of the world, and the confusion of tongues in Babel, 416 years after the flood, which corresponds to the year 2133 of the world, as established, and it seems very reasonable to me because it is an average between the two calculations that Boturini himself gives in the mentioned place, that is, the common one of the Hebrews and Latins and that of the Seventy. According to the first, the confusion of tongues occurred in the year 1873 of the world; and according to the second, in the year 2497, and so the year 2133 in which I establish it, according to the system of the Indians, is an average between the one and the other.

They would include this event of the confusion of tongues on their charts, painting a round hill on the front of which a medal is seen placed, and a face is engraved on it like that of an old man with a long beard, and outside the medal there are many tongues that surround it and form a border. This mode of painting it in the form of a hill agrees well with the information that ancient and modern travelers give us, who affirm that they have seen the remains that have been left of it, and on the authority of these, Father Augustín Calmet asserts in his dissertation on the tower of Babel, at the beginning of his commentary on Genesis, and in his Bible Dictionary under the entry Babel, that this tower was massive inside and seemed more like a mountain than a building.

In our times an irrefutable monument still exists, as well as the constant and perfect knowledge that these people had of the construction of this famous tower and the craft of its construction, as they are descendants of those who attempted to put into practice such an arrogant project. This is the famous Tower of Cholollan, built by the Olmec nation, one of the first that inhabited the country of Anahuac, with the same proud purpose of making their name famous, and in our days a considerable portion of their ruins still exists in that city of Cholollan, one league from la Puebla de Los Angeles, in the figure of a massive hill with the ascent on the outside.(1)

In this confusion of tongues, they say that seven families found themselves to be of the same language, which was Nahuatl, and today it is known as the Mexican language, and as they understood each other among themselves, they joined together, and together they undertook their pilgrimage through various lands and countries, at random and without a certain destination, until finding land that seemed suitable and appropriate for them to settle, and having walked for one age, which among them was the space of 104 years, crossing mountains, rivers, and arms of the sea which they indicate on their charts, they arrived at the place where they made their first settlement at the northern part of this kingdom, which they call Tlapallan, which is interpreted as the Bermeja [red land], because the land was red, and in fact on all the modern maps they give the name of Mar Bermejo [Red Sea] to the sea which they locate between the eastern coast of California and the western coast of the provinces of New Mexico and Sonora, and the river that flows into it through the northern part they call the Colorado [Red] River. In subsequent times they called this city Huehuetlapallan, which means the old Tlapallan, as opposed to another one that was founded many years later with the same name, as we will say later on.

The mountains, rivers, valleys, and seas through which they traveled are next to impossible to indicate individually which they were, because lacking their maps of destination and dimensions, and as they were not familiar with the use of the needle and the compass,(2) it is not easy to say for certain. The birth of the sun was their only guide; this is not indicated on all the charts, and on those on which it is found, it is not sufficient to infer the location of the countries, nor the certain land through which they walked.

But in all, the uniformity of the itinerary charts of so many different nations who wanted to preserve the memory of their origin and pilgrimage to these lands, the universal assertion of all the interpreters of these charts who were descendants of those very people, the existence of many places and lands that even to our days maintain the same names, the widespread knowledge that the Spanish found in all these peoples of pointing out their ancient fatherland at the northern part of New Spain, the existence of the settlement of Tlapallan, whether it was the first or the second town of this name (there is some variation in this as, I will say later), and finally, the failure to find any trace that they may have come from somewhere else are fully convincing that the coming of these seven families (which I suppose were already numerous then) from the countryside of Sennaar to these regions, was through the Tartary, to enter to the northernmost part of the continent of America, some companies following the course on dry land and others along with Peninsula

49

of California, from where they traveled to the continent by crossing the strait in between.

On the charts they indicate the site where they departed from this other side, which they call Culhuacan, which means place of the snake, in which they subsequently founded a settlement of the same name which still remains, and it is the first one on the dry land, situated in front of the mentioned Peninsula of California,(3) and they preserved the memory of this settlement of Culhuacan, but later the Toltecs founded a famous city of the same name, which became the court and capital of a kingdom that was also called Culhuacan, of which the relics likewise remain in our days in a small settlement that retains the name, close to Mexico City, on the banks of the Chalco lagoon, as the other one is on the banks of the California sea.

Boturini says,(4) in his mentioned book, that Fernando de Alba Ixtlixochitl, in his historical narrations, mentions the names of the heads or fathers of these seven families who joined together in the scattering of Babel, and took a pilgrimage from the countryside of Sennaar to these regions. I have all the historical narrations of Alba, copied from the ones that the mentioned Boturini gathered, and I have not found this information in them. It seems to me that he was mistaken, and I confirm it from his own expressions, because he says that seven Toltecs who were present at the construction of the tower, seeing that they could not understand the others, left with their wives and children, and after having traveled in Asia, they came to settle in the land of Anahuac; and this is to confuse the seven families of the scattering of Babel with the seven who rebelled against their sovereigns after these peoples were already established in the northern part of these regions, and having fled, seeking other lands in which to settle, they came to establish their monarchy in Tollan and the whole territory that now comprises the jurisdiction of the Royal Audience of Mexico, and the mentioned Alba recorded the names of these family heads, as I will say later on.

The rivers, straits, or arms of the sea that they describe on their charts to have crossed in their entire extensive pilgrimage from the countryside of Sennaar until reaching California are without a doubt the same ones that have been discovered lately, which are shown on the most modern maps, and every day we see that new lands are being discovered on this side, that just as they have enlightened us that California is not an island, I expect that they verify these regions to be continents with those that were believed to be so far apart, and separated from them only by short straits as the Indians affirm.

The manner in which they had to pass through these straits, sea arms, and rivers shown was in square rafts formed of reeds or light poles, and in flat canoes to which they gave the name of Acalli, which means house of water, and they paint them that way, and on them they paint the persons traveling, some sitting down and others lying down or stretched out along the raft or canoe. But on none of the many maps I have seen do they show how they controlled them, because no person is seen swimming to guide it, nor can an oar or paddle be seen with which to steer it from on top, nor have I found any information whatsoever on this in the manuscripts. But it is not credible that they would throw themselves to the whim of the waters, nor that they could travel without oars or towing, and so we must suppose that in one way or another they did it, even though they do not describe it, unless they used their arms in place of oars, which suspicion I am led to by seeing, as I have said, that of the persons whom they paint on the raft, some are sitting down and others lying down, and on such a chart I have seen those who seem to have their arms extended outside the raft, with which they may be depicting that they used their arms as oars to guide the raft.

Having reached the place that seemed most comfortable to them for their habitation, they founded their first city, to which they gave the name of Tlapallan, which means red, and later they called it Huehuetlapallan, that is Tlapallan the old, to distinguish it from another one that was more modern. They indicate their findings in a year of the same character or hieroglyph of a flint, which according to the tables seems to have been the year 2237 of the world, because it is the first one that is found in the tables indicated with the character of a flint, ten centuries having gone by since the confusion of Babel. They say that this city is still in existence in our times, although reduced to a small population known as Huetlapallan de Cortés, because they assert that up until the time this conqueror [Cortez] penetrated to it, perhaps motivated by the information about them, they always preserved in their memory that this had been the first city that they founded after their exile.

But it seems to me that there may be a mistake in this, and that Cortez did not reach this ancient city, but rather the other one by the same name that the Toltecs founded later; because the location of the former, as affirmed by the interpreters themselves is far to the north, beyond the Apache nations, where Cortez is not known to have gone.

It seems that the other one is more toward the southern coast, not far from the mouth of the Colorado River, and he may have gotten to here. And so once established in that, their first settlement, they started to multiply, and in these early times it was a very populous city. Afterwards they started spreading throughout that whole vast region, and founded many other settlements from which the great Chichimec empire was formed, to which they gave the name of Chichimecatlali, that is, land of the Chichimecs. Some say that the reason for taking this name of Chichimecs was because the main leader who led them from the countryside of Sennaar was named Chichimecatl. Others want this to have been their first king, after they settled on this continent, and after some companies of people who penetrated various parts of the continent had separated from them. Others think variously, as we will say further on. Of this empire, then, Huetlapallan was the famous court, and from it the people would leave at various times in bands or companies and populate very extensive regions, each one taking a different name, according to the chief or father of the family who was ruling it, becoming different nations over the course of time with different languages or dialects. In this way, according to the beliefs of these natives and their history, all the inhabitants of this new world have their origin and beginning from these seven families, and this city of Huehuetlapallan has the glory of having been the first settlement that was founded in it after the flood, and the cradle of all its inhabitants, the memory of which those of the New Spain always preserved, calling it their old fatherland.

Footnotes, Chapter II

(1) The hill of Cholollan, or Cholula, as we say today, which in fact is artificially made, is, according to Clavijero, 500 French feet high, equivalent to 194 rods; but this historian denies that the purpose of its construction was the same as for the tower of Babel, and supposes that it was a great temple, as the so-called pyramids of Teotihuacan, which are also artificial hills.

(2) The Mexicans described concentric circles, especially in the representations of the sun, with so much precision that it would be difficult to decide that they were unacquainted with the compass.

(3) Boturini imagined that the Toltecs colonized the western coast of North America, having crossed the narrow straits which separate that continent from Asia; and that continually migrating to the south, some of them penetrated into California, and others reached the more central provinces situated to the north of Mexico. He was of the opinion that the Aztecs, the ancestors of the Mexicans, were those who settled in California, who, like the children of Israel, beginning their migration by crossing the Red Sea, (for the Gulf of California was otherwise named Mar Bermejo [Red Sea] by the Spaniards, perhaps with the design of veiling by an equivocal adoption of names the real history of the Mexicans), proceeded on their pilgrimage to the land of Anahuac. He also presupposes a long journey undertaken by the Toltecs through Tartary from central Asia, such as other authors have believed that the Jews of the lost tribes took to arrive at America. To this supposition it may be objected that Montezuma assured Cortez, in the presence of all his nobles, that his ancestors had arrived at Mexico from a country situated towards the rising sun; that Sahagun declares in the general preface to his History of New Spain that a colony which had navigated the ocean in early ages disembarked in the port of Panaco, which is situated on the shores

of the Mexican Gulf; that the native traditions of the people of Guatemala, (who claimed, as being descended from the Toltecs, consanguinity with the Mexicans,) recorded that their ancestors were Jews who had quitted Palestine, or that part of Arabia which is contiguous to the Red Sea, and had crossed the Atlantic to America; that Votan is said to have come from the old to the new continent; that that Quetzalcoatl, when meditating his return to the country from which he came, proceeded in an easterly direction, and arriving at Coazacoalco, a province of New Spain which borders on the Atlantic Ocean, there embarked. To the reasons which have been enumerated for dissenting from the opinion of Boturini and Echevarria that America was colonized on its northwestern side by tribes crossing from Tartary, and that the ancestors of the Mexicans were descended from them, we shall add another, which, if it be of a negative description, will still be found to possess as much weight as any of the foregoing; it is contained in the following passage, which is taken from a work of Torribio de Benavente Motolinia, preserved in manuscript in the library of the Escorial, who there says that the inhabitants of Taxcala and many other provinces of New Spain had a tradition that their ancestors had migrated from a province situated to the northwest of Mexico, but that that tradition, wanting the corroborative evidence of the Mexican language being spoken in any of the provinces discovered by the Spaniards as far north as Sibola, was not entitled to credit, and that it was therefore to be inferred that the Mexicans were "of a strange and unheard-of race." Those of Texcoco, who in antiquity and lordship are none other than the Mexicans, are today called Aculuaques, and their whole province together is called Aculua; and this name came from a valiant captain they had, a native of the same province, who was called Aculi by name, which is the name of the bone that goes from the elbow to the shoulder, and from the same bone they called the shoulder aculi. This captain Aculi was like another Saul, valiant and tall of body, so much so that from the shoulders up he stood above all the people, and there was no other like him. This Aculi was so spirited and vigorous and renowned in the wars that the province of Texcoco Aculuaca was named for him. The Tlaxcaltecs who received and helped to conquer the New Spain for the Spanish are of the Nauales, that is, of the same language as the Mexicans, and they say that their ancestors came from the northwest, and to enter into this land they sailed for eight or ten days; and the most ancient who came from there had two arrows, which they kept as precious relics, and they had them as a principal sign to know if they were going to win the battle, or if they should retreat in time. These Taxcaltecs were a warring people, as will be discussed later on in the third part; when they went out to battle, two captains, the most outstanding in effort, would carry those arrows, and in the first encounter they wounded the enemies by throwing them from afar, and they would strive to death to recover them, and if they injured and spilled blood with them, they considered victory to be certain, and they would all become very spirited to triumph, and with that hope they would strive to wound and conquer their enemies; if with the mentioned arrows they didn't injure anyone or spill blood, the best thing they could do was retreat, because they had it as a certain omen that it was going to go bad for them in that battle. Returning to the purpose, the most ancient of the Tlaxcaltecs have to [come] from that part of the northwest, and there they point and say that the Nauales came, which is the main language and people of New Spain, and many others say and feel this same thing. Toward this same northwest part they are already conquered and four languages discovered, as far as the province of Cibola, and I have a letter from this same year, as from that part of Cibola they have discovered an infinite multitude of people, in which the language of the Nauales has not been found, where they seem to be a strange and unheard-of people. Aristotle, in the book De Admirandis Naturae, says that in ancient times the Carthaginians sailed through the strait of Gibraltar toward the west on a sixty-day voyage, and that they found pleasant, delightful, and very fertile lands; and as that voyage was much followed, and many stayed there and became dwellers, the Carthaginian senate ordered under penalty of death that no one sail and no navigation was to come to these lands or islands. They could have been those that are before San Juan, or Española, or Cuba, or perhaps some part of this New Spain; but such a great land so sparsely populated everywhere, but it seems to bring an origin from other strange places, and in some indications it even seems to be from the distribution and division of the grandchildren of Noah. Some Spanish, considering certain rites, customs, and ceremonies of these natives, judge them to be of the generation of Moors; others, because of some causes and conditions that they see in them, say that they are of Jewish generation; but the common opinion is that they are all gentiles, for we see that they use it and have it for good. If this narration were to leave the hand of your illustrious lordship, two things I beg as alms for the love of Our Lord: one, that the name of the author be said to be a minor friar and no other name; the other, that your lordship order it examined in the first chapter that is celebrated in your villa of Benavente, for very learned persons gather in it; because there are many things, after being written, that I didn't have time to reread, and for this reason I know that something awful and poorly written is going out. I beg our Lord God that his holy grace always dwell in your soul and enliven your excellent lordship. Done in the Convent of Saint Mary of the Conception of Teozaan, on the day of the glorious Apostle Saint Matthew, in the year 1541 of the human redemption. Introductory epistle of a minor friar to the Illustrious Lord Antonio Pimentel, Sixth Count of Benavente."

(4) Boturini, book 16, n. 11 and 12.

CHAPTER III

Information given on two memorable events that were the origin of two fables.

With the city of Huehuetlapallan having been settled, and its dwellers having increased significantly so that they no longer fit in it, they started to extend throughout all its contours, being divided into towns and neighborhoods, and the great Chichimec empire started to arise, from which so many powerful monarchies later came. The houses they lived in, in the city as well as in the other settlements, were none other, at that time and many centuries afterwards, even when they already had kings and governments, than the caves that they found made by nature, in the likeness of which they would form others, and these were all their habitations. They lived on fruits, vegetables, and hunting, and their clothing was the skins of the same animals that they hunted, formed like a truss that they called Maxtli, with which they precisely covered the most shameful parts of their body.

Three ages after the foundation of their capital city of Huehuetlapallan, they make mention of a singular event, the memory of which remained so vivid among them that they took it as an era in the historical narration of those in the future. They say that in a year that was indicated with the hieroglyph of seven rabbits, the sun remained suspended in its course for the space of one natural day, creating excessive heat such as they had never experienced, and this caused such an abundance of mosquitoes that they could find no relief. They fabricated a fable afterwards on this event, saying that when the mosquito saw the sun so suspended, he went to the sun and told him: Lord of the world, why are you so suspended and pensive and don't do your job which is your obligation? Do you want to destroy the world with your fire and reduce it to ashes, becoming deaf to the pleas of men? Go, move and fulfill the charge of the office you hold. But inasmuch as the sun, for his own reasons, did not move, the mosquito approached him and, biting him in a leg, obliged him to move and to continue his accustomed rotation.

One age among them consisted of 104 years, and thus the three ages that they say had passed since the founding of their city until this event comprise 312 years, which, counting from the year 2237 of the world in which that founding was established, the three ages come to an end in the year 2549, which was indicated with the hieroglyph of a flint, as is seen in the tables, but with them expressly saying that the character of the year in which this suspension of the sun occurred was that of seven rabbits, it seems that it should be placed in the year 2555 of the world, which is the first year after the three ages that is indicated with this hieroglyph. This event that the Indians preserved in their history is very similar to what the scripture tells us in chapter 10 of the Book of Joshua, in the time as well as in the duration of the suspension of the sun, for according to what it says in number 13 of the same chapter, So the sun stood still in the midst of heaven, and hasted not to go down about a whole day. With regard to the time, most authors indicate it with little difference compared to the Indians: See the scholarly dissertation of father Calmet at the beginning of his commentary on the Book of Joshua, where he places this suspension of the sun in the year 2553 [the book says 2550] of the world, which is only two years different(1) from the calculation of the Indians.

One thousand seven hundred sixteen years after the flood, and eight ages after the suspension of the sun, in a year that they indicate with the same hieroglyph of a flint, they mention having suffered another terrible calamity of some furious hurricanes that tore down a multitude of trees in the mountains and toppled the rocks, and thus wreaked destruction on men, many thousands of them dying, the only ones who escaped being those who remained enclosed in their caves, and when the storm was over, they say that on coming out of the caves they found the land covered with monkeys, an animal that they hadn't seen and didn't know until then, and since at the same time they missed such a large number of people who had perished with the hurricane, they invented another fable that the men had become monkeys, and in later times ignorance believed it so much that to this day there is no lack of those of the foolish masses who affirm it, and they added that these were the lazy and the vagabonds who were turned into monkeys in punishment for their idleness. They believed that they knew how to talk and that their failure to talk was so that they would not be made to work.

According to the comparison of the tables with their calculations, it appears that this event should be set in the year 3433 of the world. They say that most of the giants who inhabited the country of Anahuac perished in this calamity, and that only a few escaped of those who had penetrated the deepest into the land, and they were living toward the banks of the river Atoyac, between the city of Tlaxcala and that of Puebla de los Angeles.

Some of our Spanish authors who wrote of things of the Indies and who came to have knowledge of there having been giants in these countries strive, with sacred and profane authorities and with reason , to prove the real existence of them in this new world as well as in the old world. But I, following the method proposed, and separated from discourses and speculations, simply mention what I find in the histories of these natives. All accounts assert their existence and their having lived in various parts of the continent. Whether their origin is the same as that of the other nations who populated it, that is, those seven families who joined together at the scattering of Babel, or whether it is different, is not easy to find out. Some of the national historians give the same origin and say that in the extensive pilgrimage of the seven families from the countryside of Sennaar, some companies of them went ahead, who, because they were more corpulent and stronger, walked more rapidly and arrived in these regions before the others; that the rest followed their tracks and through the signs of their long trek they arrived many years later and found them already established in these parts. Boturini seems to give them a different origin, because he says that they are among the descendants of Cain, the son of Noah, and in the confusion of tongues they spread through various parts, and some of them traveled until settling in America. However it was, what is certain is that when the main body of people coming from those seven families after their extensive pilgrimage through Asia arrived in these lands, they found the giants already established in them, who in many places would not let them pass and prevented them from occupying the land. And because afterwards I will again touch on this matter when I discuss their total extinction, it is sufficient now to say that this calamity and destruction that the giants suffered with the hurricanes was very acceptable to the other dwellers of these regions, because being fierce, barbarous, and brutal people (as they describe them), who lived only on what they stole, doing them many other damages, they kept these other people in constant movement to try to repel them and take cover from their insults. This was the origin and beginning of their militia and where they started to become soldiers and captains.

The sudden appearance of the monkeys (an animal that they had not known until then) immediately after the hurricanes had obviously been an effect of the winds; either their impetus blew them to these lands from the other neighboring lands they inhabited, where they had remained until then, or this animal, fleeing from the elements as by instinct, went to seek more protected places to take shelter in. But I am not persuaded that the invention of these two fables on the two events mentioned was an invention of these times, but of later times, in which the Toltec nation distinguished itself in ability and talent; because at the same time that they were very wise and industrious, they were also very hard working and such enemies of idleness and laziness (which is the vice attacked by the morality inferred from both fables) that they would relentlessly pursue the lazy and the vagabonds, throwing them out of their cities and settlements, and so I wouldn't hesitate to believe that in the same way they invented other fables which I will tell about in their own places about other facts, as true as they are fabulous, to reprehend various vices, they invented these about these certain facts of their history in order to condemn laziness. And these as well as the other fables were afterwards adopted by ignorance in their material sense with a blind credulity, to which the superstitious persuasion of their hypocritical priests contributed a great deal, as will be seen later on.

Footnote, Chapter III

(1) [This footnote is from the book.] "Five," it should say; but in the Museum manuscript, as well as in ours, it says "two," undoubtedly by mistakes of the copiers. – E.

CHAPTER IV

Of the council that they held for the correction of their calendar and adjust-
ment of the times, and information is given of two other fables that they
invented of the origin of the sun and the moon.

With the destruction of the giants, these peoples ended up at rest, now free of such bothersome enemies who obligated them to live in constant fear, and they started to dedicate themselves with greater diligence to the cultivation of the land and to the observation of the heavenly bodies.

They do not tell us in detail what the system was that they followed nor the order that they kept at that time in their calendar, but it is on record that having attentively observed from earliest times that the natural year started at the same time as the fields started to be populated with new plants, that the earth maintained its greenness until the cold of winter withered and destroyed it, and that once these were over it would again dress in new shoots, they set the course of the natural year from one new production to the other, and they gave it the name of Xihuitl, which means the new grass, numbering the years and measuring the solar course by the sprouting of the grass, and the name Xihuitl, which they gave to the year at that time, is the name that it always kept and preserved until our times, the Nahuatl language not having any other with which to explain it. And, being taught by the repeated experience, as many times as years that went by, that the variety of seasons, natural conditions, and productions of the earth originated from the invariable order and regulated movement of the stars, they started to dedicate themselves to the observation of the stars, and especially to the sun and the moon, whose magnitude to their view facilitated the observation of their movement.

I do not mean by this that until these times they had lived in such ignorance that they were totally unaware of the course of the heavenly bodies and their influences on the earth, whose productions and diversity of seasons become apparent even to the irrational; but rather that at about these times some men among them started to stand out, who were more speculative and attentive in the study of the stars, who dedicated themselves to working the annual calculations. And with the rotation of the moon through its visible daily mutations being more perceptible to them, they worked out their year by it, dividing it into new moons of twenty-six days, which they divided into two

59

equal parts, each thirteen days long. They counted the first from the day that the moon appeared in the sky and they called it Mextozoliztli, that is, wakefulness of the moon. Once the thirteen days were over, they would start the second part, which they called Mecochiliztli, that is, sleep of the moon. I have not found any author to tell how many of these new moons made up the year, but it is unquestionable that they had them instead of months, and so after their correction they did not give any other name to the month than that of Metztli, which means the moon; and even in their new regulations they continued the count of the days of thirteen on thirteen, as will be seen, preserving the division of the new moon that they did at the beginning, although in a different form. Some also believe that even as early as these times they were already numbering the years by olympiads, that is, of four on four, indicating them with the four hieroglyphic symbols of the elements, which they later used for their calculations; and this seems reasonable that it was that way, at least in those times immediately before the correction and regulation, which I am going to talk about. But nothing can be assured with certainty, and it isn't even known exactly what the system was that they were following, nor how far their knowledge had come when the correction was done.

What they tell us is that nine centuries after the hurricanes, in a year that was indicated with the hieroglyph of a flint, which according to the tables seems to have been the year 3901 of the world, a great meeting was convened of astronomers in the city of Huehuetlapallan, which by then was a famous and numerous settlement, to make the correction of their calendar, or reform their calculations, which they knew to be in error according to the system that they had followed until then.

This meeting was attended not only by the many wise astronomers who lived in that city, but by a great many others who came from the other settlements, which by that time they already had in considerable number, having spread a great deal throughout all that region. And having conferred at length on the errors that they had recognized in their calculations, in that meeting it was established that the duration of the world should be divided into four spaces or ages, that each one had to expire through violence of one of the four elements. The first one, from its creation until the flood, in which such great calamity had been suffered at the unleashing of the waters; and so they called this age Atonatiuh, which literally means sun (or day) of water, and allegorically space of time that ended with water. The second, from the flood to the hurricanes, in which at the terrible impetus of the winds they had suffered the second calamity, and thus they called it Echecatonatiuh, which literally means sun (or day) of air, and allegorically, space of time that ended with air. The third age, which they were in, they said had to end with furious earthquakes in which mankind would suffer the third calamity, and thus they called it

Tlachitonatiuh or Tlaltonatiuh, which means sun (or day) of earth or space of time that is to end with earthquakes. And that after this, the fourth and last age of the world would follow, which was to end by violence of fire, in which everything would be consumed, and thus they called it Tletonatiuh, which means sun (or day) of fire or space of time that would end with fire.

The words Tonatiuh, which means the sun, or tonalli, which means the heat of the sun, were the first words they used to explain the day, such that they counted as many days as suns; and even though afterwards the word Tlacotli, which means day, or Cemihuitl, which means the space of a day, were invented, they always remained in little use, and up to our times the common people generally do not understand nor is it understood by other words than those of tonatiuh or tonalli.

They later extended these same words to mean a period, as is seen in those mentioned above, in the same way that they used the word Xihuitl, which means the new grass, to name the year, as I have already said, and the words Metztli, which means the moon, to name the months up to this day. Of these spaces of time in which they divided the age of the world, they gave the first two, already past, a fixed duration, indicating 1716 years for each one. But in all the monuments that I have become familiar with, I have not found anywhere that they indicate or predict the duration of the two future ages. However, I am persuaded that they believed that it was to be the same as that of the two past ages. In subsequent times they report having suffered another great calamity of horrendous earthquakes, which we will discuss later on, but they indicate it as 633 years after the hurricane, and no report is found of any other universal one up to our times. Therefore, if we are to believe their prediction and establish the duration of the third age based on it, it would have been much smaller than the two previous ages.

The Gentleman Boturini, in his mentioned work in book 1, page 3, talks about this division of the times, placing the periods variously. He puts the first, sun (or day) of (the) water, from the creation to the flood; from the flood to the earthquakes, sun (or day) of (the) earth; from this time to the hurricanes, sun (or day) of (the) air; and the last, sun (or day) of (the) fire. I confess and have always confessed his great intelligence and profound knowledge in this history, acquired with unspeakable work and continuous study, which was based on an uncommon erudition in every class of good letters. I likewise confess that the first enlightenment that I had on this subject, and the little bit that I can speak of it, I owe to his verbal instruction and to the documents that he gathered with so much work and diligence, because even for those that I have added to in order to be able to write this history, I owe the information to him. But just as I cannot adjust to his system that I talked about in chapter 2, I cannot follow him in this point, nor in others that we will see.

I have three reasons not to follow him in this point; the first is that in all the manuscripts I have, I find these periods placed in the way that I have placed them, except in two of them, which are, the one, some very succinct historical notes of an anonymous author, which are of little moment and have other obvious errors; the other is the Chichimec history by the celebrated Fernando de Alba Ixtlilxochitl, which is truly very authoritative on the matter, for from this same author I have the historical narrations of the Toltec nation, in which he puts them as I have placed them, and it is noteworthy that this work is, to me, the most appreciable one of this author, because he claims to have taken them from the very historical charts that he was able to interpret, and thus they are very detailed and expressive, and at the end of the fifth narration he brings a catalog of old and well-educated individuals and of monuments that he used to perfect his interpretation, refuting the errors of the Spanish authors, especially Gomara, who talks about this division of ages and places the period of sun (or day) of (the) earth in second place, as does Boturini. In addition to this, in the mentioned narrations Alba expressly discusses this subject, and in their Chichimec history he includes it in the first chapter succinctly and in passing, as preliminary knowledge to enter his topic, and he could have been mistaken.

The second reason that I have to not follow him is that the periods placed as Boturini places them are in opposition to the same historical and chronological narration of the events, as is seen in the previous chapter; for the first calamity that they mention after the flood is the hurricane, which destroyed so many people that they believed they had turned into monkeys, and this is the period Echecatonatiuh, or sun that ended with air, and many centuries afterwards they make mention of the earthquake, which is the Tlaltonatiuh, or sun that ended with earthquake. Therefore I am persuaded that the Gentleman Boturini was mistaken, as he was in other things, which isn't surprising, having written that book without having the documents in view that he had gathered for the formation of his history, and thus he says that in the prologue that this his work is a restoration that the memory is making of what is deposited in it; and he wrote the mentioned book strictly from memory, of which I am a witness, and I saw him write it in my own house, where I had him as my guest. Rather I am amazed, and will always be amazed by his great retention with which he was able to report not just such an accumulation of knowledge, but what's more, so many words, names, and phrases from the Mexican language, so strange to him, and which he did not possess, except those words and their meanings that he had learned in the manuscripts that gathered.

The third is that, as we are going to see, these natives later used the hieroglyphs of the four elements as the key of all their calculations and calendars, and they placed fire in the first place, earth in second, wind in third, and water in fourth; and the reason for having placed them in this order was because they considered fire as the most sublime and powerful; after it and at a lower level of power, the earth; less than the earth is the wind, and finally water, and in proportion to the power of each one, they believed the destruction caused by nature should be, until fire, as the most powerful, annihilates everything.

So counting these same elements in reverse order, the period of the calamity caused by water should be placed first; then, that of the wind; in third place, that of the earth, and finally, that of fire; and with its not being that way, this order is reversed against all the reasons that I have explained, and I do not find any in all their monuments that indicates or persuades this reversal.

Gomara(1) acquired some knowledge of this division of ages, but so confusing and distorted that he well declares that he got it from a common person, not at all educated in his history, or he was lacking in understanding the true meaning of the information. Because understanding the word Tonalli to be the material sun, he tells us that these people believed that there had been five suns, that the first perished in the waters, the second by the sky falling upon the earth, the third was consumed in the fire, the fourth ended with air, and that when the fifth appeared, the Gods died, with other fables that he mixes, the belief of which was very possibly introduced among some of the common and ignorant people, for we have plenty of examples of this in our century, in spite of the greater enlightenment which it has reached. Listen to the common people, how they talk, when it concerns eclipses, comets and other phenomena, the course of the stars, the shapes and colors of the clouds, the rainbow and other such things, and it will be found that they are steeped and infatuated in an infinity of fables and ridiculous stories. For when it comes to history, ancient information and wondrous cases, there is nothing more common in each nation and in each people, even the most refined, making no exception for the courts, in which the common people are not preoccupied by innumerable fables and incredible foolishness. It could also be that the Indians purposely deceived anyone who tried to learn anything from them, as they did in many other things, and this was very common in those early times immediately after the conquests, of which Fernando de Alba himself gives us some examples in the mentioned fifth narration.

Before going on, it has seemed appropriate to me to give information here of another famous fable that they invented about the origin of the sun and the moon. These peoples had a high concept of the sun, considering it as the center of fire, the most highly esteemed of the elements among them. They looked at it as the source of light that they believed was one with it, as the father of all the living and moving beings, and as the main active principle in all the productions of the earth, and so to celebrate it they invented a heroic fable, saying that the Gods, being pleased with the virtues that some mortals were practicing in a high degree, wanted to reward them to stimulate the others to imitate them.

For this, they say that in a large field, in the middle of which there was a bonfire or mouth that was vomiting formidable flames, they called and gathered together all the wise, virtuous, and valiant of the earth, and they told them that those who had the courage and strength to cast themselves into that bonfire would be transformed into Gods and divine honors would be given to them. The proposal having been heard by the men, they paused and started to dispute among themselves as to who should throw himself first. While they were arguing, the God Cinteotl, the God of the Corn Fields, whom they also called Inopintzin, that is, the orphan God, alone and without parents, approached one of the contestants who was very old and was suffering from buboes or Gallic disease, tolerating his pains with great patience and perseverance, and he said to him: "What are you doing here? How is it that you don't hurry to cast yourself to the flames, while your companions hold back in useless disputes? Throw yourself into that bonfire to put an end to your troubles, which you tolerated for so many years with such heroic perseverance, and you will perpetually enjoy your divine honors." Encouraged with this hope, the sick man, dragging himself however he could, approached the bonfire and threw himself into it. Great was the shock and admiration caused in all those present by such a generous act, and it was much greater to see that his body was slowly melting and being transformed into the flames themselves, until no trace of him was left. At this time they saw a very beautiful and corpulent eagle come down from the sky, and going inside the bonfire and using his claws and his beak to grasp the ball of flames that the sick man had been transformed into, he carried it up to place it in the sky.

Encouraged by this example, one of those wise men who was present, wanting to attain that happiness, also threw himself into the bonfire, but its flames having already employed the greatest vigor in the transformation of the sick man, their activity was much less, and so they were only able to reduce him to ashes that remained visible at the bottom of the bonfire, and the wise man was transformed into the moon and placed in the sky, but in a lower place than the sun.

Boturini feels that these fables were the work of the second age that he calls the age of the heroes, which corresponds to these times of which we are speaking, when among these Indians some started to stand out who were wiser, more prudent, and more courageous, who, by ruling their families with justice, moderation, and discretion, became respected, being joined by the vagabonds and orphans, whether motivated by the fame of these heroes or obligated by their own needs, they gave them their liberty, giving them obedience, from where the kingdoms and monarchies began. But I am persuaded that the invention of these fables was in later times, because from the fables themselves it is seen that idolatry had already arisen and they paid homage to various deities, and it is constant in all their histories that neither in these times nor in many afterwards did they worship any other deities than the Creator God, as will be seen further on.

Footnote, Chapter IV

(1) Crónica de la Nueva España [Chronicles of the New Spain], chapter 52[?].

CHAPTER V

Of the way in which they divided time, and the system that they established to count the signs [centuries in book].

This division being made of the duration of the world into the four ages mentioned, those of the great meeting entered to adjust their calculations and correct their calendar, dividing the time into ages, centuries, indictions, [the book says indictional centuries] years, months, days, and nights, and although they did not achieve the subdivision of the hours, they indicated the four seasons of dawn and midday, of evening and midnight.

They called the age Huehuetiliztli, which means old duration, and it consisted of two centuries. They called the century Xiumolpia or Xiuntlalpilli; both words meant tie, or bunch of years, and it consisted of four indictions, not of fifteen but rather of thirteen years that they called Tlalpilli, which means knot or tie. Each Tlalpilli being thirteen years long, the century was fifty- two years, and the age, one-hundred four.

They called the year Xihuitl, which, as has been said, means the new grass, and they divided it into eighteen months of twenty days, which together made up three-hundred sixty days, at the end of which they added five more days which they called Nemontemi, which means tragic or fatal, for the reason that I will tell later; and knowing that even with all this it did not equal the annual course of the sun, they invented the leap years, adding one day more every four years, which was counted among the Nemontemi or fatal days. They continued to count the days by thirteen on thirteen, according to their ancient method of new moons, but without adjusting to the appearance of the moon; rather, these periods of thirteen days served them as weeks, and so each year had twenty-eight weeks and one day, and the great exactness of their count lay in this extra day, which, in the revolution of one indiction, made up an entire week,.

All the skill of their calendars is founded on the continued repetition of four symbols, or hieroglyphs, that were not the same everywhere, although the system was one and the same. First I will give the explanation of the calendar as it was ordered and noted by those of the empire of Texcoco, the kingdom of Mexico and other neighboring kingdoms, and afterwards I will tell of the variation that existed in others.

The symbols that were used in the mentioned monarchies for numbering their years were these four: Tecpatl, which means the flint; Calli, the house; Tochtli, the rabbit; and Acatl, the reed cane, and they showed them in the way that is seen in the illustrations which follow.(1) The material meanings of the words are those mentioned, but the allegorical meanings that they wanted to explain in these symbols were the four elements that they knew to be main elements of every material compound and in which all had to be resolved.(2)

They gave supremacy to fire, considering it as the most noble of all, and they symbolized it in the flint, undoubtedly because even though fire results from the striking and rubbing of other rocks and even of a piece of wood with another, none gives it more easily than flint. In the later times of their idolatry and false religion, they celebrated this element by idolizing it as deity under the name of Xiuhteuctli. In other, simpler times they were satisfied to give it the first place among the four initial characters, which they made key of all their astronomical and chronological calculations.

In the hieroglyph of the house they wanted to signify the element of the earth, and they gave it the second place in the initial characters. In the time of idolatry they also idolized it as deity, celebrating it with various names and in different figures, especially that of their famous god Tlaloc, whom they said was the minister of the supreme Tezcatlipoca, a symbol of Divine Providence.

In the rabbit they symbolize the element of air, and the writers are very much in disagreement in giving the reason for having chosen this animal as a symbol of the wind. Some say that because of the sharpness of its sense of smell, others that because of its swiftness in running, others that because it announces the wind by coming out of their holes to frolic when there is to be air. The Gentleman Boturini, in his mentioned book, says that perhaps it is because the word Tochtli, which means the rabbit, was derived from the word Toca, which means the wind walking or running. I believe that he was mistaken in this, because Toca is not the same as Otoca. The words Otoca and Otlatoca mean to run; but Toca means only to bury, and for these meanings I turn to Friar Alonso de Molina in his celebrated and highly regarded ancient vocabulary, and undoubtedly the derivation of the word Tochtli from the word Toca for bury would be more natural and genuine, because the rabbit lives always buried in the underground caves, which it digs for its habitation. Finally, if I am allowed to guess the reason the Indians had to symbolize the wind in the rabbit, I would say that perhaps it was because in those primitive times they did not distinguish it from the hare, fast as the wind in its running, as many of the ancient naturalists symbolized them, having both species as just one, and thus Pliny the Second (Hist. Animal. book 8, chapter 25) says that "in Spain there is a species of hares that they call rabbits." Eliano (book 13 chapter 15) and Estrabón give them the same name, calling them "lepusculos" [Translator: Latin for little hares] because they are smaller than the hares. They also idolized as deity this element of the wind in the idolatrous time, with the name of Quetzalcohuatl, and they represented it in various ways, one of which was the sacred sign of the Holy Cross, for the reasons that I will give later on.

The fourth initial character, which is the reed cane, which is what the word Acatl properly means , is a hieroglyph of the element of water, and naturally so, because this plant is such a lover of water that reeds are regularly the sign of finding water. They also celebrated it afterwards among their deities with the name of Chalchiuhcueitl.

Footnotes, Chapter V
1st part

(1) [This footnote is from the book.] In the information about the author I already indicated that I have hopes of replacing these illustrations that are missing in the manuscript. – E.

(2) [This footnote is from the book.] Modern chemistry has rejected this theory of the four elements. The substances that are now considered such, because means to break them up have not been found, are no less than 54; but there is no chemist who asserts that they cannot be broken up; and therefore, and because of the rapid progress that science is making, it is very probable that each day the number of the elemental substances or bodies will increase. – E.

(3) [This footnote is from the book.] At the end of chapter 8 of this book. – E.

(Beginning of second section of Chapter 5, taken from Book)

And so they chose these four symbols to be the general key of all their astronomical calculations, and to order all their calendars with them. They would number the years with them, repeating them in the order that they are given, without ever admitting any variation or alteration, but varying the figure from one to thirteen, and thus they would indicate perfectly well and without equivocation all the years of a century. As we have said, they divided the century into four indictions or Triadecaterides, indicated with the four symbols mentioned, so that in every century the first indiction was indicated with the flint, the second with the house, the third with the rabbit, and the fourth with the reed. See the tables,(3) in which each column is one century of 52 years divided into four equal parts of thirteen years, that each one corresponds to one of the four symbols with which it starts and ends indicating the thirteen years of its indiction in this way. They started counting the thirteen years of the first indiction of the century, which had to be indicated with the first character of the flint, and they said this:

(End of Kingsborough excerpt)

(Beginning of second section of Chapter 5, taken from Book)

First year	One Flint
Second	Two Houses
Third	Three Rabbits
Fourth	Four Reeds
Fifth	Five Flints
Sixth	Six Houses
Seventh	Seven Rabbits
Eighth	Eight Reeds
Ninth	Nine Flints
Tenth	Ten Houses
Eleventh	Eleven Rabbits
Twelfth	Twelve Reeds
Thirteenth	Thirteen Flints

Here we see how the first indiction was indicated with the hieroglyph of the flint with which it begins, and it finishes showing its thirteen years, with only the number varying from one to thirteen. Once the first indiction was over, they counted the second one continuing on from the first, indicating it with the second hieroglyph, which is the house, and which by order is followed and counted like this:

First year	One House
Second	Two Rabbits
Third	Three Reeds
Fourth	Four Flints
Fifth	Five Houses
Sixth	Six Rabbits
Seventh	Seven Reeds
Eighth	Eight Flints
Ninth	Nine Houses
Tenth	Ten Rabbits
Eleventh	Eleven Reeds
Twelfth	Twelve Flints
Thirteenth	Thirteen Houses

Thus they would indicate the second indiction, which started and ended with the hieroglyphs of the house, with only the variation of the number from one to thirteen, and they continued counting the other two indictions in the same way, indicating them with the rabbit and reed hieroglyphs; and once the last indiction was completed, and with it the century, they started to count another one in the same order.

For this they would form their calendars of centuries in various figures: some in circles, like that of illustration number 1; others in a spiral, like that of illustration number 2; others in a square, like that of illustration number 3; representing, in this way of showing them, the permanent succession of the centuries one after another; and so they would put a snake around some, biting its own tail, as can be seen in illustration number 4, which is a calendar of the Mexican nation, which Gemelli Carreri brings (volume 6, page 65) in his trip or Vuelta al mundo [Return to the world], which was undoubtedly from Carlos de Siguenza, to denote that the end of one century was the beginning of another that had to run and stop in the same order as the one that ended.

The way of indicating the number was by putting some very thick dots, round like balls, in the box of each hieroglyph or over it, and thus they would write the number as seen on illustration number 3; so that in seeing the symbol of the flint, for example, with four dots, it is the year of four flints, which is the fourth year of the second indiction and the 17th year of the century. In seeing the house with eight dots on top of or underneath it, it is the year of eight houses, which is the eighth of the third indiction and the thirty-fourth year of the century, and so on with the rest. But generally they did not put these figures on the wheels or paintings that served them as calendars, because for the intelligent their order was sufficient to understand the number that corresponded to each hieroglyph. Not so on the historical charts and other writings, in which they would note the year in which the event or action in question occurred; and thus in these, above or below the hieroglyph of the year they would put the mentioned dots that served as numerical figures, and on some they would add the hieroglyph of the month and the day on which the event occurred in the same order. And we should note that they formed most of the ancient calendars, for the century as well as the year and months, in circles or squares, running from right to left, the way the orientals write, and not as we are accustomed to in forming similar figures, running from left to right, following the method in which we write. But they did not maintain this order in the figures that they would paint and use as a hieroglyph in them, but rather they would put some looking to one side and others to the other. They would go along indicating the centuries that went by and naming them according to the most particular public events that happened in them, such as plagues, wars, uprisings, and other similar events, and they would paint the hieroglyphs that portrayed these events in boxes that they would form and place in the upper part of their calendars, as seen in illustration number 1, where each box is equivalent to one century.

The gentleman Boturini, who worked very much in understanding and explaining this calendar, whom the public must have gotten out of the most obscure darkness, in which this precious remnant of ancient history lay, as the invention of so many exquisite and considerable monuments that he gathered at the expense of imponderable effort,[1] and to whom I confess I totally owe my first enlightenment and instruction of the main points of this History, told me on several occasions, and he confirms it in the work that I have quoted at folio 122, that they would indicate each century with one of these four characters: because with the first century beginning with the character Ce Tecpatl, the second begins with Ce Calli, the third with Ce Tochtli, and the fourth with Ce Acatl; and for this reason, with any character of these initial characters being placed in the history, four Indian centuries of fifty-two years each must pass, which makes two hundred eight years, before that character

71

can be found again in the future.

I already touched on this point in the second chapter, talking about the year in which, according to the calculations of the Indians, it is appropriate to establish the confusion of tongues in Babel, and now it is necessary for me to touch upon it again here, as well as in its own place. Because having ingenuously confessed the singular scholarliness of the gentleman Boturini, his instruction in this history at the cost of nine years of continuous work, walking a large part of New Spain with many inconveniences, and that I am not only indebted to him for the first enlightenment that I had of it, but also for most of the instruments that I have used for this work that he was planning to write, those who read it and compare it with his book will necessarily feel considerable discomfort with the explanation that I give, as it is different and discordant from the one that he promises. Therefore I feel compelled to satisfy this objection by sincerely declaring the reasons on which I am grounded.

I have labored in this work with considerable diligence, always revolving around the same principles that Boturini establishes, and I learned from him. I have used not only the very manuscripts and documents that he gathered, but also the same chronological tables that he had started in his own hand. However, I do not understand or grasp the calculation that he was figuring of this period of two hundred eight years, resulting from four centuries of fifty-two years each, indicated with the four initial characters in such a way that the first starts to count from Ce Tecpatl, one flint, the second from Ce Calli, one house, the third from Ce Tochtli, one rabbit, and the fourth from Ce Acatl, one reed, such that if one of these is found in this history indicating some era, it is necessary for two hundred eight years to go by to find it again in the tables.

Because I cannot understand anything else, either from the figures of their calendars or from the explanation that the Indian authors whose manuscripts he gathered made of them, other than the concept that every century started its first indiction with the hieroglyph of the flint in the first number and ended it with the same symbol in the number thirteen. The second started with the hieroglyph of the house in the first number and ended with the same one in the number thirteen. The third started with the hieroglyph of the rabbit in the first number and ended with the same one in the number thirteen, and the fourth started with the hieroglyph of the reed in the first number and ended with the same one in the number thirteen. And with one century thus being completed, counting was started in the following century in the same order without any difference, indicating the first year of the century with the flint in the first number, Ce Tecpatl, without ever finding that any century begins with Ce Calli, nor with Ce Tochtli nor with Ce Acatl, because in that case one of two things would be necessary: either completely omit the previous indiction or invert the order of the initial characters, and neither is admissible. Not the first, because with the first indiction omitted, the second century would no longer be fifty-two years long, but rather of thirty-nine, resulting from the three indictions of thirteen each. The third century, if the first two indictions were omitted, would be just twenty-six years long, and the fourth, just thirteen, with the three indictions omitted: and the period of two hundred eight years would always be adulterated..

The second is not admissible, because inverting the order of the symbols completely destroys the artifice of the wheels and squares formed with these figures and surrounded by the snake that bites its own tail to denote the invariable succession of the years, counted in the same order and indicated with the same hieroglyphs.

The flint was the first and main hieroglyph of these four, as a symbol of fire, esteemed among them as the most noble of the four elements; and thus having to count the age of the world from its creation, they indicated the year in which it was created with the symbol of the flint in the first number. This is so certain that all their histories unanimously establish it that way.

No less certain is the fact that all the ways they had to figure their centuries are reduced to three, as I have already said, which are the circle, the spiral, and the square, as is seen in illustrations number one, two, and three, and the latter was used very little, and no calendar will be found in any figure other than those mentioned. And the fact that these figures served to count not just one century, but all the centuries in the same successive order, is proven with evidence: first because, as demonstrated in illustration number one, over the calendar wheel they would place the past centuries in their boxes, from which some lines come down that come to stop at a point right where the years of the century should start being counted, which is shown on the wheel, and this means, as the interpreters explain, that each of these boxes represents a century and that it was counted in the same way that the wheel shows.

But even though it could be said that the figures of the circle and the square only served to count a century, so that if it was of the flint character, starting to count it with this symbol in the number one, or if it was of the house character, rotating the wheel or the square and starting to count with this hieroglyph in the first number, and so on with the other two, the rabbit and the reed; this was not so to indicate many successive centuries. This presumption[2] is evaporated by the second figure of the character, in which it is seen that indicating the first century, and counting its fifty-two years from the symbol of the flint at the first number to that of the reed at the number thirteen, which are the four indictions as I have explained them, each one indicated with one of the four hieroglyphs, it continues to indicate the following centuries in the same order. So all were counted in the same way, that is, starting with the symbol of the flint in the first number, and not as Boturini says, that each century starts to count its years with one of these four symbols successively.

Besides, the excellence of these calculations lies in the uniform and constant rotation of the four symbols, repeated successively in the same order, with the variation of numbers from one to thirteen, and all the authors without exception agree on this. In this uniformity lies the exactness of the calculation, and knowing exactly the year indicated in each century depends on this, and all this crumbles in Boturini's system, because by starting to count the second century, for example, with the house character in the number one, the second indication could in no way be omitted, because, as we have already seen, the centuries would not be fifty-two years long, which is the first thing that everyone uniformly agrees on. And so, in order to preserve the number of fifty-two years, it was necessary to invert the order of these symbols in the annual succession, because by ending the first century with a year indicated by the reed character, it is necessary to skip the flint to start the following century with the house, and thus the invariable order of these symbols is destroyed, along with the quantity of four on which they were based, as I have explained, and which Boturini likewise confirms in his mentioned work at folio 4.

Second, by indicating the first year of the second century with the symbol of the house in the first number, the first three indictions of the second century would end up exactly the same in the sign as the last three indictions of the first century; the first three of the third with the last three of the second; the first three of the fourth with the last three of the third; the first two of the third with the last two of the first, etc., which is a horrible confusion, with which it would be almost impossible to set the chronology of the events. To understand the strength of this reasoning it is necessary to understand the way they indicated it on their historical charts.

I have already said that the past centuries appeared in the way that is shown on illustration number 1. And so they would indicate the main event, which they would take as an era, such as a war, a plague, the founding of a town or something similar, and they would put in as many other century figures as centuries had passed since that era until the event that they were going to mention, which they would paint over the figure of the century in which it had happened, as is seen in the mentioned illustration, letter A, which is the founding of the town of Cohuacicamac. This wheel is a calendar of the Mexican nation, over which one of the natives, or someone who understood their calculations, tried to establish the years that had gone by since the founding of that town and of the other three that follow in the boxes indicated with the letters B, C, D, until the year 1654, in which the mentioned adjustment appears to have been made; and here one can see the way in which he does it. He sets the founding of Cohuacicamac in the year of two reeds, the character of which he puts above the figure with two thick dots, which in fact was, according to my tables, the year 1195 of the common era, as he notes with our numbers below the figure. In the following box indicated with the letter B he puts the founding of Apasco, one century later, in the year of the same character of two reeds, and therefore he does not repeat the sign of the year, which was in fact that of 1247, as he notes below in our numbers. He does the same thing in the following two boxes, each one of which means one century, indicating the founding of Tepayocan and Chapultepec in the years 1299 and 1351 respectively, which were indicated with the same hieroglyph of two reeds. Afterwards he counts another six centuries ending in the year of the same character, until the year 1663, which is shown on the wheel in the second box going to the right. Then he takes off the nine years that were lacking to reach the year 1654 in which the adjustment was made, as he notes in the margin, saying in their language axcan ypanxihuitl, 1654. So to indicate the year in which the event had occurred that they were taking as an era, they would figure it and put above, as this one does, or at the side, as seen in illustration number 4, or below, the symbol of the year with the dots that served them as a figure, as seen in the mentioned illustration, letter A, in which there is a bunch or bundle of reeds with two thick dots above the hieroglyph of the event that it denotes, which means that it was in the year of two reeds, and they continued indicating the centuries with respect to the sign of that first year that they were representing.

In this supposition, according to Boturini's system, it was extremely difficult to find out what year of ours it corresponded to; because if the century that is indicated was of the sign of the flint, it would be the second year of the third indiction of Tochtli and twenty-eighth year of the century; if this were of the sign of the house, the year would be the second of the second indiction and fifteenth year of the century; if this were the year of the sign of the rabbit, it would be the second year of the first indiction; and if it was of the sign of the reed, it would be the second year of the fourth indiction and year forty- one of the century; and for each one to know the character or hieroglyph of the century, it was necessary to form tables, at least from some fixed era of a known character, or for all these centuries to have some sign that would show the character with which they were indicated and started to count their years, and I have not been able to find this in any of the charts that I have become familiar with.

On the contrary, following the system that I conceive, it is known at the fixed point that the year it indicates at this point and which serves us as an example was the second year of the third indiction of Tochtli, and twenty-eighth of the century; and from there counting the nine centuries that it indicates of fifty-two years each, which make up four hundred sixty-eight years, I will say that four hundred sixty-eight years had gone by until the year of two reeds, where the lines of said centuries are going to expire on the wheel that this author formed for his guidance, probably of that century in which he was living. Consequently, it is known exactly that from the founding of Cohuacicamac to that of Chapultepec, which is the one that appears in box D, 156 years went by; and according to this author this was also in the year of two reeds, because over the main hieroglyph he does not put a character of years, and continuing the numbering of centuries, with the lines he comes to the year of two reeds on the wheel; from which we know that he is counting from one century to another from this sign.

It could be felt that Boturini was persuaded that way because of his having found many of these calendars that start the century with the symbol of the rabbit in the first number, if one didn't see that he explains this by attributing this custom to the Mexicans, of whom he says at folio 125: I finally report that the Toltecs put the character Ce Tecpatl at the head of their calendar; the Mexicans, Ce Tochtli; and it may be that some begin it with Ce Calli; and others with Ce Acatl; which has given rise to so much confusion among the Indians themselves. I will put all of them at peace in the General History, where the most notable eras and the common tables of those calendars will be given.

It is clear that the Mexicans started the numbering of the years of the century by the symbol of the rabbit, which is Tochtli, in the first number; but the cause of this is that their arrival to these regions was in a year of this character, and this era being so celebrated, therefore they took this symbol for the beginning of their century, because they would indicate the most notable events of their monarchy in relation to that very illustrious era of their first settlement in these parts, but not because in their antiquity they were any different from the Toltecs in the ordering and method of their calculations, because this invention of the Mexicans was not more ancient than the one mentioned; all this variety between the Toltecs and Mexicans did not consist of anything other than the fact that the Mexicans were starting to count the century when the Toltecs were already in the middle of it, and thus the first and second indiction of the century in the Mexican calendar were the third and fourth in the Toltec, and the third and fourth of the Mexican were the first and second of the following century in the Toltec calendar; but the years were the same, indicated with the same hieroglyphs and numbers, just as if among the nations of Europe someone wanted to start their year with the month of July because of some illustrious event that occurred in that month, in which case the first six months of the year in that nation would be the last six months among the rest, and the last six months of that year would be the first of the following year in the other nations; but the months would still be the same, that is, in January it would be January everywhere; in February, February, and in July, July; although in one nation January is at the first of the year, and in another, July is. In the same way, among Toltecs and Mexicans the year of the flint, the house, the rabbit, etc., would be the same, with the only difference that among the Mexicans the year of the rabbit was the first of their century, and among the Toltecs the year of the flint was the first.

The fact that the years preserved the same character and number from one to another is verified by all the monuments of this history, in calendar wheels as well as in historical charts, in which some authors interpreted those that the Toltecs made, others, those that the Mexicans painted, others, those of the Tlaxcaltecas and Huexutzincas, others those of the Tecpanecas, etc., and nevertheless, they precisely agree with each other in the hieroglyphs and numbers of the years, as we will see; for now, to illustrate this truth, I will just put an example here of each one.

Illustration number 4 is a calendar of the Mexican nation, and so the head and tail of the snake are joined together over the box holding the rabbit, which was the symbol with which they started their century, counting the first indiction from one to thirteen. Then the year of the reed followed in the same way, and so the center of the wheel shows the event that appears on the wheel, which is the coming of certain peoples to their kingdom, symbolized in one as a turban, which is the adornment of the kings, and three human footprints going to it, and below, the years of this movement are indicated; in front of the box of the reed next to the twist in the snake on the outside circumference is the same hieroglyph of the reed with a thick dot. This is followed by that of the flint, with two dots, and then the house, with three, which means that those people came to the kingdom in those three years of a reed, two flints, and three houses. Here we see how the Mexicans indicated the years of the century in the same way, in the same order, and with the same figure as the Texcocans, with no variation other than that of their making the first year of the century that which is the first year of the third indiction of the Texcocans.

With regard to the events of history, one of the most celebrated and unquestionable is the prediction that all these nations had that in a year that would be indicated with the hieroglyph of a reed, some white, bearded people would come to these lands from the east and would take possession of it. After they learned of the coming of the Spanish to San Juan de Ulua in the year 1519, the Mexicans, Texcocans, Tlaxcaltecas, and Huezutzincas, and finally, all of them, unanimously agreed that the time of the prophecy's fulfillment had arrived, because the year was indicated with the hieroglyph of a reed. This is such an obvious fact that since then it became public, and many of our historians mention it; and from it one is convinced with evidence that in spite

of the diversity of calendars among these nations, with regard to the hieroglyphs and numbering of the years in each century they perfectly agreed,
although some started the century with the sign of the flint and others with
that of the rabbit, and thus the only difference was that this year 3 was the first
year of the second indiction and fourteenth year of the century on the
Mexican calendar, and among the Texcocans it was the beginning of the
fourth indiction and the fourteenth year of the century.

From here another infallible proof is inferred against Boturini's
system: because let us suppose that the Mexicans started to count their
century with the symbol of a rabbit, which was the one that corresponded to
the first year of the third indiction of a Toltec century, indicated with the flint
character. In such a case the first and second indication of the Mexican
century would be indicated with the symbol of the rabbit and the reed, which
were the ones that corresponded to the last indictions of the Toltec century,
and the last two of the Mexican would be indicated with the two symbols of
the house and the rabbit, which were the symbols that should correspond to
the first two indictions of the following Toltec century, if the Toltec century
were to start to count its years with the second sign of the house; and here is
another abyss of confusions: because in the infallible supposition that we
have established to agree on the hieroglyphs and numbers, it would follow:
first, that the Mexicans inverted the order of these symbols, putting the house
after the reed, which shouldn't be, but rather the flint. Second, that this
Mexican century indicated the four indictions with just three hieroglyphs,
confusing the last with the first, both indicated with the symbol of the rabbit,
with the flint totally omitted. Over the centuries these confusions and absur-
dities would keep increasing, in such a way that it would be impossible to get
out of the chaos. And, what shall we say if the Mexicans were to go about alter-
nating these same symbols to indicate their centuries in the way of the
Toltecs, as it seems must be said in following Boturini's system? This is a difficulty so insurmountable that it is enough to destroy it. With everything, I am
not flattering myself on my good sense.

I would have liked to be able to propose these difficulties to Boturini to
hear his answers, and it may be that some mind superior to my limited one
can compose them. Meanwhile I am proposing what I understand, without
presumptions of censure, so that the reader may be instructed and take whatever side he likes. But I warn that in the tables that Boturini himself formed
with his own hand, which are the same ones that I have perfected and am
publishing, each column comprises one century of fifty-two years divided into
four triadecaterides of thirteen years, and each century starts its first year
with the hieroglyph of the flint in the first number. So every fifty-two years
this initial character is found, and consequently, what he asserts in the
mentioned folio 122 is contradicted, that "with one of these initial characters

put in the history, it is absolutely necessary that four Indian centuries of fifty-two years each go by before it can be found thereafter, and even though the same characters Ce Tecpatl, Ce Calli, Ce Tochtli, Ce Acactl are found in them, they are not pertinent, especially when the ancient histories paint the character of something notable to represent an era." I cannot conceive how, with the hieroglyph being one and the same without any variation either in its figure or in its number, one that was the head of a century could be distinguished from one that wasn't. Based on this system it has not been possible for me to work out any calculation or determine the time in which the events of this history have occurred. I have come up with them all through the system that I have explained and will continue to explain, correctly, as it seems to me, as we will see.

Footnotes to Chapter V
Second part

(1) The efforts of this antiquarian were indeed great to gather the Mexican monuments and manuscripts from which he formed his museum, and as his reward the viceroy of Mexico declared the most unjust persecution upon him. See the Government Journal of March 12 of this year, in which Mr. Carlos Bustamante gives a report of the illegalities committed with him, removed from the trial that was formed against him, and the original exists in the General Archives. In consideration of those who cannot consult it, here I will extract the essential elements.

Boturini came to Mexico for the purpose of collecting 1,000 pesos annually at the Royal Treasury, money the King of Spain granted to Lady Manuela de Oca, Silva y Moctezuma, countess of Santibañez. As this errand left him much free time, he dedicated himself to investigating the evidence of the appearance of the Virgin of Guadalupe that would be contemporary to the event. He was a great devotee of hers, and so for this purpose he traveled through many provinces, sleeping, as he asserts, in huts of miserable Indians, perhaps forewarned of nighttime on the roads, and suffering imponderable labors. Because of these investigations he came to gather so many ancient documents, charts, and paintings that he conceived the idea of writing a general history of Mexico. In consideration of his devotion he requested an obtained from the Council of St. Peter of Rome a commission to crown the Holy Virgin in that city with a crown of gold, as was the custom in Italy. Having presented that commission to the Accord, and having obtained the pass, Boturini started to collect contributions for the creation of the crown; and when he was the most involved in his project, the Viceroy Count of Fuenclara arrived, and from Jalapa he ordered that the dispatches that Boturini had printed and circulated for the collection of the contributions be gathered up, and that a trial be formed for him, which was in fact formed. Among various charges that were made against him, the main ones were that of having proceeded to this questorship, having offered to do the coronation at his expense, and having carried it out after he was denied permission by Archbishop Viceroy Juan Antonio Bizarron, because the commission had not been passed from the Council of Rome through the Council of the Indies, as required by law 2, title 21, book 1 of its Compendium, which could not be derogated by the pass from the Accord of Mexico. Boturini gave various arguments in his own behalf, but this did not free him from being imprisoned, as the prosecutor requested, and having all of his papers seized, including the manuscripts, charts, and paintings that made up his museum, the index of which the reader can see in his Idea de una Nueva Historia de la America Septentrional [Idea of a New History of North America]. The prison was later reduced in size, putting him in a small, dark cell, where he survived on alms; and finally, and in spite of the report that was given in his favor by the judge who knew of his cause, Judge Valcarcel, apologizing for his proceedings and attributing them to an indiscrete devotion and to an imprudent zeal, he was sent off to Spain by the Viceroy under a registration certificate. There he was set at liberty: but he never succeeded in having his museum restored to him. — E.

(2) It seems that it should say supposition; but in the two manuscripts that have been consulted, presumption is read. — E.

(3) Namely, Ce Acatl, a reed. — E

CHAPTER VI

Of the year and its months.

They divided the year into eighteen months of twenty days each, which in all made three hundred sixty days, at the end of which they would add another five days in a regular year and six in a leap year, which days were not included in any month, and these they called Nemontemi, which, as said, means ominous days.[1] Each of the months had its name, although these were not the same, not only throughout New Spain, but not even in the area of the kingdoms of Texcoco and Mexico, for in the various ancient calendars that I have gathered I find variations of some names, which I will tell about later. For this reason, and because they all allude either to their festivals, rites, and worship of their false deities, all of which started in later times, or to the observations of the seasons of the year, of the decrease of the waters, ripeness of the fruits, and similar things, which are not at the same time in all the countries of this new world, it cannot be known what the primitive names were that their wise men gave to them on the occasion when they made the correction of their calendar that we are discussing. And so that this can be seen more clearly, here I will put the names of the months that are found on one of the ancient Mexican charts that I have in my possession, from which illustration number 5 is copied, which is a calendar of one single regular year in which the eighteen months are indicated, with the hieroglyphs that explain their names, and at the end of them the five days that they added before starting to count another year. The names of the months, then, are the following:

1	Atemoztli.	Decrease of the waters.
2	Tititl.	Our mother.
3	Itzcalli.	The grass sprouting.
4	Xilomaniztli.	Offering of ears of corn.
5	Cohauilhuitl.	Festival of the snake.
6	Tozcotzintli.	Small fast.
7	Hueytozcoztli.	Big fast.
8	Toxcatl.	That interpret effort.
9	Exolqualiztli.	Meal of green beans.
10	Tecuilhuitzintli.	Festival of the young gentleman.

11	Hueytecuilhuitl.[2]	Festival of the greater lords.
12	Micailhuitzintli.	Festival of the dead children.
13	Hueymicailhuitl.	Festival of the dead adults.
14	Huepaniztli.	Sweeping time.
15	Pachtzintli.	Festival of the small Pachtli.
16	Hueypachtli.	Festival of the big Pachtli.
17	Quecholli.	Festival of the peacock.
18	Panquetzaliztli.	Flags or banners of feathers.

The five globes that they would show in the last box meant the five days that were added in each year that was not a leap year, which were not included in any month.

These are the most common and general names that they gave to the months of the year, and their meanings, although in the month of Atemoztli, which I have put for the first of the year, they varied in their tradition. Boturini, following some of the authors whose writings he gathered, interprets it as Altar of the gods; and a manuscript I have of Fernando de Alba, which Boturini was undoubtedly instructed in, says that the name is taken from a festival that they made to Tlaloc, god of the rains, and although he does not deduce the etymology, it seems that the word Atemoztli is made up of the three words Atl, which means water, Teotl, which means god, and Moztli or Momoztli, stone or altar of sacrifice. Others interpret the word Atemoztli as decrease of the waters, making it a compound of Atl, which means water, and Temoztli, a participle of the verb Temo, which means to lower or to decrease, and this version seems more natural to me because in no vocabulary, nor in the common use of speech, have I found anyone who says that Moztli or Momoztli means stone or altar of sacrifice. Nevertheless, I confess that the hieroglyph with which they showed it was one of these altars, as seen in illustration number 5. But this does not persuade me that the name means it, but rather that they put it there because of the festival that they made to the god Tlaloc in this month; but the name of the month related to the season of time, in which, because it corresponded to our month of February, they were more aware of and familiar with the decrease of the waters in the rivers, lagoons, and ponds in which they fished: and so I have followed this translation rather than the other one, because as will be seen with other months, although they had other names because of the festivals, they kept the name that corresponded to its season, such as Zilomaniztli, Xocotlhuetzi, which they gave to other months as I am going to say, because in some parts they varied and some months were known by different names in this way.

The fourth month, which we have called Xilomaniztli, or offering of tender corn, the Mexicans called Atlacahualo, which means leave the water, and it was a phrase to explain that the fishing was over. In other places they called this month Quahuitlehua, which is interpreted as plantings of tree cuttings, or time when the trees sprouted: but I have not been able to find out where they get this etymology from. Others write Quahuitlehuac, and interpret it as tall tree: I don't know where they get that from either, nor what they mean by it. The true meaning of the word Quahuitlehuac is burning of the trees or of the mountains, because it is made up of the word Quahuitl, which means the tree and figuratively the mountain, and of the word Tlehua, which means to burn or to put fire to something; because in the mountainous site and locations they would clear the lands to do their general planting of seeds at that time.

The fifth month, which we have called Cohuailhuitl or festival of the snake, the Mexicans also called Tlaxipehualiztli, which means skinning, because of a cruel festival that was celebrated by skinning many captives.

The sixth month we have called Tozcotzintli, which they interpret small fast, and the seventh, Hueytocoztli, which they interpret big fast. Some authorities call the sixth month Totzotzontli, and the seventh, Hueytotzotzontli, but they give them the same meanings of small and big fast. Others call them Toztli and Hueytozontli and translate these words sting of veins or small bleeding and big bleeding, because in these months the thighs, chins, arms, and ears were pierced for penitence and mortification, accompanied by fasting, in observance of the god Centeotl, who was the God of the corn.

The twelfth month, which we have named Micailhuitzintli, or festival of the dead children, they also called Tlaxochimaco, which means mat of flowers, by allusion to another festival that they held in honor of the God of war.

The thirteenth month, which we have called Hueymicailhuitl, or festival of the dead adults, they also called Xocotlhuetzi, which means ripeness of the fruits, because this month coincided with our October, which is the time when the corn ripens in these countries.

The fifteenth, which we have called Pachtzintli, or festival of the small Pachtli, they also called Teotleco, which means return or rise of the Gods, because they pretended that they had been out of the city the month before, as we will discuss when we talk about their superstitions and rites.

The sixteenth month, which we have called Hueypachtli, or festival of the big Pachtli, they also called Tepeilhuitl, which means festival of the mountains. I have always found all the other months with just the names that I have indicated for them, without the least variation throughout the whole collection of lists and ancient and modern wheels that I have become familiar with.

At folio 49 Boturini puts the catalog of these names, taken from the work of Father Martin de Leon in his book entitled El camino del cielo [the road of heaven], and at folio 50 he puts the catalog brought by Gemelli Carreri in his Giro del mundo [Tour of the world], volume 6, chapter 5, page 64, because, as he has confessed in the prologue of this work, he found himself without the materials that he had gathered to write it, and they had been seized from him in Mexico, and even without some notes that he was carrying with him and lost on the trip, and so he wrote from memory. But not being able to preserve in memory the names of the months, he uses two other catalogs that he found printed in these authors, in which Father Leon starts counting the year with the month Atlcahualo, and Gemelli, at Tlaxipehualiztli, because, as Boturini himself asserts at folio 47, a considerable variety is found among the Indian authors as well as among the Spanish in counting the months and assigning which was the first among them: because as all their annual calendars were in a circle, and they did not indicate the intercalary days, at least in the ancient ones that I have seen, it is not easy to find out which months they began with, and each one has made his own lists, beginning with the one that seemed best to him, as happens with the symbols of the days, of which I will speak later.

Although it does not oppose the sure number of the months or substantially confuse their system, this variety alters the time of the sacrifices, ceremonies, and many events of history. This is not all, because to write it indicating the eras of the events with the greatest possible precision it is necessary to expend a great labor in reconciling their variety to compare not just their years with ours, but some months and days with others. For this, in so much obscurity and confusion, after becoming familiar in great detail and over time with all the lists, catalogues, and calendars, ancient and modern, and all the manuscripts that have come into my hands that can instruct me in the matter, I have chosen the one that I have put down and from which illustration number 5 was copied, just as I found it among Boturini's papers, in which the intercalary days are noted after the last month, because it is the one that is most adapted to the natural order of the meaning of the names of the months, and the symbols in which they wrote them down, taken either from the actions that they would perform in them or from the effects of the time in which they fell: which does not happen in the one of Father Leon, putting Atlcahualo as the first month, which he interprets as stopping of the waters. I do not know what he would mean with this expression; for if it is the rains being suspended, it does not occur in these countries except around the end of October, and there is no one who says that the year begins with this month. What Atlcahualo means is to leave the water because it is made up of the word Atl, which means the water, and the word Cahua, which means to leave; and thus it literally means leaving of the water, because, as I have said, they stopped fishing, and therefore it is a mistake to indicate it as the first month of the year; that although there is a great variety among the national authors in assigning a certain fixed day of our days on which they started to count the days of their year, because some say on February 2nd, others on the 10th, others on 26th, 27th, or 28th of February, others in March, indicating various days, and one or another goes up to April 10th, I have not found anyone who goes beyond that, and this was not the time when they would leave fishing (nor do they today), but rather in May, because that is the month when it starts to rain very often in these countries, and the dirty and unsettled water starts to enter the lagoons, and the rivers grow and prevent the people from fishing. Besides, they couldn't give it the other name that they give it of Xilomaniztli, which means offering of tender corn, because in February there is no corn, and in May there is, for it is normal for a few small waters to fall at the beginning of February, and with this juice they would sow and still sow some corn in the lands that are not very cold, which today they call Candlemas corn, and with the first ears or tender cobs that are gathered in May they would make this offering as of first fruits.

The month Itzcalli, which means the sprouting of the grass, they indicate as the last month, which corresponds to January; and in this month there is just frost and cold, which do not give place for the grass to sprout. The grass starts to appear in April, and thus with the year beginning in February, Itzcalli was the third month, which corresponds to April.

He calls the sixth month Etzalqualiztli, which he interprets as meal of green beans, and it is an obvious error, because Etzalqualiztli means meal of certain corn porridges that they call Etzali. The other name that they gave to it, and with which I have indicated it, which is Exolqualiztli, does not mean meal of texocotl [Mexican hawthorn] either, but rather meal of exotl, which the Spanish, hispanicizing the word, call ejotes [green beans], and they are the tender pods of the frijoles or beans, which in Spain we call green beans; and even though today this could take place not just in the sixth month, which corresponds to July, but in almost all the months of the year, this is because they have been diligent in the cultivation of the seeds in these recent times, and with the mildness of the climate and abundance of water, today they plant it in the gardens during all the months to have this dish all year. But the general plantings of this bean, of which they raise very numerous harvests, because it is one of the seeds of greatest consumption in this kingdom, are not done until the end of June or beginning of July, and the crops are harvested at the end of October or beginning of November, and so they are in the pods in the season of being eaten while tender from the middle of September or middle of October, which corresponds to the ninth month. And if Exolqualiztli were a meal of texocotl, as he translates, it was more exemplary still, because the texocotl are a fruit similar to the haw of Spain, and the earliest that are seen are around November, but they are not tender until they are well chilled; but around July they are never seen because it is the time when these trees start to flower.

The name Tecuilhuitzintli, which he puts in the seventh place, he translates small festival of the Lord, and it isn't that, but rather festival of the young gentlemen, because it is made up of the words Tecuhtli, which means gentleman2, Ilhuitl, which means festival, and Tzintli, which is a reverential and diminutive term that refers to the Tecuhtli; and thus it means festival of the little gentlemen or of the young gentlemen.3

The following month, which they call Hueytecuilhuitl, he translates festival of the great Lord, and it is not that, but rather festival of the great lords, or of the old gentlemen, because Huey means big, and Tecuilhuitl, of the gentlemen; and if the Huey, great, isn't meant to apply to the gentlemen, but rather to the festival, it will mean great festival of the gentleman.

Gemelli's catalogues, which he puts at folio 50, is taken from the illustration that this author brings in the place that I have mentioned, which is undoubtedly a copy of some ancient calendar of the Indians that came from Carlos de Siguenza, and the same one that I give in this work indicated with the number 4, having corrected the errors that Gemelli's has. In it, a century of 52 years is described, and the progression of many others that can be counted upon it in the same order, and in another smaller circle that it has in the center, the eighteen months of each year are described with their own hieroglyphs. In Gemelli's copy, some are inverted and the names are dislocated, and they are obviously indicated with our common numbers from one to eighteen, beginning with Tlaxipehualiztli; but he does not admit any doubt that these were put there in later times, and not in the times of the Gentilism of the Indians, who never knew about the Arabic numbers that we use; and so this does not prove that Tlaxipehualiztli was the first month of the year among them, but rather that the person who copied it held this opinion and added the numbers. Nor does it prove that Carlos de Siguenza was of this opinion: but I have positive foundations to persuade me that he held the same opinion that I assert, because most of my calculations, as we will see throughout this work, agree with those of Siguenza, which could not happen if he held the opinion that Tlaxipehualiztli was the first month, which I establish as the fifth; because these one hundred days of difference would be obvious in the comparison of the eras, as happened in those of Fernando de Alba, who constantly asserts Tlaxipehualiztli as the first month of the year in his narrations. In each narration this author varies in his calculations, perhaps because of not having formed tables, and he falls into a thousand anachronisms, which, although they do not destroy the truth of the events, nevertheless detract from their harmony. And with the same obstacles being found in this opinion of Gemelli's catalog, with little difference from that of Father Leon, because of the symbols and meaning of the names of the months not agreeing with the season to which they correspond, I could not adapt to it, and I took the one that I have here established for the reasons that I have expressed.

Father Torquemada[4] also puts Atlcahualo as the first month of the year, and asserts that it began in February.[5] To overcome the difficulty that arises and that we have discussed in the other two names that they would give to this month and its meanings, which are Quahuitlehua and Xilomaniztli, he interprets the first, saying that it means the sprouting of the plants, because at that time, once the cold and frost have passed, the spring starts. This interpretation is entirely arbitrary, because the word in no way means that. Besides this, it is obvious that the cold is not lacking even in February in this country, nor do the trees start to sprout[6] nor does spring come until the middle of the following month.

To the other name Xilomaniztli that they gave to this month, he cannot escape applying his own meaning to it of offering of ears of corn, which is the tender corn; but he says "that this was not because they offered it then, as some have meant, because even then there are no sown fields, as everyone knows, and it is well known throughout all this land; but rather because in this province of Tlaxcala sowing is started in the highlands around this month of February, which was the first of their year; and in thanksgiving for having let the time come to be able to sow the fields of their sustenance they had to make this offering of the grain of the corn, which they kept on the cob and called (as I have heard many times), Xilotzintli." I have copied his words, because they themselves show the futility of the solution to the difficulty, and at the same time they prove my assertion that they started their year in the month of February and in it they did their first plantings of early corn; but not that Xilomaniztli was the first month, nor that by saying its very name offering of tender corn one is to understand hard corn because they kept it on the cob, nor to believe by conjecture that they had to do it in thanksgiving for the sowing time to have arrived, but because Xilomaniztli was not the first month, but rather the fourth, and fell in our May, in which there already was, as today, tender corn of that which is sown in February. Nor does the word Xilozintli, which he said he had heard to name the ears of corn, prove anything, because what this means is corn on the cob, but not offering of corn. Finally, not satisfied himself with his solution, he concludes the paragraph with these words: "Whether it is the one or the other, they call this their first month in the manner said." He would have come out of all the difficulty by following the opinion that I follow of those who put Atemoztli as the first month of their year.[7]

Footnotes, Chapter VI

(1) The Bishop Granados in his American Afternoons wants Nemontemi to be the name that they gave to the year; but this is an error, and all the historians of Mexico give it the meaning that our author gives it. It

seemed appropriate to mention it here, so that the mentioned work, which is out in everyone's hands, can be read with caution. — E.

(2) In the manuscript of the Museum it reads Hueymicailhuitl; and the copyist did not notice that the thirteenth month has this same name. — E.

(3) [Translator's note: The word caballero, translated here as gentleman, also means horseman in Spanish.] With horses not being known here at that time, it is clear that the author takes the word caballero in the sense of noble or person of distinction, in which it was used very much in his time; and although it is falling into disuse among us, we still say, in referring to an individual who is well born or has noble qualities, He is a "caballero." — E.

(4) Volume 2, book 10, chapter 34.

(5) Clavijero follows the same opinion, and he calls it Atlacahualco.

(6) This is not always so, at least in Mexico. Precisely in this year of 1836 the trees of the Alameda [poplar grove or poplar-lined promenade] started to sprout in the month of February. It is true that in this place they are cultivated diligently; and as the author's negative statement must refer to the general rule, this prevails, in spite of there being some exceptions. — E.

(7) See the Abbot Clavijero, pages 416, 417, and 418 of the Spanish translation. — E.

CHAPTER VII

Continuation of the material from the previous chapter.

Regarding the meaning of the names of the months, it is known that at least not all the names are or can be the original, primitive names that were given to them, or the names were not given to the months on the occasion when the correction of the times was done; for at that time there is no information in all the ancient monuments that I have become familiar with that they worshiped any divinity other than the Creator God, whom they called Tloque Nahuaque, nor that there were human sacrifices, nor skinning of people, nor offerings of fruits, nor did they know the fast; because all their worship and rites arose many years later, in the same way and by the same steps that ignorance introduced idolatry throughout the world, disrupting the true meaning of the hieroglyphs and converting them into deities.

Each one of these months consisted of twenty days, and each day also had its name, but arranged in such a way that the twenty names were contained in four groups of five each, characterized with the four main hieroglyphs Flint, House, Rabbit, and Reed, and of the five that each group contained, the one characteristic of it went first. See illustration number 6, which is a copy of one of the charts that I have, the one which I have indicated with the letters A, B, C, and D outside the last circle for easier understanding. In it the hieroglyphs are seen with which they indicated the twenty days of each month, all divided into the four groups, from A to B of the flint, from B to C of the house, from C to D of the rabbit, and from D to A of the reed. The names of these twenty days were these:

1. Tecpatl.	Flint.
2. Quiahuitl.	Rain.
3. Xochitl.	Flower.
4. Cipactli.	Snake of knives.
5. Checatl.[1]	Wind.
6. Calli.	House.
7. Cuetzpallin.	Lizard.
8. Cohuatl.	Snake.
9. Micuitl.[2]	Death.

89

10. Mazatl.	Deer.
11. Tochtli.	Rabbit.
12. Atl.	Water.
13. Itzcuintli.	Dog.
14. Ozomatli.	Monkey.
15. Malinalli.	Twisting.
16. Acatl.	Reed.
17. Ocelotl.	Tiger.
18. Quauhtli.	Eagle.
19. Cozcaquahtli.	Owl.
20. Ollin.	Movement.

Nor am I persuaded that these are the original names that were given to the days of the month at the time the correction was made, although some authors assert that they were hieroglyphs of as many fixed stars that they came to calculate, after having gotten to know and understand the movement and revolution of the six wandering planets,3 in which they placed various gods and demigods, the interpretation of which Boturini offered to do in his mentioned work to the satisfaction of the learned. I confess with naivety that I have not been able to find any document that instructs me on the subject to be able to do it; and with everything, even if I could do it as he promised, I would never believe that this was a work of these times; in which they did not worship gods or demigods, and it may be that at that time they did not even give any name at all to the days, being content to divide them into the four groups of five indicated with the four main symbols, as has been said.

I find all the monuments that I have become familiar with and all the calendars used by the inhabitants of these kingdoms which I am discussing to be in agreement with this list of the names of the days of the months, except the next to the last, which I have put as Cozcaquauhtli, which varies and has been replaced with Temeztlatl, which means corn-grinding stone; and not only do I find the same names on all of them, but also placed in the same order, although in the meanings of some there is some variation, such as in Tecpatl, which they translate as knife or arrow. In fact, on some wheels they paint it with these figures, because both the knife and the arrow were carved from flint, which is what Tecpatl4 means.

They translate Cipactli as Espadarte [Translator's note: possibly Espadante, or swordfish, in the original manuscript], which is a type of wide and long fish, similar to the sturgeon, and in fact it is also found on some wheels painted with this figure. Boturini interprets it as the first father.

Malinalli is translated by some as broom, because to show it they would paint two twisted cords, which on some charts look like a broom; but the meaning of the word is twisting, and it comes from the verb malina, which

90

means to twist.[5]

They interpret Ollin as weather or climate, and Boturini, in his mentioned work, section 7, folio 45, writes it as Ollin Tonatiuh and interprets it as movement of the sun, which is in reality what it means, but in none of the many wheels that I have seen and that I have in my hands have I found the word Tonatiuh added, but just Ollin, which means movement, and that is how I have translated it.[6] In the rest I have not found any variation in the meanings.

What there is considerable variation in is in the beginning of the lists of these names which are not in a circle or wheel, because some start with Cipactli, others with Cuetzpallin, others with Ocelotl, etc. This has arisen from the fact that those who copied these names from the wheels did not come to understand the artifice of the wheels in the ordering of their calculations and use of their weeks, as we will later see, and for that reason some have said that they counted their weeks of five days each, because of seeing the division of the twenty days into the four groups indicated with the four main hieroglyphs. Thus Torquemada calls them 7 quintanas, because he did not come to understand the artifice of what we are here calling weeks, even though he knew that they counted the years and the days of the months by thirteen on thirteen; and although these periods cannot properly be given the name of week or septimana because they were not seven days long, they were what they had in the place of our weeks. The ordering of the twenty days of the month in this way was to precisely continue their count in the succession of the years, because these twenty names always kept the same successive order, not only within the same year, but also in the progression and transition from one to another with particular harmony, but they were not always counted in the same way.

If the year was of the character Tecpatl, the first day of each month was indicated with this character, and they continued noting the rest of the days with the following hieroglyphs in the order in which I have put them; so that the twentieth day of each month was Olli [Ollin?]: see the wheel on the mentioned illustration number 6 and start counting from the letter A. If the year was of the second hieroglyph Calli, they started to count from this character, and all the first days of each month were given this name, and they continued noting the remaining days with the following hieroglyphs until ending at Checatl: see the wheel and start to count from the letter B. If the year was of the third character Tochtli, they started counting the days from this character and ended at Mazatl: see the wheel counting from the letter C. And if it was the year of the fourth character Acatl, they started to count the days of their months from this character until ending in Malinalli: see the wheel counting from the letter D. In the eighth chapter I am putting in a table in four columns, which clearly shows the order that they followed in the placement of the twenty days of each month, according to the character of the year and the intercalary days for the transition from one year to another, without varying the order and repetition of the hieroglyphs.

Once the eighteen months of the year were over, it was necessary to add another five days in a common year, and six in the leap year, to complete it. They did so, and the five days that they added in the common year they indicated with the five names that followed in order, so that in the supposition of being the year of Tecpatl, it has already been said that all the first days of the month were given the name of Tecpatl, and they continued counting the twenty, which ended in Ollin: and so, once the last month was over, they would indicate the five intercalary days with the five names that followed in order, and they were these:

Tecpatl.
Quiahuitl.
Xochitl.
Cipactli.
Checatl.

With this, in the following year, which they had to indicate with the second main hieroglyph, which is Calli, they started from this character to count the days of their months, because that is the one that followed in order on the list of the days; so that all the first days of each month were called Calli, and all the twentieth days Checatl, as has been said, and once the eighteen months were over they would count their intercalary days with the hieroglyphs that followed in order and which are these:

Calli
Cuetzpallin.
Cohuatl.
Micuiztli.
Mazatl.

And so in the third year, which should be indicated with the hieroglyph Tochtli, they started with it to count the days of their months, because it was the one that followed in order on the list of the days, ending them at Mazatl, and at the end of the last one they would count their five intercalary days with the names that followed in order, which are these:

Tochtli.
Atl.
Itzcuintli.

Ozomatli.
Malinalli.

Then the fourth year, which should be noted with the fourth main hieroglyph, started the day of the month with it, and the month ended in Malinalli, and so on, without interrupting the order of their days or of their years, according to their calculations; and thus as the first days of each month were indicated with the initial character that the year had, so also were the five intercalary days that corresponded to it: so that in the year of Tecpatl, this was the initial character of the five intercalary days, and in the year of Calli it was Calli, and so on in the other two.

In the fourth year, which was indicated with the character Acatl, they did leap year and added six days, as has been said (and afterwards I will explain the way in which they did it), of which they would indicate the five with the five hieroglyphs that followed in order, and the sixth and last, with the same sign as the fourth, but varying the number as corresponded to the day of the week. To understand the way in which they did this it is necessary to first explain the system they followed in the count of their weeks, their formation and successive order.

Footnotes, Chapter VII

(1) The Abbot Clavijero writes Ehecatl. — E.

(2) This is undoubtedly an error of the copyists, because later on both manuscripts read Micuiztli, and Clavijero writes it that way. — E.

(3) Astronomers today know about eleven planets; Uranus being discovered in modern times, announced in 1781 by Herschell, whose name is customarily given, Ceres by Piazzi in 1801, Palas by Olbers in 1802, Juno by Harding in 1803, and Vesta by Olbers in 1807. — E.

(4) See Clavijero, volume 1, page 419 of the Spanish translation. — E.

(5) Clavijero, in the mentioned place, says that Malinalli is the name of a plant, but he does not say what plant it is. — E.

(6) Clavijero also writes Ollin Tonatiuh. — E.

(7) Volume 2, book 10, chapter 36.

CHAPTER VIII

Of the weeks and their days.

The word semana [week in Spanish] comes from the Latin septimana, which means a period of seven mornings or seven days. In this rigorous sense it is certain that the Indians did not have weeks, but they did have a period equivalent to them in the use of the calendar. This was that of thirteen days, preserving the ancient memory of their new moons in this number, as I have said in Chapter III, although they did not keep the same order that they had then of counting them, from the appearance of the moon. These days of their weeks did not have a particular name, but rather, just as among us, on the ecclesiastical calendar all the days are called holidays, and we just distinguish them by the numbers with which we count them as second, third, fourth, in the same way they counted the days of the weeks from one until thirteen, and they added the number of the day of the week to the name of the day of the corresponding month; so that in the supposition that it was the year of the first sign or character of the flint, it has already been said that all the months had to start to count their twenty days by this name until ending in Ollin, movement. Let us now suppose that the first day of the first month was also the first of their weeks, as it in fact was in the first year of each century, and in such a case they would say it like this:

1 day.Ce Tecpatl.	1	Flint.
2 days.Ome Quiahuitl.	2	Rains.
3 days.Yey Xochitl.	3	Flowers.
4 days.Nahui Cipactli.	4	Snakes.
5 days.Macuili Checatl.	5	Winds.
6 days.Chicuazen Calli.	6	Houses.
7 days.Chicome Cuetzpalin.	7	Lizards.
8 days.Chicuey Cohuatl.	8	Snakes.
9 days.Chiuhnahui Micuiztli.	9	Deaths.
10 days.Matlatli Mazatl.	10	Deer.
11 days.Matlatlionce Tochtli.	11	Rabbits.
12 days.Matlatliomome Atl.	12	Waters.
13 days.Matlatliomey Iztcuintli.	13	Dogs.

With this the week was now complete in its thirteen days; and even though seven more days are needed to complete the month, they did not continue adding the figure, but rather they started over to count the days of the week from the number one, joining the number to the names of the following days of the month in this manner.

14 days.Ce Ozomatli.	1	Monkey.
15 days.Ome Malimalli.	2	Twistings.
16 days.Yey Acatl.	3	Reeds.
17 days.Nahui Ocelotl.	4	Tigers.
18 days.Macuili Quauhtli.	5	Eagles.
19 days.Chicuazen Cozcaquautli.	6	Owls.
20 days.Chicome Ollin.	7	Movements.

In this way the month was completed, having gone through all twenty hieroglyphs in the twenty days of the month, and they would start the second month by counting from Tecpatl again, which we suppose was the character of the year, joining this and the others to the numbers of the days of the week that followed; and thus in the supposition that we are doing, they started counting their second month from the eighth day of the week, with respect to which the last day of the previous month is the seventh, and this is what they called them:

1 day.Chicuey Tecpatl.	8	Flints.
2 days.Chiuhnahui Quiahuitl.	9	Rains.
3 days.Matlatli Xochitl.	10	Flowers.
4 days.Matlatlionce Cipactli.	11	Snakes.
5 days.Matlatliomome Checatl.	12	Winds.
6 days.Matlatliomey Calli.	13	Houses.

Having finished the week this way, they started to count another week from the first number to the number thirteen, joining them to the names of the days of the following month, and so on, so that even though all the months started to count their days with the flint character in the year of this sign, the number added to it varied continually, according to the day of the week that it corresponded to; because in the first month, in the supposition that we are making of its being the first year of the century, the first day would be Ce Tecpatl, one flint; in the second it would be Chicuey Tecpatl, eight flints; in the third, Ome Tecpatl, two flints; and thus the number varied according to the day of the week, but this did not keep the first of the month from being indicated with the flint.

We have already established in the previous chapter that the regular year had three hundred sixty-five days, and the leap year, three hundred sixty-six days. The regular year consisted of twenty-eight weeks and one day, and the leap year, the same twenty-eight weeks and two days. If it weren't a leap year, the thirteen remaining days in the thirteen years of each indiction or triadecateride would make up a full week, and the thirteen years of each indiction would make up three hundred sixty-five full weeks; and thus each indiction would start to count the first day of its first year on the first of the week. But this did not happen except in the first indiction of each century, which always started counting the days of its first month by its main character of the flint at the first number because it was the first day of the week. The second year, with the house character, started counting by it at the number two because of the day that was left over in the previous year, its twenty-eight weeks being complete, and it was the first day of the subsequent week. With this the third year, with the rabbit character, started counting its days with the character at the number three of the week, because of the two that were left over from the two previous years; and in the same way the fourth year, with the reed character, started counting its days by it at the number four of the week, because of the three remaining days of the previous years.

At the end of the fourth year of the reed character they did a leap year; and thus once its twenty-eight weeks were complete, two days remained, which, along with the three remaining days from the three previous years, made up five days of another week; and thus the following year, with the flint character, started to count its days by the number six, which was the number that corresponded to the week, and they continued counting in this same order until the end of the first indiction, which in its thirteen years comprised three hundred sixty-five weeks and three days, because of the days that they had added in the three leap years that they had had in the three years of the reed sign. These three days were counted in their order and without variation, joined to the hieroglyph of the last three intercalary days as the first, second, and third days of another week; and thus the first year of the second indiction, indicated with the house symbol, started counting from it the days of its first month, but at the number four, which was the number that corresponded to the week.

Once the second indiction was complete, and in it its three hundred sixty-five weeks, another three days remained, corresponding to the three leap years that it included, which, along with the three of the first indiction, were six days of another week, and thus the third indiction of the rabbit character started counting its days with it, but at the number seven, which was the number that corresponded to the week. At the end of this third indiction another three days were left over, corresponding to the three leap years that the indiction includes, and along with the six previous remaining years, they make up nine days of another week; and thus the fourth indiction, with the reed character, started counting its days with it, but at the number ten, which was the number that corresponded to the week.

The fourth indiction included four leap years in the four years of the mentioned reed character that are found in the indiction, and thus at the end of it, the three hundred sixty-five weeks being complete, four days were left over, which, along with the nine left over from the previous indictions, make up thirteen days, which is a full week; and thus the last day of the year, the last year of this indiction, which was also the last of the century, coincided with the last day of the week, and in this way the following century, like the previous one, started counting its days with the first flint character, at the first number, because it was the first day of the week.

For the most perfect understanding of the exquisite fineness of this calculation and count, here I am putting in a table that comprises one of their centuries, divided into its four indictions, indicating the days of the week in which each year started and finished counting its days, joined to the corresponding symbols of the days of the month, with the leap years indicated with an asterisk in the margin, so that the curious who want to get to know for themselves the calculations and counts that I have formed to fix the eras of the main events of this history and the correspondence of their months and days with ours can do so easily with this table and the two that follow of the days of our months on which each one of theirs started, and the order in which they placed the names of the twenty days of each month, according to the character of the year in conformity with the explanation that I have given in this and in the previous chapter.

The mentioned tables do not serve to find out the years in which the events occurred which are mentioned in this history because the general tables that go at the end of this volume are for that, on which, counting the years that they assert to have passed from one event to another, of those that they took for illustrious eras, and paying attention to the hieroglyphs with which they indicate the year in which it happened, it is easy to learn what year it was in our calculations, as we have seen and practiced in chapters 2, 3, and following to find out the year of the flood, of the confusion of tongues, and other mentioned events. So the use of these other tables is to find out the days of the months in which some events happened which they recorded with great precision.

For example, they say that the death of Ixtlixochitl occurred in the year of four rabbits, in the month of Micailhuitl, the eighteenth day indicated with the symbol of the snake in the number four. So look in the first column of the first table for the year of four rabbits, and you will find that it is the fourth year of the fourth indiction, and in the second column, in front of it, you will find that it started counting the days of its first month with its characteristic symbol of the rabbit in the first number; and thus it was the first day of the week. In the second table look for the month of Micailhuitl, and you will find that it is the twelfth month of its year. In this supposition eleven of their months and eighteen days had gone by of the year of four rabbits, which made two hundred thirty-eight days, which make eighteen weeks and four days; and now it is verified here that it was the fourth day of the week. Look at the third table of the order in which they placed and counted the symbols of the days of the months according to the character of the years, and in the third column you will find the one that they kept in the year Tochtli, which is the rabbit, in which the eighteenth day was indicated with the symbol of the snake, which is Cohuatl; and now it is verified that in this year the eighteenth day of the month of Micailhuitl was the fourth day of the week, and therefore they record it with the symbol of the snake at the number four. Finally, to quickly find out the day of our months to which it corresponded, look in the second table for the month of Micailhuitl, and in the opposite column you will find that it started on the tenth day of September: and so the eighteenth day of the month of Micailhuitl was September twenty-eighth.

FIRST TABLE

Table of an Indian century of fifty-two years, divided into four Tlalpillis or indictions of thirteen years, with the days of the week on which each year started and finished counting, joined to their proper symbols.

First Tlalpilli or Indiction.

Years	Started Counting	Finished Counting.
1 Flint.	1 Flint.	1 Wind.
2 Houses.	2 Houses.	2 Deer.
3 Rabbits.	3 Rabbits.	3 Twistings.
*4 Reeds.	4 Reeds.	5 Movements
5 Flints	6 Flints.	6 Winds.
6 Houses.	7 Houses.	7 Deer.
7 Rabbits.	8 Rabbits.	8 Twistings.
*8 Reeds.	9 Reeds.	10 Movements.
9 Flints.	11 Flints.	11 Winds.
10 Houses.	12 Houses.	12 Deer.
11 Rabbits.	13 Rabbits.	13 Twistings.
*12 Reeds.	1 Reeds	2.Movements
13 Flints.	3 Flints	3.Winds

98

Second Tlalpilli or Indiction

Years	Started Counting	Finished Counting.
1 House.	4 Houses.	4 Deer.
2 Rabbits.	5 Rabbits.	5 Twistings.
*3 Reeds.	6 Reeds.	7 Movements.
4 Flints.	8 Flints.	8 Winds.
5 Houses.	9 Houses.	9 Deer.
6 Rabbits.	10 Rabbits.	10 Twistings.
*7 Reeds.	11 Reeds.	12 Movements.
8 Flints.	13 Flints.	13 Winds.
9 Houses.	1 House.	1 Deer.
10 Rabbits.	2 Rabbits.	2 Twistings.
*11 Reeds.	3 Reeds.	4 Movements.
12 Flints	5 Flints.	5 Winds.
13 Houses.	6 Houses.	6 Deer.

Third Tlalpilli or Indiction

Years	Started Counting	Finished Counting.
1 Rabbit.	7 Rabbits.	7 Twistings.
*2 Reeds.	8 Reeds.	9 Movements.
3 Flints.	10 Flints.	10 Winds.
4 Houses.	11 Houses.	11 Deer.
5 Rabbits.	12 Rabbits.	12 Twistings.
*6 Reeds	13 Reeds	1 Movement.
7 Flints.	2 Flints.	2 Winds.
8 Houses.	3 Houses.	3 Deer.
9 Rabbits.	4 Rabbits.	4 Twistings
*10 Reeds.	5 Reeds.	6 Movements.
11 Flints.	7 Flints.	7 Winds.
12 Houses.	8 Houses.	8 Deer.
13 Rabbits.	9 Rabbits.	9 Twistings.

Fourth Tlalpilli or Indiction.

Years	Started Counting	Finished Counting.
*1 Reed.	10 Reeds.	11 Movements.
2 Flints.	12 Flints.	12 Winds.

3 Houses.	13 Houses.	13 Deer.
4 Rabbits.	1 Rabbit.	1 Twisting.
*5 Reeds.	2 Reeds.	3 Movements.
6 Flints.	4 Flints.	4 Winds.
7 Houses.	5 Houses.	5 Deer.
8 Rabbits.	6 Rabbits.	6 Twistings.
*9 Reeds.	7 Reeds.	7 Movements.
10 Flints.	9 Flints.	9 Winds.
11 Houses.	10 Houses.	10 Deer.
12 Rabbits.	11 Rabbits.	11 Twistings.
*13 Reeds.	12 Reeds.	13 Movements.

SECOND TABLE.

Table of the days of the months of our calendar on which the Indians started counting the days of their months in each year.

Indian months

1 Atemoztli started on	February 2.
2 Tititl.	February 22.
3 Itzcalli.	March 14.
4 Xilomaniztli.	April 3.
5 Cohuailhuitl.	April 23.
6 Tozcotzintli.	May 13.
7 Hueytozcoztli.	June 2.
8 Tozcatl.	June 22.
9 Exolqualiztli.	July 12.
10 Tecuilhuitzintli.	August 1.
11 Hueytecuilhuitl.	August 21.
12 Micailhuitzintli.	September 10.
13 Hueymicailhuitl.	September 30.
14 Huepaniztli.	October 20.
15 Pachtzintli.	November 9.
16 Hueypachtli.	November 29.
17 Quecholli.	December 19.
18 Panquetzaliztli.	January 8.

THIRD TABLE

Of the order of which they placed the names of the days of the month according to the year; and it is the following:

Year Tecpatl	Year Calli	Year Tochtli	Year Acatl
1 Tecpatl.	1 Calli	1 Tochtli.	1 Acatl.
2 Quiahuitl.	2 Cuetzpalin.	2 Atl.	2 Ocelotl.
3 Xochitl.	3 Cohuatl.	3 Itzcuintli.	3 Quauhtli.
4 Cipactli.	4 Micuiztli.	4 Ozomatli.	4 Cozcaquauhtli.
5 Checatl.	5 Mazatl.	5 Malinalli.	5 Ollin.
6 Calli.	6 Tochtli.	6 Acatl.	6 Tecpatl.
7 Cuetzpalin.	7 Atl.	7 Ocelotl.	7 Quiauitl.
8 Cohuatl.	8 Itzcuintli.	8 Quauhtli.	8 Xochitl.
9 Micuiztli.	9 Ozomatli.	9 Cozcaquauhtli	9 Cipactli.
10 Mazatl.	10 Malinalli.	10 Ollin.	10 Checatl.
11 Tochtli.	11 Acatl.	11 Tecpatl.	11 Calli.
12 Atl.	12 Ocelotl.	12 Quiahuitl.	12 Cuetzpalin.
13 Itzcuintli.	13 Quauhtli.	13 Xochitl.	13 Cohuatl.
14 Ozomatli.	14 Cozcaquauhtli.	14 Cipactli.	14 Micuiztli.
15 Malinalli.	15 Ollin.	15 Checatl.	15 Mazatl.
16 Acatl.	16 Tecpatl.	16 Calli.	16 Tochtli.
17 Ocelotl.	17 Quiahuitl.	17 Quetzpalin.	17 Atl.
18 Quauhtli.	18 Xochitl.	18 Cohuatl.	18 Itzcuintli.
19 Cozcaquauhtli.	19 Cipactli.	19 Micuiztli.	19 Ozomatli.
20 Ollin.	20 Checatl.	20 Mazatl.	20 Malinalli.

Intercalary	Intercalary	Intercalary	Intercalary
1 Tecpatl.	1 Calli	1 Tochtli.	1 Acatl.
2 Quiahuitl.	2 Cuetzpalin.	2 Atl.	2 Ocelotl.
3 Xochitl.	3 Cohuatl.	3 Itzcuintli.	3 Quauhtli.
4 Cipactli.	4 Micuiztli.	4 Ozomatli.	4 Cozcaquauhtli.
5 Checatl.	5 Mazatl.	5 Malinalli.	5 Ollin.

CHAPTER IX

Continuation of the material from the previous chapter, and the errors which our writers have incurred are mentioned along with the reasons for them.

I have already mentioned previously the variety that is found among the writers I have about assigning the name that they gave to the first day of the month, and consequently the order in which the rest of the month followed, some indicating Cipactli on the list of months, others Micuiztli, others Ozomatli, and others Cozcaquauhtli. I have also said that this variety has arisen from not having perfectly understood the system of these calculations, that everything revolved around the four main hieroglyphs of the flint, house, rabbit, and reed, and not having come to thoroughly understand the method and count of their weeks; such that even the gentleman Boturini, with all his diligence, did not come to understand it, and expressed that to me many times; seeing that it was still necessary to work very hard for it. Nor would I have come to understand it without his enlightenment, and working upon his instruction and principles I have come to understand its artifice; and thus in the work that the mentioned Boturini[1] printed and quoted it says that these twenty names and their figures were symbols of as many fixed stars, the main ones that they came to discover, and their calculation likewise served the astronomers to demonstrate the position of the signs, and the chronologists to put the symbols of the days in order; and he simply asserts that the first symbol of the days of the month is Cipactli, which, on most of the charts that he gathered, is seen painted with the figure of a fish, like a serpent armed with knives, like spears of arrows. He battled very much with its interpretation, and it seemed better to him to take it from the etymology of its word, which he says is a shortening of the words ce, ipan, and tlatli, and means the father superior to all, as Cipactonat, the father superior to the sun; and thus Cipactli is the first father of all the human generation, that is, Adam.

Of course I agree that giving twenty days to the month was because of the number of the main fixed stars of which they had knowledge, because some of their authors and interpreters assert that; but I have not found a way to adopt the idea that the hieroglyphs with which they indicated these twenty days symbolize those stars.

I do not understand the etymology that he gives to the name Cipactli and the meaning of the three words of which he makes it a shortening, ce, ipan tlatli,; because ce means one, ipan or apan, upon, and tlatli or tlactli, the body of man, and thus the three words would mean, one upon the body of man, and allegorically, according to the style of the Nahuatl language, an entity superior to man.

It is true that one of the lessons that I learned from him was that, with all the names of the Nahuatl or Mexican language being significant, as they are, the safest road to resolve any question was to turn to its meaning, and I have followed this doctrine in not a few passages of this history, always with good results. However, acceptance is suspended on this point for the reasons already mentioned, and because among such a number of monuments that I have become familiar with, they all assert the perfect knowledge that these people had that they had all come from one man and one woman, and even though they give the woman the names of Tlotil, Oxomozco, and Teoyaomiqui, I don't find that they give any name to that universal father; and if they had wanted to signify it in the word Cipactli, it would be natural for them to let us know with this other equivalent. Besides the fact that on as many lists as I have seen of these names, all of them unanimously give Cipactli one of the two meanings that I have already mentioned, which are snake or serpent of Knives and "Espadarte" [espadante, or swordfish?]. If I were to look for another meaning for it in the Nahuatl language, it seems to me that I would get it more naturally from the words Cihua, bread, and tactli, the woman who overcame or brought down the man, alluding to Eve's suggestion; or from the words Cihua and pachihuiliztli, the fulfillment of the woman, or the woman who was filled, in harmony with the name Oxomozco that they gave her, the pregnant attractive woman, and it wouldn't be contradicted by the hieroglyph with which they most commonly showed Cipactli, which was a snake or serpent armed with points.

But whether it means the first father or the first mother, it is a very weak argument and a very long proof that for this reason Cipactli would be the sign or character of the first day of the month; and so I cannot agree on it, because not only do I find no reason to convince me, but rather positive repugnance and opposition in the system of the Indians, as I am going to explain.

If Cipactli is the first character of the days of the month, then the system is not intelligible, nor the adjustment of their calculations possible, nor do I believe that Boturini had any other reason to be persuaded to it than having found it in first place in most of the lists of the names of the days of the month that he gathered, because of the Indian authors I have not found any who says that, and all these lists are formed after the conquest, taken from their calendars formed in wheels or squares, and because of the lack of instruction and understanding of those who copied them in the method followed in the count of their weeks, they placed the names in this order, giving Cipactli the first place, some in the days of the months, and others in the days of the weeks, making it like Sunday among us; and here you will see how they incurred the error.

These natives formed the calendars in circles or squares, some of which contained one century, others one year, and others one month.

The hieroglyphs of the first were just the four main ones of flint, house, rabbit, and reed, which, repeating them continually in the same order and adding the figure from one up to thirteen, formed the four triadecaterides which make up the century, each one thirteen years long, which in all make up fifty-two years; and even though there are only four hieroglyphs, with the variation of the number they distinguished them perfectly, without there being any mistake, and once a century was over they continued counting others and others in the same order, as we have seen in illustrations numbered 1, 2, and 3; so that on the same calendars they could count many centuries, and this was the reason why they formed them in these perpetual or continuous figures; this is shown by the snake that surrounds the whole circle biting its own tail, as seen in illustration number 4.

In the calendars of just one year they were governed in the same way, placing in the circle the hieroglyphs of the eighteen months, which, as everyone already knew, were twenty days long, in which they indicated the intercalary days and showed them with fixed dots, as seen in illustration number 5. They practiced this same thing on the wheels that they formed of just one month, placing the hieroglyphs of the twenty days in the twenty boxes into which they divided the wheel, as seen in illustration number 6, and in the blank that was left above each one between the last two circles they indicated the days of the week corresponding to the month that they were showing. So we see in that illustration that there is a single dot above the word Cipactli, denoting the number 1; over the word wind there are two, over the house, three, and so on until the word reed, which is numbered with thirteen dots; and even though there are seven boxes left to go through to complete the circle, with that many more hieroglyphs corresponding to the seven days remaining to complete the month, they do not continue putting the figure up to twenty, but rather, above the following box containing the hieroglyph tiger it starts again with the number 1 until flower, which is indicated with seven dots; so if the month meant to appear on this wheel was in a year with the flint character, this month (like all the others of this year) started counting its days with the flint, although here it is found at the number 5, because this shows that in this month shown, the first day of the month coincided with the fifth day of the week. If the month shown was in a year of the house character, it started, like all the other months of the year, on this name to count its days even though the house hieroglyph is found at the number 3, because this shows that the first day of the month shown coincided with the third day of the week; and I say the same thing if the year was of the rabbit and reed character, because even though these are found at the numbers 8 and 13, they would not stop being the first days of the month, and these numbers show the days of the week with which they coincided.

Here one can clearly see the cause of the error in those who formed the list of the names of the days of the month in columns, copying them from the wheel that came into their hands, for not being well instructed in the system of these natives, although they understood that this wheel indicated the days of the month, they did not understand that the numbering attached to the names of their days indicated the days of the week, and so they started their lists, some with one, some with another, depending on which one was indicated with the first number, believing that it was the first day of the month, without taking into consideration the week of thirteen days.

Others who acquired the knowledge of this count of the weeks of thirteen days, and did not find the method and order with which they followed them, making the figure of the day of the week agree with the hieroglyph of the month, said that Cipactli was the first day of the week, as Sunday is among us, without realizing that with the week having only thirteen days, and with twenty days in the month, the symbols of which they had to go through precisely in each month, in the course of a year there would necessarily be a week in which Cipactli absolutely did not appear. This is clearly seen in illustration number 2, whose author, or whoever put in the numbers found between the lines, followed this opinion, as it says in a little row that is in the last circle in the center, where the hieroglyph of the twenty days of the month are placed; and to show the perpetual and invariable progression of these periods of thirteen days, he uses the same figure of the spiral, and starts with Cipactli, over whose box he puts the number 1, and he continues counting up to thirteen, which ends with Acatl. He starts the second week with Ocelotl, which ends in Micuitztli, and in it Cipactli gets the number 8. He starts the third in Mazatl, where I have placed an A for reference, and concludes it in Quiahuitl, where there is a B; and here we now see one week in which Cipactli absolutely does not appear. So the first day of the week can be wrong, since there is not just one, but many weeks in the course of the year without this character appearing in them with any number, as seen in those weeks that start on the mentioned wheel in the places that I have indicated with the letters C, D, E, F, G, and H. This is the origin and the reason for the obstacles and confusions incurred by the writers who tried to give the explanation of these wheels.

Father Torquemada, having reported in the mentioned place about the way in which they followed the count of their years and months, says in chapter 37 that they had another third count of this manner. "They had twenty characters or medals of various forms and paintings, the first of which they called Cecipactli, which is 'espadarte' [espadante or sword fish?]; the second, Cecelotl; the third, Ceacatl; the fourth, Cexochitl; the fifth, Ceacatl, and they would proceed in this way up to twenty, and they would say that each one of these characters ruled for thirteen days, that all of them together make the number two hundred sixty, and some tried to say that these thirteen days were weeks for these Indians, but this is not so, but rather the number of days that the sign or character at the beginning ruled. In this divinatory and illicit account they interposed the characters of the count of the year, those four characters that were mentioned above, that is, the reed, flint, house, and rabbit, where they counted the hebdomad [week of seven] of their years, which are the fifty-two. It should be advised that this count is very harmful and very superstitious and full of idolatry. Some praised it very much, saying that it was ingenious and that it had no blemish or error; but they said this because they didn't understand to what end this count was directed, nor did they understand the multitude of superstitions, festivals, and idolatrous sacrifices that were contained in it, and they called it the calendar of the Indians, not noticing that this count does not extend to all the days of the year because it only has two hundred sixty days of circle and turn, and then it returns to its beginning; and thus it cannot be a calendar, nor was it ever, because they do not have the circle of the three hundred sixty-five days that the year contains, which it must have for the proper count of the festivals, and this was unknown by those who said that this divinatory art was a calendar."

I have wanted to copy this entire piece so that the reader can form an opinion of what the origin has been of so much obscurity and confusion in this matter, which has been none other than not having come to understand the exquisite fineness with which these people ordered their calculations. There is no other author of ours up to now who has written so much of the ancient history of these nations as Father Torquemada. He gathered much information, and he says in various parts of his writings that he dealt with persons instructed in it, that he saw their historical charts, that he had various wheels of these calendars; and in the previous chapter he talks about one of them with a whole explanation given by Father Toribio Motolinia, who was one of the first monks of his order who came to these kingdoms, and he says that he was amazed by the strange curiosity of these natives, and it removed the doubt he had before starting to write of how one could have information of their things, and mention with precise detail what happened a thousand years ago as they do. In spite of all this, because he did not come to understand the counting of their weeks, he opposes the assertion of those who said that it was very ingenious and did not contain any error, and he establishes as infallible that it is divinatory, that it is not legitimate, that it is very harmful and superstitious, and what is more important for our purposes, he leaves us entangled in a thousand confusions, because after having told us in the previous chapter that a year among these peoples consisted of three hundred sixty-five days, now in this that he calls the third count only two hundred sixty days were included, and he does not tell us how the one hundred fifty remaining days were counted; for although he asserts that once finishing its circle and returning to its beginning, not being able to complete another circle within the same year, it necessarily had to be continued in the following year, and afterwards in the other years with considerable alteration in each one of them, because of the diverse way of starting the count. And finally, although this count is aimed at ordering their idolatrous festivals, it had to be adjusted to their calculations, and it was well for us to be told how they followed it and adjusted to them to order their festivals each year.

It is certain that the twenty characters or medals of various forms and paintings are the twenty days of the month, whose names were joined to the numbers of the week, in the same way that we join the names of the days of the week to those of the month in our calendar, saying, for example, Friday the first, Saturday the second, Sunday the third, etc., and in the successive progression of counting by thirteen on thirteen, the seven of them would coincide at least once with the number 1, and sometimes twice, depending on the number at which the year began, in the same way that in our calendars each one of the days of the week becomes the first day of the month two or three times in a year, with the difference that among us, because of the number of days of the week being shorter and the months being unequal, for some have thirty and others have thirty-one days, there is no set way of assigning how many times each day of the week becomes the first day of the month; but as among these natives the number of the days of the week was greater, and all the months were equal with twenty days, it was necessary for seven of the twenty days of the month to coincide twice with that number of the week with which the year started counting the days of its first month, and once with the others.

As he did not come to understand this count of the weeks, and saw Cepactli at the number 1 on some wheel or list, he says that this was the first of the twenty characters, and that they called it Cecipactli, perhaps because the one who explained it in Mexican wrote it that way, joining the number 1, which in this language is Ce, with the name of the day, which is Cipactli; and counting thirteen from this day forward, he then found Ocelotl at the first number, and called it Ceocelotl, and so on with the rest. See illustration number 6, and start to count from Cipactli by thirteen on thirteen, and it will be found that the first thirteen are completed with Acatl, and therefore the number one should coincide with Ocelotl, and so it will be called Ce Ocelotl to count another week which will be concluded on Micuiztli, and thus the first number will coincide with Mazatl: and so it will be called Ce Mazatl, not Ce Acatl, as this author says (which is a known error because he repeats this sign twice) to start another week which will conclude on Quiahuitl: and thus the first number will coincide with Xochitl, and will be called Ce Xochitl, and counting the thirteen days from it, it will end with Malinalli, and so Acatl will be the first day of the week, and it will be called Ce Acatl. Here we clearly see the five characters that he names Cecipactli, Ceocelotl, Cemazatl, Cexochitl, Ceacatl, and those who accept the superstitious count in which each one rules for thirteen days, which are nothing more than the days of the month to which the number one, Ce, has been joined, because of having been the first days of the week on the wheels or lists from where this information was taken, did not understand the artifice of the count.

Other writers give information of this type of weeks that the Indians used, but they do not explain how they counted them. The one who became most enlightened about them was Francisco Lopez de Gomara in his Cronica de la Nueva Espana [Chronicle of the New Spain], who in chapter 191 explains very clearly how they would count them, joining the number of the days of the weeks to the characters of the days of the months, and even to the indictions into which the century was divided, counting the years of thirteen on thirteen. He gives them the name of weeks, but he also puts Cipactli as the first character of the days of the month; and even though he says that they did not always start with it to count the days of the week, but rather as it came, he does not explain nor does he seem to understand the artifice of this count in the progression of all the years of a century.

The Gentleman Boturini said repeatedly, and rightfully so, that he had not yet come to perfectly understand this system; and truly this has been one of the points that has taken me entire years of work to come to understand in the way I have explained it here, which is the genuine way adapted to this system. In this way all the difficulties in which the interpreters got entangled trying to explain them are resolved; because it is incontestable that the key to this system are the four symbols flint, house, rabbit, and reed, which Boturini, following those interpreters, called initial characters: and if each one didn't start counting the days of its months according to the symbol of the year, they would lose this term, because they are called initial characters for no other reason than because the days of the year were counted starting with them , and consequently the days of each one of its months. I do not share Boturini's opinion that Cipactli was the symbol of the first day of each month, when he himself corrects Gemelli, who said that Cipactli, Micuiztli, Ozomatli, and

Cozcaquauhtli are symbols of the first days of the year; Boturini changes it, saying: It is denied that any day of the year started with these four symbols. And further down, revising the assertion of Gemelli, who said that Cipactli corresponds to Tochtli, Micuiztli to Acatl, Ozomatli to Tecpatl, and Cozcaquauthli to Calli, he says these formal words: Nor do any of these correspond to the character of the year, and it is infallible that if the character of the year is Tochtli, Tochtli must also be the symbol of the first day of the year, and the same thing is understood of the others.

Here we see an obvious contradiction; because if it is infallible for the character of the year to be the symbol of the first day of the year, which is that of its first month, then infallibly it must be the symbol of the first day of all of its months; because having gone through the twenty symbols in their order during the first twenty days of the year, comprising the first month, it must appear again as the initial character of the second month3, and so on with the others. Then Cipactli can never be the first day of the month, because if there cannot be any year that is indicated with this character, but just with the four main characters, and if it is infallible that the first day of each month is to be indicated with the character of the year, Cipactli can never be the symbol of the first day of the month.

I have another reason to suspect that Boturini had not come to a perfect understanding of this system and of the order that they followed in counting their weeks, and it is that in paragraph 5, folio 43. Speaking of the vestiges that are found in the town of San Juan de Teotihuacan of an ancient temple of the Toltecs dedicated to the sun, he says that the Indians of Chiapa counted seven wandering stars corresponding to the days of their week, and he adds: On the wheels and tables of the Toltec symbols of the days of the year I find after the Triadecateride the septenary number so distinguished in Holy Scripture; and as a consequence of this, in paragraph 7, folio 45, he puts the catalog of the names of the days of the month, starting with Cipactli; and counting the first thirteen, which end in Acatl, he puts some dots below with which he separates them from the other seven remaining, which he counts from Ocelotl, numbering them from one to seven. In the margin of the first thirteen he puts this inscription: Triadecateride; in the margin of the other seven, Septenary; at the end he takes their sum and puts twenty as the number. From here I infer that he did not come to understand the artifice of the weeks: because even if Cipactli were the character of the first day of the month, and the first month of the year were to start with it, in the second month it would vary in number and appear on the eighth, to conclude the week of thirteen days at Micuiztli and start the following in Mazatl. Here the system of the Triadecateride and the septenary is already destroyed: because at the beginning of the second month six days would remain, counted from eight to thirteen; then the Triadecateride would follow and at the end there would be another day left by itself, which is the twentieth, indicated with the name of Xochitl, which must be joined to the first number to start the following week. In the third month Cipactli would appear at the number two, and already in this month the two quantities of 13 and 7 would be lacking entirely; because to end the week of thirteen days in the first part of the month, twelve symbols would be counted which would end with the number thirteen at Malinalli and it would start over with Acatl at the first number until ending with Xochitl at the number eight. So this month would have the quantities of twelve and eight, and not of thirteen and seven, and in the same way they would keep varying in the rest of the months if one were persuaded (which I don't believe) that all the months should be counted in this order, that is, first the thirteen days and then the seven. Besides, I haven't found any monument that says that: this would be a count with two kinds of weeks, which would entirely destroy the whole system.

In addition to this, there is the other reason of consistency, because it should be pointed out that they also used the mentioned four main symbols to indicate the four times of the year, but varying them according to the character of the year. See Boturini's mentioned work, paragraph 10, folio 54. If the year was that of Tecpatl, flint, with this hieroglyph they would indicate the spring, with that of house, the summer, with that of rabbit, the autumn, and with that of reed, the winter. If it was the year of house, this symbol indicated the spring, the rabbit, the summer, the reed, the autumn, and the flint, the winter. If it was the year of the rabbit, this indicated the spring, the reed, the summer, the flint, the autumn, and the house, the winter. And if the year was of the reed, this indicated the spring, the flint, the summer, the reed, the autumn, and the rabbit the winter. So the character of the year always retained the initial position in the course of the seasons2; how much more should it have that position in the order of the days of the month! This is most regular and in conformity with said system.

See illustration number 7, which is a copy of an ancient chart of those that Boturini acquired, which seems to be from the Mexican nation, noted in our characters by a Mexican, because it says that it contains the fourth triade-cateride of the century, which among the Mexicans had the house sign, which was the second among the Toltecs. The mentioned wheel contains twenty years, the thirteen of the mentioned sign and seven of the subsequent sign of the rabbit; and in the center circle the twenty days of the month are shown. This wheel is made only to show the four times according to the character of the year; and thus in the boxes of the outer circle the symbols of the years are painted in their order, showing the four seasons as I have explained; and for their better understanding the letters V, E, O, and I have been placed underneath to signify verano3 [spring], estio [summer], otoño [autumn], and invierno [winter]. Finally, if Cipactli were the character of the first day of the month, we would then have another initial character that is not in proportion to nor adapts to this system, either in its meaning, or in its order, or in its quantity.

Footnotes, Chapter IX

1. Idea de una nueva historia general [Idea of a new general history] 7, folio 44.

2. If this illustration cannot be printed, because so far it has not been possible to find it in spite of the efforts that have been made, readers can see it marked with the number 2, which is fortunately preserved and offered to them now to appear at the end of the book. Undoubtedly the differences in the two illustrations were very slight, because everything the author says here with reference to the number 6 is found in the number 2. — E.

3. Translator's note: The copy I am translating from has the word character instead of month, but that doesn't make sense to me, so I have taken the liberty to change the word to month. RRC.

4. [Translator's note: This following footnote does not apply in the translation, as it refers to the author's use of a French word instead of the Spanish word for season. The translation into English is unaffected and is correct and accurate the way I have given it. RRC.]

Gallicism which may have been in use in Veytia's time, and would have been brought by the French who went to Spain with Phillip V, because he was the monarch of that nation. Today no one would translate the French word Saison, speaking of the times into which the year is divided, with sazón, but would say estación instead. — E.

5. Translator's note: In modern Spanish the word verano means summer, but it comes from the Latin vernum, which meant spring, and that is obviously the intended meaning here. RRC.

CHAPTER X

About the Leap Years.

One of the most universal events and one on which the national historians most agree is the invention of leap years. They all concur in it, and those who explain their calendars report that it took place on the occasion of the meeting of wise astronomers who gathered in Huehuetlapallan for the adjustment of their times and correction of their calculations; because having divided the year into eighteen months of twenty days each and having added five more days onto each year, and seeing that even with this they were not exactly even with the course of the sun because of the not-quite six hours remaining that they became aware of, they decided to add one more day every four years; but the information they give us of how they did it is very scant and confusing, and there is some variation among the authors of those manuscripts in assigning the character of the year when the leap day occurred. Most, and those with the best reputation, assert that it took place in the year of the fourth character reed, and this is the most regular and in conformity with their system.

The way they did it on the astronomical calendar and consequently on the usual calendar (not on the ritual, as I will say later) was by indicating this extra day with the same hieroglyph and name as the last day of the month or of the last intercalary day, but varying the number according to the day of the week with which it coincided. I said of the last day of the month or of the last intercalary day because there is variety in this among the authors: some say that they invariably did it in the hieroglyph Malinalli, and others say that they did it in Ollin. But so that it is understood with all clarity, I will give examples of both.

It is already established that all the years started to count the days of their months with the hieroglyph that was characteristic of the year, and so the fourth year started to count the days of its months with the reed sign, and continuing to name the subsequent days with the names that we have already said. According to the order in which they appear in the tables of chapter 8 in the fourth column, the twentieth day of each month was called Malinalli, or twisting. Let us now suppose that the last day of the last month of the fourth year of the century coincided, as it in fact did, with the twelfth day of the week;

they would indicate this by saying: Matlatliomome Malinalli, twelve twistings. If the leap day was assigned to this character, as the first historians say, the next day they would name with the same sign Malinalli, but varying the number of the day of the week, and so they would call it: Matlatliomey Malinalli, thirteen twistings, and they would continue counting the five intercalary days like this:

Ce Acatl.	One reed.
Ome Ocelotl.	Two tigers.
Yey Quauhtli.	Three eagles.
Nahui Cozcaquauhtli.	Four owls.
Macuile Ollin.	Five movements.

In the hypothesis of the second authors, they counted the five intercalary days in the order of the week, indicating them as I have said, with the five names of the reed quinary, and they called them:

Matlatliomey Acatl.	Thirteen1 reeds.
Ce Ocelotl.	One tiger.
Ome Quauhtli.	Two eagles.
Yey Cozcaquauhtli.	Three owls.
Nahui Ollin.	Four movements.

And having to add the extra day, they gave it the same name as the fifth intercalary day, but varying the number according to the day of the week; and thus they would indicate the leap day in this year with the same symbol of movement, but with the number five, which was the one that followed in the order of the week, and so they would call it Macuile Ollin, five movements, if the leap day was done on the last intercalary day, as the other authors believed, counting from the last day of the month indicated with the hieroglyph Malinalli at the number twelve, in the supposition that we are presenting.

I have not been able to find any documents to convince me to take a side between these two opinions; but whether the leap day coincided with the last sign of the days of the months, or with the last of the intercalary days, it is obvious that they formed it at the end of the year of the fourth character Acatl, and that this year with its five intercalary days ended in the sign Ollin on the same day of the week, as is seen in the two examples that I have given, and in one way or the other the fourth year of the century ends on the fifth day of the week, and this day was called Macuile Ollin. The following year, which was indicated with the hieroglyph of the flint, started with the flint to name the days of its months, without interrupting its order; but in the supposition that we are presenting, the first day of the new year would be the sixth day of the week, and so they would name it Chicuacen Tecpatl, six flints, and from there they would continue counting their week up to thirteen, joining the numbers to the names of the days of the month in the way already explained.

I have already established in Chapter VIII that the days that were added in the leap years formed an entire week in the revolution of one century of mine of fifty-two years each, because being added as they were in the years of the fourth sign, Acatl, in each one of the first three indictions or triadecaterides of the century there were three years indicated with this character, which make nine, and four of the fourth, which complete the thirteen days of a week. In this way the one thousand four hundred sixty-one full weeks which made up a century were fit in; because each regular year had twenty-eight weeks and one day, which, if there were no leap years, would complete an entire week in the revolution of one indiction of thirteen years; so that the last day of the last year would coincide with the last day of the week, and the year following the triadecateride that followed in order would start to count its days with the first number of the week.

But because of the leap years it would happen that the second indiction, which was of the sign Calli, started to count the days of its first year with this character, but at the number four, which was the number that corresponded to the day of the week, because of the three leap days that had been included in the previous triadecateride in their order in the respective week.

The third indiction, of the character Tochtli, started to count the days of its first year with it, but at the number seven because of the six days that had been added in the two preceding indictions, three in each one, included in the numbering of the weeks.

It happened in the same way in the fourth indiction, which, because of the three additional days that had been included because of the leap days in the previous indiction, which along with the sixth of the other two indictions made nine days, started to count the days of its first year indicated with the character Acatl with this sign at the number ten. In this last indication there were four leap days in the four years of the sign Acatl, and therefore, at the end of it there were four extra days, which, along with the nine of the three previous indictions, made thirteen, and it was an entire week; and in this way the last day of the year, the last year of the century, coincided with the last day of the week; and thus the following century started over to count its days from the first of the week like the previous one. See the table in chapter VIII.

If it is true, as the national writers assert, that these astronomers invented the leap year from such remote times, they cannot be denied the epithet of wise men, when among such polished and cultured nations as those of Europe, they didn't invent it until the times of Julius Caesar in the year 709 of the founding of Rome, which, according to the most accepted calculation, was forty-five years before the birth of Jesus Christ2. But whether these natives made this discovery in the year 3901 of the world, one hundred thirty-four years before the Virgin birth, in this meaning which we have been talking about, or whether they made it in subsequent times, what is certain and leaves no room for doubt, according to their charts and calendars, is that in the year 1519, when the Spanish arrived in these parts, this calculation was already established and common among them and leap years were already in use.

Among the manuscripts that I have gathered, deserving singular attention are those of the illustrious Fernando de Alba Ixtlilxochitl, the grandson of the last emperor of Texcoco, which flourished around the end of the 500s [1500s?] and the beginning of the 600s [1600?]; and in one of his narrations that seems to be written in the year 1600 he mentions it. To support the truthfulness of his entire narration, at the end of it he gives a list of the individuals whom he consulted to form it, in addition to his education and the understanding that he had in the explanation of the hieroglyphs of his historical charts, which was so well known that his fame in this kingdom endures today. He indicates individuals of known quality and education and who were one hundred years old and older with whom he communicated, who very well went back to the time of their gentilism; and he quotes the writings of others who were already dead.

Among them he quotes Alonso Axayacatzin, the son of Quauhtlahuatzin,3 the next-to-last king of Mexico and the nephew of Moctezuma, who in his gentilism and at the time of the arrival of the Spanish was the head archivist of Texcoco, a job which was only given to the princes or infantes of Mexico and Texcoco. He had charge of the archives in which the historical charts were kept, as well as other things that contained treaties between the powers, division and distribution of lands among the vassals, and all the other instruments that were necessary to properly govern their republic, as I will mention later on. These archivists were very well educated men in understanding these charts because people went to them to decide any of these points.

This Axayacatzin was one of the first who received the Catholic faith and customs of the Spanish; and having learned to write in our characters, he formed two narrations of the history of his antiquity, according to the education which he had, because of the employment that he had and the charts that he kept, one in his Mexican language and another in our language. The mentioned Alba as well as other writers had a great appreciation for these narrations, and therefore the Gentleman Boturini sought them with great diligence, but without effect; and although I have looked for them with great diligence at his direction, I have not been able to find them either.

The authority of these national writers is very strong to persuade us that the leap years were established at that meeting of wise men; but even if that weren't the case, it is imaginable that this calculation was already common in the year fifteen nineteen when the Spanish came to these countries, and consequently it was invented some years before the conquest; and so they are praiseworthy and deserving of the name of wise in astronomy, and accurate in their observations, being worthy of the greatest admiration because of having done this without the aid of spectacles, telescopes, compasses, or any other instrument, because in everything I have read of their histories, ancient as well as modern, I have not found the slightest information that they used any instruments for them, nor did they know the compass or the ruler for the formation of their circles and squares in their calendars. But this will not be difficult to believe for anyone who has been in these countries, where it is frequently seen that the Indians who tend to be painters, masons, carpenters, and other similar arts practice them without using the compass, or the ruler, or any other instrument with which to adjust their measurements, except small sticks and little strings, and with them they produced their artifacts in the proper proportion. I am talking about those who work well, as everywhere there are good craftsmen and bad.

I have not found this information of the invention of the leap year in any of our Spanish authors, who in their writings talk about or somewhat touch upon the ancient history and customs of these Indians, according to what each one may have had and the way he understood it, which is generally scant, confused, and distorted from its true understanding and explanation. They substantially agree in that these natives had their calculations worked out; that they formed their wheels or squares that served them as calendars, in which the centuries of fifty-two years appeared, divided into four indictions, each one of thirteen years, indicated with the hieroglyphs of the flint, the house, the rabbit, and the reed, that their years consisted of eighteen months of twenty days each, which in all made three hundred sixty days, at the end of which they added the five intercalary days; and finally some, like Herrera, Gomara, Solis, and Torquemada, had some enlightenment of the use of their weeks, although they were not correct in their understanding. But with regard to the invention of the leap year, I have not found anyone who touches upon it: but rather Torquemada[4] positively affirms that these people did not attain the leap years; and in another part,[5] talking about the great talent of the emperor Nezahualpiltzintli, he says that "even on leap day he tried to fall and get it right, it seeming to him that the festivals were being prolonged."

Gemelli Carrera, who wrote his work entitled Viaje de vuelta del mundo [trip back from the world] at the end of the last century, establishes its existence,[6] gotten from the illustrious Carlos de Siguenza y Gongora; but his explanation is very succinct and short, and leads more to confusion than clarity; because it seems that instead of adding the day in each fourth year as the leap day, he subtracts it; and he did not come to understand the artifice, and he confused the way they formed it in the astronomical year with the way they formed it in the ritual year; in the same way that he was mistaken on the information that Boturini corrects; which is not surprising in an individual who, in passing, and in the short time that he was in Mexico, did not do little in jotting down the great knowledge that Siquenza communicated to him, and especially not having a perfect command of our Spanish language to give a proper explanation.

It is not probable and I am not persuaded that from the times when they did the correction of their calendars, the calendar ended up in all its perfection as has been explained, but it did end up with the error adjusted and the system established of the century of fifty-two years, divided into the four indictions of thirteen years each, indicated with the repetition of the four signs flint, house, rabbit, and reed, and the year divided into eighteen months of twenty days each, and the establishment of the addition of the five intercalary days in the three years of the first three signs and of six in the fourth sign; but I believe that the names of the months and days came many years later; and even if they had names since that time, they are undoubtedly not the names that they got later, as we have mentioned. But as it was necessary for me to give information in this place about this meeting of wise men who made the correction of the times and invented the leap year, it was also necessary and appropriate for me to put a whole detailed explanation here of their calendars. First, because this is one of the most curious matters in this history, worthy of public knowledge and the appreciation of the learned, and because it is necessary to the integrity of this work. Second, so a person can understand the manner they observed in the formation of their leap years, which without all this explanation could not be well perceived. And third, because with my having to indicate the eras of the events of this history, according to the calculations of these natives and their monuments, it was indispensable to first give the whole plan of their system, so that once instructed, the reader can be aware of the calculations that I have done for the comparison of their years with ours, and for this purpose I have put the three tables of the century, months, and days in chapter VIII, and here, for the most complete information, I am putting an entire calendar for one year (in the way we form our calendars), which indicates the ninth year of the fourth indiction or triadecateride of Acatl, copied from one of those that Boturini gathered, which I have chosen because, being the fourth character, it serves for the explanation that has been given of the leap year. With these, along with the general tables that are going at the end of this book, one can achieve a perfect understanding in this subject of their calendars, which in my opinion is a work of exquisite fineness and well expresses the talent and capacity of its inventors, whom some mistakenly consider to be uncultured and barbarian.

MEXICAN CALENDAR

Corresponding to the ninth year of the fourth indiction (leap year), indicated with the hieroglyph of nine reeds, and compared to ours.

ATEMOZTLI, MONTH I

Days of the months	Days of theweek	Signs of theDays	Corresponding to
1	7	Acatl.	February 2
2	8	Ocelotl.	February 3
3	9	Quauhtli.	February 4
4	10	Cozcaquauhtli.	February 5
5	11	Ollin.	February 6
6	12	Tecpatl.	February 7
7	13	Quiahuitl.	February 8
8	1	Xochitl.	February 9
9	2	Cipactli.	February 10
10	3	Checatl.	February 11
11	4	Calli.	February 12
12	5	Cuetzpalin.	February 13
13	6	Cohuatl.	February 14
14	7	Micuiztli.	February 15
15	8	Mazatl.	February 16
16	9	Tochtli.	February 17
17	10	Atl.	February 18
18	11	Itzcuintli.	February 19
19	12	Ozomatli.	February 20
20	13	Malinalli.	February 21

TITITL, MONTH II

Days of the months	Days of the weeks	Signs of the Days	Corresponding to
1	1	Acatl.	February 22
2	2	Ocelotl.	February 23
3	3	Quauhtli.	February 24
4	4	Cozcaquauhtli.	February 25
5	5	Ollin.	February 26
6	6	Tecpatl.	February 27
7	7	Quiahuitl.	February 28
8	8	Xochitl.	March 1
9	9	Cipactli.	March 2

10	10	Checatl.	March 3
11	11	Calli.	March 4
12	12	Cuetzpalin.	March 5
13	13	Cohuatl.	March 6
14	1	Micuiztli.	March 7
15	2	Mazatl.	March 8
16	3	Tochtli.	March 9
17	4	Atl.	March 10
18	5	Itzcuintli.	March 11
19	6	Ozomatli.	March 12
20	7	Malinalli.	March 13

ITZCALLI, MONTH III

Days of the months	Days of the week	Signs of the Days	Corresponding to
1	8	Acatl.	March 14
2	9	Ocelotl.	March 15
3	10	Quauhtli.	March 16
4	11	Cozcaquauhtli.	March 17
5	12	Ollin.	March 18
6	13	Tecpatl.	March 19
7	1	Quiahuitl.	March 20
8	2	Xochitl.	March 21
9	3	Cipactli.	March 22
10	4	Checatl.	March 23
11	5	Calli.	March 24
12	6	Cuetzpalin.	March 25
13	7	Cohuatl.	March 26
14	8	Micuiztli.	March 27
15	9	Mazatl.	March 28
16	10	Tochtli.	March 29
17	11	Atl.	March 30
18	12	Itzcuintli.	March 31
19	13	Ozomatli.	April 1
20	1	Malinalli.	April 2

XILOMANIZTLI, MONTH IV

Days of the months	Days of the week	Signs of the Days	Corresponding to
1	2	Acatl.	April 3
2	3	Ocelotl.	April 4
3	4	Quauhtli.	April 5

4	5	Cozcaquauhtli.	April 6
5	6	Ollin.	April 7
6	7	Tecpatl.	April 8
7	8	Quiahuitl.	April 9
8	9	Xochitl.	April 10
9	10	Cipactli.	April 11
10	11	Checatl.	April 12
11	12	Calli.	April 13
12	13	Cuetzpalin.	April 14
13	1	Cohuatl.	April 15
14	2	Micuiztli.	April 16
15	3	Mazatl.	April 17
16	4	Tochtli.	April 18
17	5	Atl.	April 19
18	6	Itzcuintli.	April 20
19	7	Ozomatli.	April 21
20	8	Malinalli.	April 22

COHUAILHUITL, MONTH V

Days of the months	Days of the week	Signs of the Days	Corresponding to
1	9	Acatl.	April 23
2	10	Ocelotl.	April 24
3	11	Quauhtli.	April 25
4	12	Cozcaquauhtli.	April 26
5	13	Ollin.	April 27
6	1	Tecpatl.	April 28
7	2	Quiahuitl.	April 29
8	3	Xochitl.	April 30
9	4	Cipactli.	May 1
10	5	Checatl.	May 2
11	6	Calli.	May 3
12	7	Cuetzpalin.	May 4
13	8	Cohuatl.	May 5
14	9	Micuiztli.	May 6
15	10	Mazatl.	May 7
16	11	Tochtli.	May 8
17	12	Atl.	May 9
18	13	Itzcuintli.	May 10
19	1	Ozomatli.	May 11
20	2	Malinalli.	May 12

TOZCOTZINTLI, MONTH VI

Days of the months	Days of the week	Signs of the Days	Corresponding to
1	3	Acatl.	May 13
2	4	Ocelotl.	May 14
3	5	Quauhtli.	May 15
4	6	Cozcaquauhtli.	May 16
5	7	Ollin.	May 17
6	8	Tecpatl.	May 18
7	9	Quiahuitl.	May 19
8	10	Xochitl.	May 20
9	11	Cipactli.	May 21
10	12	Checatl.	May 22
11	13	Calli.	May 23
12	1	Cuetzpalin.	May 24
13	2	Cohuatl.	May 25
14	3	Micuiztli.	May 26
15	4	Mazatl.	May 27
16	5	Tochtli.	May 28
17	6	Atl.	May 29
18	7	Itzcuintli.	May 30
19	8	Ozomatli.	May 31
20	9	Malinalli.	June 1

HUEYTOZCOZTLI, MONTH VII

Days of the months	Days of the week	Signs of the Days	Corresponding to
1	10	Acatl.	June 2
2	11	Ocelotl.	June 3
3	12	Quauhtli.	June 4
4	13	Cozcaquauhtli.	June 5
5	1	Ollin.	June 6
6	2	Tecpatl.	June 7
7	3	Quiahuitl.	June 8
8	4	Xochitl.	June 9
9	5	Cipactli.	June 10
10	6	Checatl.	June 11
11	7	Calli.	June 12
12	8	Cuetzpalin.	June 13
13	9	Cohuatl.	June 14
14	10	Micuiztli.	June 15
15	11	Mazatl.	June 16

16	12	Tochtli.	June 17
17	13	Atl.	June 18
18	1	Itzcuintli.	June 19
19	2	Ozomatli.	June 20
20	3	Malinalli.	June 21

TOZCATL, MONTH VIII

Days of the months	Days of the week	Signs of the Days	Corresponding to
1	4	Acatl.	June 22
2	5	Ocelotl.	June 23
3	6	Quauhtli.	June 24
4	7	Cozcaquauhtli.	June 25
5	8	Ollin.	June 26
6	9	Tecpatl.	June 27
7	10	Quiahuitl.	June 28
8	11	Xochitl.	June 29
9	12	Cipactli.	June 30
10	13	Checatl.	July 1
11	1	Calli.	July 2
12	2	Cuetzpalin.	July 3
13	3	Cohuatl.	July 4
14	4	Micuiztli.	July 5
15	5	Mazatl.	July 6
16	6	Tochtli.	July 7
17	7	Atl.	July 8
18	8	Itzcuintli.	July 9
19	9	Ozomatli.	July 10
20	10	Malinalli.	July 11

EXOLQUALIZTLI, MONTH IX

Days of the months	Days of the week	Signs of the Days	Corresponding to
1	11	Acatl.	July 12
2	12	Ocelotl.	July 13
3	13	Quauhtli.	July 14
4	1	Cozcaquauhtli.	July 15
5	2	Ollin.	July 16
6	3	Tecpatl.	July 17
7	4	Quiahuitl.	July 18
8	5	Xochitl.	July 19
9	6	Cipactli.	July 20

10	7	Checatl.	July 21
11	8	Calli.	July 22
12	9	Cuetzpalin.	July 23
13	10	Cohuatl.	July 24
14	11	Micuiztli.	July 25
15	12	Mazatl.	July 26
16	13	Tochtli.	July 27
17	1	Atl.	July 28
18	2	Itzcuintli.	July 29
19	3	Ozomatli.	July 30
20	4	Malinalli.	July 31

TECUILHUITZINTLI, MONTH X

Days of the months	Days of the week	Signs of the Days	Corresponding to
1	5	Acatl.	August 1
2	6	Ocelotl.	August 2
3	7	Quauhtli.	August 3
4	8	Cozcaquauhtli.	August 4
5	9	Ollin.	August 5
6	10	Tecpatl.	August 6
7	11	Quiahuitl.	August 7
8	12	Xochitl.	August 8
9	13	Cipactli.	August 9
10	1	Checatl.	August 10
11	2	Calli.	August 11
12	3	Cuetzpalin.	August 12
13	4	Cohuatl.	August 13
14	5	Micuiztli.	August 14
15	6	Mazatl.	August 15
16	7	Tochtli.	August 16
17	8	Atl.	August 1
18	9	Itzcuintli.	August 18
19	10	Ozomatli.	August 19
20	11	Malinalli.	August 20

HUEYTECUILHUITL, MONTH XI

Days of the months	Days of the week	Signs of the Days	Corresponding to
1	12	Acatl.	August 21
2	13	Ocelotl.	August 22
3	1	Quauhtli.	August 23

4	2	Cozcaquauhtli.	August 24
5	3	Ollin.	August 25
6	4	Tecpatl.	August 26
7	5	Quiahuitl.	August 27
8	6	Xochitl.	August 28
9	7	Cipactli.	August 29
10	8	Checatl.	August 30
11	9	Calli.	August 31
12	10	Cuetzpalin.	September 1
13	11	Cohuatl.	September 2
14	12	Micuiztli.	September 3
15	13	Mazatl.	September 4
16	1	Tochtli.	September 5
17	2	Atl.	September 6
18	3	Itzcuintli.	September 7
19	4	Ozomatli.	September 8
20	5	Malinalli.	September 9

MICAILHUITZINTLI, MONTH XII

Days of the months	Days of the week	Signs of the Days	Corresponding to
1	6	catl.	September 10
2	7	Ocelotl.	September 11
3	8	Quauhtli.	September 12
4	9	Cozcaquauhtli.	September 13
5	10	Ollin.	September 14
6	11	Tecpatl.	September 15
7	12	Quiahuitl.	September 16
8	13	Xochitl.	September 17
9	1	Cipactli.	September 18
10	2	Checatl.	September 19
11	3	Calli.	September 20
12	4	Cuetzpalin.	September 21
13	5	Cohuatl.	September 22
14	6	Micuiztli.	September 23
15	7	Mazatl.	September 24
16	8	Tochtli.	September 25
17	9	Atl.	September 26
18	10	Itzcuintli.	September 27
19	11	Ozomatli.	September 28
20	12	Malinalli.	September 29

HUEYMICAILHUITL, MONTH XIII

Days of the months	Days of the week	Signs of the Days	Corresponding to
1	13	Acatl.	September 30
2	1	Ocelotl.	October 1
3	2	Quauhtli.	October 2
4	3	Cozcaquauhtli.	October 3
5	4	Ollin.	October 4
6	5	Tecpatl.	October 5
7	6	Quiahuitl.	October 6
8	7	Xochitl.	October 7
9	8	Cipactli.	October 8
10	9	Checatl.	October 9
11	10	Calli.	October 10
12	11	Cuetzpalin.	October 11
13	12	Cohuatl.	October 12
14	13	Micuiztli.	October 13
15	1	Mazatl.	October 14
16	2	Tochtli.	October 15
17	3	Atl.	October 16
18	4	Itzcuintli.	October 17
19	5	Ozomatli.	October 18
20	6	Malinalli.	October 19

HUEPANIZTLI, MONTH XIV

Days of the months	Days of the week	Signs of the Days	Corresponding to
1	7	Acatl.	October 20
2	8	Ocelotl.	October 21
3	9	Quauhtli.	October 22
4	10	Cozcaquauhtli.	October 23
5	11	Ollin.	October 24
6	12	Tecpatl.	October 25
7	13	Quiahuitl.	October 26
8	1	Xochitl.	October 27
9	2	Cipactli.	October 28
10	3	Checatl.	October 29
11	4	Calli.O	ctober 30
12	5	Cuetzpalin.	October 31
13	6	Cohuatl.	November 1
14	7	Micuiztli.	November 2
15	8	Mazatl.	November 3

16	9	Tochtli.	November 4
17	10	Atl.	November 5
18	11	Itzcuintli.	November 6
19	12	Ozomatli.	November 7
20	13	Malinalli.	November 8

PACHTZINTLI, MONTH XV

Days of the months	Days of the week	Signs of the Days	Corresponding to
1	1	Acatl.	November 9
2	2	Ocelotl.	November 10
3	3	Quauhtli.	November 11
4	4	Cozcaquauhtli.	November 12
5	5	Ollin.	November 13
6	6	Tecpatl.	November 14
7	7	Quiahuitl.	November 15
8	8	Xochitl.	November 16
9	9	Cipactli.	November 17
10	10	Checatl.	November 18
11	11	Calli.	November 19
12	12	Cuetzpalin.	November 20
13	13	Cohuatl.	November 21
14	1	Micuiztli.	November 22
15	2	Mazatl.	November 23
16	3	Tochtli.	November 24
17	4	Atl.	November 25
18	5	Itzcuintli.	November 26
19	6	Ozomatli.	November 27
20	7	Malinalli.	November 28

HUEYPACHTLI, MONTH XVI

Days of the months	Days of the week	Signs of the Days	Corresponding to
1	8	Acatl.	November 29
2	9	Ocelotl.	November 30
3	10	Quauhtli.	December 1
4	11	Cozcaquauhtli.	December 2
5	12	Ollin.	December 3
6	13	Tecpatl.	December 4
7	1	Quiahuitl.	December 5
8	2	Xochitl.	December 6
9	3	Cipactli.	December 7

10	4	Checatl.	December 8
11	5	Calli.	December 9
12	6	Cuetzpalin.	December 10
13	7	Cohuatl.	December 11
14	8	Micuiztli.	December 12
15	9	Mazatl.	December 13
16	10	Tochtli.	December 14
17	11	Atl.	December 15
18	12	Itzcuintli.	December 16
19	13	Ozomatli.	December 17
20	1	Malinalli.	December 18

QUECHOLLI, MONTH XVII

Days of the months	Days of the week	Signs of the Days	Corresponding to
1	2	Acatl.	December 19
2	3	Ocelotl.	December 20
3	4	Quauhtli.	December 21
4	5	Cozcaquauhtli.	December 22
5	6	Ollin.	December 23
6	7	Tecpatl.	December 24
7	8	Quiahuitl.	December 25
8	9	Xochitl.	December 26
9	10	Cipactli.	December 27
10	11	Checatl.	December 28
11	12	Calli.	December 29
12	13	Cuetzpalin.	December 30
13	1	Cohuatl.	December 31
14	2	Micuiztli.	January 1
15	3	Mazatl.	January 2
16	4	Tochtli.	January 3
17	5	Atl.	January 4
18	6	Itzcuintli.	January 5
19	7	Ozomatli.	January 6
20	8	Malinalli.	January 7

PANQUETZALIZTLI, MONTH XVIII

Days of the months	Days of the week	Signs of the Days	Corresponding to
1	9	Acatl.J	anuary 8
2	10	Ocelotl.	January 9
3	11	Quauhtli.	January 10

4	12	Cozcaquauhtli.	January 11
5	13	Ollin.	January 12
6	1	Tecpatl.	January 13
7	2	Quiahuitl.	January 14
8	3	Xochitl.	January 15
9	4	Cipactli.	January 16
10	5	Checatl.	January 17
11	6	Calli.	January 18
12	7	Cuetzpalin.	January 19
13	8	Cohuatl.	January 20
14	9	Micuiztli.	January 21
15	10	Mazatl.	January 22
16	11	Tochtli.	January 23
17	12	Atl.	January 24
18	13	Itzcuintli.	January 25
19	1	Ozomatli.	January 26
20	2	Malinalli.	January 27

INTERCALARY

Days of the months	Days of the week	Signs of the Days	Corresponding to
3		Acatl.	January 28
4		Ocelotl.	January 29
5		Quahtli.	January 30
6		Cozcaquauhtli.J	anuary 31
7		Ollin.	February 1
8		Ollin.	February 17

Footnotes, Chapter X

(1) Translator's note: The Spanish says three here, but seems to be in error; from the context and the words at the end of the third paragraph of this chapter, it appears that thirteen is the author's intended meaning.

(2) Lorenza Hervas, in the letter he wrote to Clavijero which is found at the end of the first volume of Clavijero's history, talks with great praise about the calendar of the Mexicans, saying that "the genius that is discovered in it owes no apologies to that of the more enlightened nations;" that "in it the use of the symbols and of the periods of the years, months, and days is admirable;" that "in no nation of the world is there anything like this clear and admirable way of calculating time;" and that with regard to the period of their weeks "their calendar was superior to ours, for our weeks are not comprised exactly in the month or in the year." These praises in the mouths of such a

well-known Spaniard in the republic of letters, without talking about what is done by other national and foreign writers, show that our author was not concerned about the love of the country and the praises that he gives in this place to our ancient indigenous people. — E.

(3) Clavijero writes Cuitlahuatzin, and Archbishop Lorenzana, in his Prefaces to the Cartas de Hernan Cortes [Letters of Hernan Cortes], Cuitlahuotzin. — E.

(4) Monarquia Indiana [Indian monarchy], book 10, chapter 26.

(5) Book 6, chapter 46.

(6) Volume 6, chapter 5.

(7) The calendar the author mentions is not found in either of the two manuscripts, and therefore they have had to be created following the system he establishes in the foregoing chapters, putting the leap day on the last of the intercalary days. As this coincides with February 1st, this day has been repeated, just as the Romans repeated VI calends on the 24th and 25th of the same month. Otherwise the first day of the following year, which is also the 1st of the month Atemoztli, would not coincide with February 2nd, as it should according to the author's system. — E.

CHAPTER XI

Of the other three manners of calendars that the Indians used.

These natives were not governed by just the solar or astronomical calendar, but in addition to it they used three others, which were the ritual, the political, and the rural. Boturini gives the political calendar the names of civil and chronological, and the rural he called natural. These three calendars always revolved around the calculations of the solar year, varying only in some things; and thus to them they did not form separate wheels or charts, but rather they put their signs and their hieroglyphs on the same ones that they used to govern the solar year, and thus it can be said that these weren't calendars in the true sense, but rather guidelines for their government in ritual matters as well as in political and rural matters.

The ritual indicated all the festivals of the year, some of which were set and others movable; but with respect to the solar calendar, all were movable, because the ritual year only consisted of three hundred sixty-five days, and it did not have the leap days every four years, but rather at the end of its century they added thirteen days corresponding to the thirteen leap days the century included, which made up one entire week, and these days were dedicated to certain solemnities, as we shall see later on, and in this way they went back to being the same as the solar calculation and astronomical calendar; but in the course of the century, every four years they would get behind one day, and therefore, even though their set festivals were always on the same days, because of this delay they kept varying on the solar calendar. This is what Gemelli tried to explain in the place mentioned, saying that the first year of the century started on April 10, the same with the second and third, but not the fourth, which was the leap year, because this year started on April 9, and thus they would diminish one day every four years, so that the last year of the century ended on March 28, and after it they went on to count another week of thirteen days of that many leap days that had been diminished in the fifty-two years of the century, which they spent in festivals and sacrifices, and with this period they would come back to being the same with the course of the sun to start the first year of the following century on the day of April 10.

This explanation must only be understood in the ritual calendar, as I already said, and not in the astronomical calendar, in which they did not follow this order in the formation of the leap days; and even speaking about the ritual calendar, it supposes the comparison of the years of the Indians with our years, and as an established matter that the first day of the first year of their century corresponded to April 10, a point so questionable among writers, that only one of those that I have follows this opinion, because the rest follow one of the two most common, which are the 2nd of February or the 20th of March. Even in this supposition, it is an error to say that the last year of the century ended on March 28th, and it shouldn't be said to be anything other than the 27th, because afterwards having to count the thirteen days that were leap days from the 29th of March, they could not be completed until the very day of April 10th, and the subsequent year would not begin on that day, but rather on April 11th.

This difference that they had in forming the leap days on one calendar and the other has been the cause of many confusions and much variety among the writers who have tried to explain their calendars and wheels to assign the days of their festivals. This has also given rise to the variety of opinions to compare the first day of their year with the corresponding day on our calendar, and some, to avoid the difficulty, say that their ecclesiastical year did not start at the same time as the solar year, and finally each one indicates the days of their festivals as he found them noted on the wheels or calendars that he had in hand, because this ritual did not use various figures to indicate their festivals, but rather the same wheels and calendars that were done for the astronomical calculation, or to understand it better, the astronomical calendar denominated its months by the solemnities that the ritual calendar indicated; and this is why I have said that the names of the months varied in some parts according to the diversity of festivals that they celebrated; and therefore I am persuaded that these names were not given to the months at the time of the correction of the calendar, but many years later, when their idolatry reached its highest peaks, as shown on illustration number 5, and they did it in this way.

The festival of the dead children, for example, was set and had to be celebrated in the twelfth month. Let us suppose now that the year was of the first character, the flint, in which, as it is established, all the months had to begin by the nomination of its twenty days according to the order in which we have put them in the table of chapter VIII, and let us suppose that the festival were to begin on the eighth day of the month. In this case, what they did was that in the same box of the wheel in which a hieroglyph of the months had been placed, or on top of it, outside the wheel, they would place the hiero-glyph of Cohuatl, which is the snake, and it was the name of the eighth day of each month in the year of the flint, and this meant that the festival of the dead children started on the eighth day of the twelfth month. Now let us suppose that four years later they had to indicate the same festival in a year of the same sign of a flint. Then they would indicate it one day earlier with the hieroglyph Cuetzpallin, which is the lizard, because of the day of delay that they were going through with respect to the solar calendar, because of not having done the leap day at the end of the fourth year, and so the twelfth month had started one day earlier on the ritual calendar. With this it was verified that this was a set festival which was celebrated on the eighth day of the twelfth month, but because of the day of delay, they indicated it on the astronomical calendar on the seventh sign of the days of the months. For this reason I have said that with respect to the solar calendar, all the festivals were movable, although there were many fixed in the ritual calendar, because the account of this was only kept by the priests, and the priests were the ones who did the annotations on the solar calendar to advise and warn the people. When the festival was movable, they would indicate it in the same way, putting the sign of the festival (as each had its own special and well-known hieroglyph) above the box of the month, and beside it, the hieroglyph of the day on which it should be celebrated.

Some say that the ritual calendar counted the months variously, that is, that it didn't start its year in the month in which the solar calendar started it, but that they varied in assigning what was the first month of the ritual year. Some say that it started with Xilomaniztli, which is the fourth month of the solar year; others say with Pachtzintli, which was the fifteenth, which they also called Teotleco, or return of the Gods, as we have already said; but in the supposition that in the astronomical calculations there was no variation, if they used different figures for the ritual annotations, it is of little value to verify this, for as I have said, in reality it was not a different calendar, but a chart that they would form for their guidance, on the calculations of the solar year.

I say the same thing about the other two political and ritual calendars that they used: the first indicated the time of going on campaign and withdrawing from it, the months and days in which the meetings or congresses were to be done which were formed in various places, the days on which the kings gave public audience, and other similar things concerning the good government of the republics. On the ritual calendar, they noted the times in which to plant the corn, cotton, salvia, chili or pepper, and other crops that they cultivated, and the time of their harvests. But these annotations were always made by the same wheels or calendars of the solar year in the same way and in the same order as in the ritual calendar, and with less variation, because in these last two there was no concern for the formation of the leap days, but rather they would follow the calculations of the solar calendar.

Also some say that in these calendars they were starting to count the year by different months than the solar calendar, and with regard to the rural calendar, there is considerable variety in assigning the first month; but in the political, most agree that the first month was the last month of the solar calendar, which they called Panquetzaliztli, which means feather flag, and it meant that it was the time of going on campaign, because it came to be about January, which in these countries is the driest time, and the withdrawal from campaign was about the sixth or seventh [the book says second] month of the solar year, which is between April and June, because it is the time when the waters start in these countries. But however it may be, this is of little importance for our concern, and I again repeat that these were nothing more than charts for their guidance; but as some of the authors say who have written in passing about this matter, because of the confusing information that they acquired, that these natives used calendars in four different ways, without giving further explanation, I have felt it necessary to give them this name and explain what they contained for the perfect understanding of their calculations.

It is already seen that none of these last three could be ordered or arranged by the wise astronomers who met in Huehuetlapallan to make the correction and adjustment of their times, but rather many years later, because then there was no worship other than that of the Creator God, nor sacrifices of human blood, nor wars, nor even planting times; at least it is certain that they did not have them for all the seeds that they later cultivated. Even the solar calendar, as I already said, I am persuaded did not at that time have all the perfection that it later achieved, and in looking at the names of months and days, there is no room for doubt that they were put there many centuries after this correction, obligated by the needs of human life, showing the times most appropriate for their plantings, hunts, and fishing, and fleeing from those that they had learned to be harmful according to the diversity of lands, variety of climates, and conditions that are experienced in these countries within short distances, then because of the idolatry that they later fell into, inventing deities which they idolized in those times when, according to their false belief, they needed more of their help, and so even though throughout New Spain the system was one and the same, which is proven with evidence by the antiquity of this ordering or correction which we have discussed, nevertheless the symbols or hieroglyphs that they used were not the same everywhere, as I have advised in chapter VI, because the people in Oaxacac, Chiapa, and Soconusco, in place of the four main characters of Flint, House, Rabbit, and Reed, used these: Votan, Lambat, Been, and Chinax. Those from Mechoacán used these: Ino Don, In Bani, Inchon, Intehui. I have not been able to ascertain in any of them what the main character was, as the tecpatl of the Toltecs, but I find their coordination to be consistent in the way mentioned in the fragments of calendars of all the nations that I have become familiar with.

Nor have I been able to learn what the names were with which those from Oaxacac, Chiapa, and Soconusco indicated their months, but I have learned the names of the twenty days which made up each month, divided into the four main houses in the same way as the others, in this manner:

Votan.	Lambat.	Been	Chinax.
Ghanan.	Molo.	Hix.	Cahogh.
Abagh.	Elab.	Tziquin.	Aghual.
Tox.	Batz.	Chabin.	Mox.
Moxic.	Enoh.	Chue.	Igh.

Of those of Mechoacán, through a calendar fragment I have been able to learn up to fourteen names of the months, which are the following: Inthacari, In Dehuni, Inthecamoni, Interunihi, Inthamohui, Iniscatholohui, Imatatohui, Itzbachaa, Inthoxihui, Inthaxihui, Inthechaqui, Inthechotahui, Inteyabchitzin, Intaxitohui, and the five intercalary days they called Intasiabire. The four months lacking are those that corresponded to our January, February, and March, because the first sheet is missing from the manuscript, and it only begins from the day of March 22, and it ends at December 31, comparing their months with ours. In the same way they divide the names of the twenty days of each month into the four main houses, and they are the following:

Ino Don.	Inbani.	Inchon.	Inthihui.
Inic Ebi.	Inixichari.	Inthahui.	Inixotzini.
Inettuni.	Inchini.	Intzini.	Inichini.
Inbeari.	In Rini.	In Tzoniabi.	Ini Abi.
Inethaati.	In Pari.	In Tzimbi.	Intaniri.

With regard to the manner in which these people of Mechoacán counted their weeks, I have not found any information, because the mentioned fragment of their calendar is undoubtedly formed in later times after the conquest, and it only numbers the days of our months, indicating them and comparing them with the mentioned names of months and days successively repeated in the same order. Looking at those of Chiapa, the Gentleman Boturini, in his mentioned book, says that they would count seven errant stars corresponding to the seven days of their weeks. I do not know where he got the information from, nor was I able to find any information among his manuscripts to instruct me on this.

CHAPTER XII

Of the giants first inhabiting the land of Anahuac, which is the land today called New Spain.

At the time that this congress of wise astronomers was held in the city of Huehuetlapallan for the correction of the calendar, these peoples already had a considerable number of settlements, not just in the vicinity of their primitive city, but in all that region in which they were already very much spread out, especially toward the coasts of the sea. But as the Toltecs were the historians who preserved this information for us, they do not name any settlement other than their main city, which they say was called Tlachicatzin, the founders of which were all wise men and skilled craftsmen in all the arts that they knew and practiced up to that time, and so they were given the name of Toltecatl, which in the Mexican language means craftsman, and it seems that by this time the Toltecs were ruling themselves by their lords and judges, independently of those in Huehuetlapallan. This was now the court and capital of the empire, and they called it Chichimecatl because the main leader who ruled them, or the first king that they elected to govern them (the writers differ in this) was named Chichimecatl.

Others say that his name was Chichen or Cichen, which means rough and rigid man, from which they took the name of Chichimecatl; and priding themselves on a great nobility, they were proud and arrogant, and they maintained this same nature from this time up until our times. Some say that they did not take the name of the leader, but of the city that they founded called Chichen; but besides the fact that this is contrary to their common style, which was to take the name of the leaders and not of the towns, I do not find in any of the history that mention is made of such a city, either in ancient times or in later times, but I do find that in the same way the Egyptians called their kings Pharaohs from the name of a Pharaoh, the Persians, Shahs, and the Romans, Caesers, so these peoples would give their monarchs the title of great Chichimecatl, proof that they did not take this name from the city, but from that first leader or king; and so Chichimecs in all times have taken and continue to take great pride in their nobility, antiquity, and supremacy of their empire, holding themselves as superior to the other nations and as fathers of all of them.

Some have also said that they were given the name Chichimecatl because of the cruel custom of sucking human blood, as the barbarians of these nations do in our times, and they infer the entymology of the word Chichina, which means to suck, and Mecayotl, which means blood relationship, as if we were to say those who suck their own blood or the blood of their own kind. But the thought does not please me, first because in none of the Indian authors and the multitude of writers that I have become familiar with do I find any mention that even in their most remote antiquity they used this cruelty of living on human blood, nor many centuries later, but on the contrary, we will see in the discourse of this history that even when the sacrifices of human blood were introduced, they were abhorred and detested by the Emperors of Texcoco, who were the ones who boasted, and rightly so, of descending from the Chichimecs, preserving in them the illustrious blood of their monarchs, because this barbarous custom of living on human blood of the Chichimecs who today inhabit the northern lands of this America arose much later among them and for the reasons that I will say later, and so there are no writers whatsoever of theirs affirming that they were given the name of Chichimecatl because of this custom, but just the two opinions that I have mentioned, some saying that they took it from a king or leader of theirs, and others that they took it from a city.

The second, because the name is not Chichimecayotl, but rather Chichimecatl; and if the rigorous entymology is to be taken of this word, its meaning is he who sucks cord, making a compound of the verb Chichina, which means to suck, and the word Mecatl, which means cord. Third, because even though it is said that in their compound names they shorten the words, which is true, and that Mecatl is a shortening of Mecayotl, there is no evidence for this other than a simple discourse, and even being so, I will not concede that the meaning that they give to the word Chichimecatl is inferred correctly, because even supposing that Mecatl is always a shortening of Mecayotl, it is necessary to know that the first meaning of the word Mecayotl is blood relationship; and so following the information of the Indian authors who say that Chichen was the name of their leader or family father, I would say that the word Chichimecatl would be interpreted better by saying that it means the blood descendants of Chichen, or the relatives of Chichen, and it seems to me that this entymology of Chichimecatl is more natural and genuine, relatives or descendents of Chichen, than the other one that has been dragged up and does not agree as well with their histories. But I would rather go along with those who say that their leader or first king was named Chichimecatl, and they took it from him, because this was the most common thing among them, as we will see in the discourse of the history.

So those among them who were of a peaceful and humble nature, inclined to the study and observation of the stars for the practice of their arts, did not come face to face with the others, and so they resolved to separate as they did, and they founded their city of Tlachicatzin, where they established their government with total independence from the Chichimecs. At their example, other people started doing the same thing, who, under the leadership of a chief they would appoint, would separate and form their settlements, and they would do this not just in these times, but even many centuries later, as I have already said, they didn't have houses but caves, some that they found made by nature, and others that they would construct in imitation; and this separation, over the course of time, gave rise to the variety of nations that was found and still exists in this new world, different in names, customs, and rights, and with a variety of languages and dialects, some of which were formed by corruption of the legitimate Nahuatl language, which the authors unanimously agree was the primitive language, and others by later invention of men, obligated by human needs, with a variety of tones and accents, some of which do not have letters or syllables with which to be able to explain them, because some words are nothing more than a mute guttural or nasal sound with the mouth closed or open, and in none of the languages known so far among these peoples have we found the perfection, harmony, elegance, and richness of words, phrases, and explanations that are found in the Nahuatl or Mexican language.

Although the populations in that region had extended far and increased greatly, they do not say that any people had left that region to populate other countries until a few years after the adjustment of the times, in which they say that certain companies left from maritime settlements and came to settle on the banks of the Atoyac river between Tlaxcallam and Quetlaxcopan, an ancient settlement which was situated where the city of Puebla de los Angeles is today, of which nations I will later speak. First I need to give information that the Indians preserve and mention for this purpose. They say, then, that before these nations came to settle on the banks of the Atoyac, this area was already populated with giants, who were the relics of those who had escaped from the calamity of the hurricanes. They assert that these had been the ancient inhabitants of these banks, but most of them perished in the calamity of the hurricanes, and that the few who escaped had propagated until these times, in which those who had remained now found themselves without hope of continuing their generation because they were left with no women at all. They give them the name of Quinametli, and in plural Quinametzin; they don't give the measurement of their bodies, but they much ponder their stature, and for good reason, because from the many bones that have been gotten and are found every day in this land where they were living, it is known that they were very corpulent. I have seen many of these bones and I have some in my possession, including one which is perfectly well known to be the head or upper part of the thigh bone that they call the cea, and according to

137

its proportion, the body which it served must have been more than three yards tall; I got this from the hill of Cahualapa on the road from Tecali [Aecali in the book]. I also have a molar which was taken from other fragments of bones on the banks of the Atoyac river close to the town of Malacatepec on lands of my estates, which by proportion must have had a body four yards tall; and I have known of very reliable persons who have seen others that because of their integrity were known to be the bones that they were, and by their proportion to have served very tall bodies.

The knowledge of the ancient inhabitants of these lands having been giants is so common in all the authors who have written of things of the Indies that hardly any will be found who does not mention that at the time of the arrival of the Spanish in these countries they found that information universally received and confirmed among the natives; but even if it weren't so, the multitude of bones(2) that subsequently have been found and are discovered every day in the very land in which they assert their populations to have been (and there is no animal to whose body they could belong) and at the same time not finding others like them or similar in other lands that they did not inhabit verifies this information that the Indians preserved for us, and the find of entire skeletons that have been discovered in these recent years, which very reliable persons testify to have seen(3), entirely removes any doubt.

The Indian authors assert, as I have already said in Chapter III, that these were the first inhabitants of the land of Anahuac, now known as "New Spain," and I have also mentioned the difficulty of verifying whether they were originally from the same seven families that joined together in the confusion of tongues, or of a different origin. Some of the national authors, including Fernando de Alba Ixtlilxochitl, who is very well educated in his ancient history, says in one of his narrations that these giants were of the same progeny as the other Indians, and descendants of those first seven families who came from the dispersion of Babel to populate these lands, and therefore I have said in the first chapter that all the peoples and nations that populated North America proceeded from those seven families.

And although the mentioned Fernando de Alba did not say so, it seems to me that in his same histories I am finding reasons on which to base it. I consider the existence of the giants to be a fact, and today it is clearly evident with the multitude of bones and entire skeletons that have been discovered in this region, and I also feel, as by faith, that they did not have progenitors other than Adam and Eve themselves, the common parents of the whole human race, and that this diversity of statures, like that of colors, comes from the various dispositions of nature, natural conditions, climate, and similar accidents, as experience shows us at every step, seeing the same parents give birth to some tall children, and others small, some white, others brown, some blond, and others with black hair, with which there is no difficulty for these giants of this new world to have proceeded from those seven first families, and all the histories of the Indians give evidence that the Toltec nation, which undoubtedly comes from them, was always exceptional in stature, so much so that even many centuries after they left their fatherland and established their monarchy in the land of Anahuac, and almost up to the times in which the Spanish arrived, the Toltecs were known for their corpulence; and all those who have entered the interior land through New Mexico, which was where they made their first settlements, affirm that there are still some nations of outstanding stature, especially in the populations of the southern coast. I have some narrations written by Father Geronimo de Zarate, a Franciscan, of the entrances that have been made through New Mexico since the year 1538 until the year 1626, in which he affirms as an eye witness because of having been in some, and spent much time on those missions to find some of these nations of outstanding stature, especially in the maritime populations, and in the account of the journey of Juan de Oñate, to California by land in the year 1604, he tells about a giant woman who was from an island called Cinoguahua, and they gave her the name of Ciñacacohota, which means woman or captainess, whose stature was one and one-half times that of a typical man of the coast, they being very corpulent themselves.

Given this supposition, the opinion of some Indian authors is not unreasonable, who assert that the giants who inhabited the banks of the Atoyac river were Toltecs, because we have already said in Chapter III, and it will be said in other places in this history, that these Toltecs were always such enemies of idleness that they totally persecuted the idle until casting them out of their settlements; and of these giants who lived in this territory it is said that they were such lazy and careless people that they occupied themselves in nothing, that they lived as brutes, totally naked, thinking only of eating and drinking, surviving by crude fishing and hunting(4), wild fruits and vegetables, because they cultivated nothing, and were drunk most of the time, and so if we are to judge by the indications, these were without a doubt some of those lazy exiled people of the Toltec settlements, who, as fugitives and slackers, came to these parts, where, because it was warmer than the climate in which they were born, or because of the idle and brutal life in which they were living, their successors gradually increased in stature until achieving the corpulence noted in their skeletons, in which there was notable variety without a doubt because in the bones that I have seen, which are very few with respect to the many that have been gotten, a considerable difference in the stature is noted in their proportions. In addition to this is what they say, that although the language of the giants and of the Olmecs, who were the first who came to settle after them, and found them in this territory, as I will say later, was not the same, they were so similar that they understood each other, and this is strong evidence for the origin of the two nations to be the same.

Finally, among the manuscripts that I have, there is one very succinct one which seems to be very old; it does not have the name of the author, but its title is History of the Toltecs. It begins like this: The first inhabitants of this land were Toltecs. After this came the Olmecs and Xicalancas, who settled toward what is now the city of Los Angeles at the banks of the Atoyac river, where they found a few giants who had escaped from the calamities of the second age etc. Then if the Toltecs were the first, and the Olmecs second, and the Olmecs found some giants, these were Toltecs without a doubt. This is corroborated with the fact that in the next line the author mentions the rebellion of the Toltecs in his fatherland, and the departure of most of their nation, travel, settlement, and monarchy until their destruction. Then these are not those first inhabitants, but rather others of their same nation who came before.

And even though we have said at the beginning of this chapter that it does not appear that, before the correction of the times, any companies had departed from their first region to settle in other countries, this does not mean that some families of these lazy outcasts exiled from the settlements wouldn't have left, that not all would come to stop in the land of Anahuac, because, in my opinion, the first inhabitants of the kingdom of Peru were from these same vagabonds. See, in the work of Inca Garcilaso de la Vega, what he says of the customs and the ancient inhabitants of that kingdom before the Inca, and they will be found to be very much in agreement with those of the giants, and it is noteworthy that in the kingdom of Peru many bones of giants have also been discovered, and the Indians of that kingdom had much knowledge, and gave it to the Spanish, of the ancient giant inhabitants of that land. See what Herrera says of the giants who in ancient times landed at the point of Santa Elena, the memory of which the natives preserved, and told to the Spanish that they were living as brutes, they ate as fifty men, and they were given to sodomy, and that fire fell from the sky and consumed them, and it seems that this was even after that land was populated by other peoples.

From everything said, one is convinced that even though it is evident that the giants were the first inhabitants of the country of Anahuac, today New Spain, their origin and ancestry was the same as the other nations that were found on this continent, that is, those seven families who joined together because of the conformity of their language, and together traveled to these parts, as has been mentioned.(5)

Footnotes, Chapter XII

(2) It is not improbable that the bones alluded to were those of elephants, or of other antediluvian species of animals too large to enter into

the ark of Noah, and therefore doomed to become an extinct species. This reflection has been suggested by an examination of a work of the celebrated Kircher, entitled 'Arca Noe,' which is illustrated with many curious woodcuts representing the different species of animals which entered into the ark, and the separate places provided for their accommodation. It was noteworthy the Moses has been guilty of a slight inadvertency in stating, in the second verse of the seventh chapter of Genesis, that God commanded Noah to receive seven of every clean beast into the ark; since we learn from the ninth verse of the same chapter that two was the number actually admitted. Discrepancies of this kind are, however, of such frequent recurrence in the Old Testament that they are scarcely worthy of observation.

(3) Acosta, book 7 of the Hist. Nat. de Ind. [Natural History of the Indies], chapter 3. Torquemada Monarquía Indiana, book 1, chapter 13.

(4) The Levitical ordinance which forbade the Jews to taste blood would have been very likely to induce them to reproach other nations with eating raw fish. The general remark is true, that whatever was forbidden to the Jews in the Pentateuch is sure to be laid by them to the charge of the heathen. As regards the accusation of sloth which they brought against the giants, it deserves to be remarked that their destruction is said to have occurred about the same time that another portion of mankind was believed to have been changed into apes; which animal naturalists have observed to be of a very lazy, gluttonous, and lascivious disposition; all which evil inclinations the prophet Ezekiel reprobates in the forty-ninth verse of the sixteenth chapter of his Prophecies, –a chapter, it must be confessed, very mortifying to the vanity of the chosen people of God.

(5) There is hardly a historian in Mexico, including Clavijero, the very sensible Clavijero, who does not accept the existence of the giants, being supported in the bones that have been found in doing some excavations; but all the wise men are now in agreement in that these colossal bones are either those of animals whose species perished, and since their true names are not known they have been given the names of Mammoths or Mastadons, or those of elephants. The Baron of Humboldt is of this opinion in his Ensayo Político de N. E. [Political Essay of N. E.], volume 1, pages 221 and 401. In the year 1828, being prefect of Tulancingo, I submitted a thigh to the Museum that was started in Tlalpam, one that was one yard and a third, and which must be in the Toluca Library. This bone was taken from the property of the Basin [or Sewer? Drain?] of the Plains of Apam, from where I was assured various others could be obtained. In Texcoco some were also found in the year 1827, as have been found in different eras in many other places. Clavijero did not

have access to Natural History as advanced as it is today, and so it is not surprising that he would deny that the bones discovered up to his time were of Elephants, based on the fact that the Indians do not mention these quadrupeds as they do the giants. – E.

CHAPTER XIII

*Of the coming of the Olmec, Xicalanca, and Zapotec nations to the land of
Anahuac, final destruction of the giants, with which they are left as owners
of the country and found the city of Chollolan.*

Some years after they made the correction of their calendar and adjustment of the times, although they do not number how many, they say that two
numerous companies of people left from the maritime settlements in search
of other countries in which to settle. The chief of one company was named
Olmecatl, and the chief of the other was Xicalancatl, and from them they took
their respective names. If these were already distinct nations, or just one
divided into two parts with two chiefs from which they later formed, is not
easy to find out. What we are told is that they left together, and some add that
another third company also came with them, and they were called Zapotecs
after the name of their chief. The information that they give of them is so
scant that it can barely made out that their coming was by sea, sailing in rafts
and flat canoes, coast to coast as far as Panuco, a port situated at the inlet of
Veracruz, which they call the Mexican heart, at nineteen degrees latitude.
There they disembarked, and going inland, they reached the territory of the
Republic of Tlaxcallan and Huexutcingo, which today comprises the jurisdic-
tions of Chollolan and Puebla de los Angeles, in which they decided to make
their settlements, its climate seeming gentle and pleasant, the land good and
fertile for their crops of corn, beans, chili, and salvia, abundant in water, with
the flow of not just the two large rivers, Atoyac and Zachuapan, but of several
other streams that water it, and finally, much mountain land populated with
timber and abundant hunting, which was one of their main sources of food.

On the banks of the Atoyac river they found some giants who lived in
those regions, more as beasts than as thinking men. Their food was the raw
flesh of the birds and wild animals that they hunted without any distinction,
the wild fruits and vegetables, because they cultivated nothing; but they knew
how to extract the pulque drink from the maguey plant, with which they
would get drunk. They went about totally naked, their hair loose and
disheveled, and even though for the hunting of fowl they used the bow and
arrow, for other prey they more frequently relied on their own swiftness and
strength, taking advantage of that and their large build to follow and catch the

143

beasts, then fight with them, and for this purpose they used large sticks, branches of trees that they would break off with as much ease as we could remove the leaves. Finally they were fierce, cruel, and proud; but even so, they peacefully received the strangers, perhaps fearful of their large number, they being so few, and showing magnanimity and generosity, they gave them permission to inhabit their lands. The newcomers started to do so, but always looking on the giants with terror and fear. The giants knew this, and it made them more insulant, and priding themselves on being lords and owners of the land, they believed they were doing the others a great favor in allowing them to settle, in recompense for which they tried to force them to serve them as slaves, bringing them food and drink in abundance, such that they no longer thought of going hunting or fishing, gathering fruits or vegetables, but rather their guests had to bring them everything, and in great abundance; otherwise they would mistreat them and punish them cruelly, and so the new settlers lived in a very hard oppression and servitude.

This wasn't the worst, but with the giants being totally without any women, even before the arrival of these nations, they had given themselves up with wild abandon to the sin of sodomy, and although these people took women with them, those barbarians never sought after them, no matter how much the men offered the women to them and delivered up their own wives and daughters(1) in order to free themselves from harm. They were bothered so much by this, and by the oppression that they were suffering, that by decree of their chiefs and main lords they resolved to get rid of the giants once and for all. For this they prepared an abundant and splendid banquet which all attended, and having eaten and drunk incredibly, everyone so drunk that they were just like logs spread out on the floor, they put an end to all of them in one day, ending up free from slavery and lords of the land. The year in which this event happened is indicated by them with the hieroglyph of the rabbit in the number one, which according to my calculation was in the year 3979 of the world.

Now lords of the land, the new settlers started to spread throughout all the territory that today is Tlaxcalla, Puebla de los Angeles, Chollolan, Atlixco, Itzucan, and on the other side to Tepeiac, Techamachalco, Quecholac, and Teohuacan, which around here they say their settlements were done by the Zapotecs; toward Atlixco and Itzucan, by the Xicalancas; and in the territory of Puebla, Chollolan, and Tlaxcallan by the Olmecs, whose primitive main settlement, they say, had been the city of Chollolan, and even though they do not indicate the year of the founding of this city, which later became very famous and is still in existence in our days, saying that it was the first one that they settled; its antiquity must go back at least to the year of the destruction of the giants, which, as I have it recorded, was the year 3979 of the world, 107 years before the Christian era, and consequently it has the glory of being the oldest in all of New Spain.

The writers tell us that each one of these nations formed their settlements separately, without mixing one with the others, and that they extended throughout all this land, especially to the banks of the two rivers Zahuapan and Atoyac. They don't say anything about the policy with which they were governed, nor do they give any information about their religion and customs, but it seems, by the later events of history that we will see, that each town had its separate lord with total independence from the others, although those who were of the same nation maintained great union and friendship among themselves, to help and succor each other in their needs. I am persuaded that these companies were also of the Toltec nation, and all their signs indicate it, because they were able and industrious people, they cultivated the earth and planted various seeds for food, at least corn, chili, and beans. It is evident in the histories that the Olmecs planted crops before the Toltecs came to settle. They did not live in caves, as did the Chichimecs, but rather in houses, as they knew the art of constructing them with such solidity and strength that in a fragment of Tlaxcaltec history that I have in my possession, written by a mestizo of Tlaxcallan named Domingo Muñoz Camargo, who lived around 1545, he asserts that he had seen the ruins of some ancient buildings of the Olmec nation that had obviously been lavish and very strong. They also knew the art of weaving, and they wove blankets and clothes of cotton and other clothing of skins of rabbits, hares, dogs, and other animals. Their language was Nahuatl, which today they call Mexican, and it is considered their mother tongue; and this was that of the Toltec nation, and I have heard it said to persons well educated in this language, that in some towns that are still in existence in our days known as being of the Olmec nation, that they do great boasting about it, such as the town of Nativitas, which in antiquity was called Yancuitlalpan, and its region close to the sanctuary of San Miguel del Milagro [St. Michael of the Miracle] in the jurisdiction of Tlaxcallan and others, and this language is spoken with much purity and elegance. Finally, when the Toltec nation came to settle, these other three joined it without repugnance or any contradiction, recognizing and being subject to their kings, laws, and government. All these reflections make me believe that these first three nations that came to establish themselves and settle on the banks of the Atoyac river were Toltecs.

Concerning the settlements of this Olmec nation, and of the other two, the Xicalanca and Zapotec, which are still in existence in our days, it is not easy to find out whether or not they are the primitive ones, much less if their names are those that were given to them in their first founding, because around these times no city is spoken of other than the great city of Chollolan, which was its trading center [emporio; the book has imperio, or empire], and they assert that it was very large and contained an innumerable population, and to this day traces are found of its marvelous extension. In it the Olmecs built a very high tower, some have said to preserve themselves from another flood, but others assert that it was for nothing more than ostentation and greatness of its population, and as a monument and reminder to those in the future that Chollolan had been the first settlement of the Olmecs, that because of its great multiplication they had already formed other settlements in its regions and were starting to divide up. This great building, whose ruins still exist in our days, is another great proof of the skill and industry of these peoples, and not less of their knowledge and education in the history of the world, which no one else other than the Toltecs are known to have preserved. The mentioned tower was ruined a few years later, as we will see; and even though the Toltec nation, when it dominated this country, erected it again, it was also ruined again, but in our times a large part of it still stands, and at its sides several fragments of great size still exist, witnesses of its ruin. In reality it should not be called a tower, but rather a hill, because it is a hill in its structure, and in this aspect it more closely resembles the tower of Babel, as I have noted in chapter II. Through several parts I have gotten to know the materials of which it is made; it is tiny stone, the kind they call pebble, and a type of very large bricks of raw clay mixed with straw(2) or dry grass, which they call adobes here; a floor or layer is of this, a little more than a half yard high, and there is another one of stones and loose earth, and thus it rises in a spiral shape. Over the piece that is still standing, the Indians later built a lavish temple in honor of Quetzalcohuatl; and when the Spanish entered into this kingdom, it was consecrated to Our Lady, whose image, of small stature, remains there in our days with much worship and veneration; some say that it was brought by a Franciscan monk to whom she appeared in Rome, and she commanded him to bring it and place it in that place. Others affirm that the one who placed it there was Fernando Cortez himself, after the punishment and killing he did in Chollolan on those who had conspired against him, as we are told by the historians ["histories" in the book] of the conquest. What leaves no room for doubt is that the worship and veneration of this holy image is great, and comes as a continuation from the early times immediately following the conquest.

Footnotes, Chapter XIII

(1) See Genesis, chapter xiv, verse 5; and Judges, chapter xix, verse 24.

(2) The advantage of manufacturing bricks with straw is not very evident; neither is it the custom of modern times. The Old Testament,

however, informs us that the Jews considered straw a necessary ingredient in brick, as fully appears by the command of Pharaoh to the Egyptian taskmasters in the seventh verse of the fifth chapter of Exodus: "Ye shall no more give the people straw to make brick as heretofore; let them go and gather straw for themselves." Sahagan, in the fifth section of the twelfth chapter of the eleventh book of his History of New Spain, says that the Mexicans kneaded sword-grass with clay to make earthenware vessels.

CHAPTER XIV

Of the great eclipse and earthquake that the Indians mention as having observed in these regions, which seems to have been that of the death of Jesus Christ.

These natives indicate another singular event in their histories with great exactness, which later served them as a fixed era for their chronological calculations. They say that 166 years after the correction of their calendar, at the beginning of the year that was indicated with the hieroglyph of the House in the number ten, being a full moon, the sun was eclipsed at midday, the solar body being totally covered, such that the earth became darkened so much that the stars appeared and it seemed like night, and at the same time an earthquake was felt as horrible as they had ever experienced, because the stones crashing against one another were broken into pieces, and the earth opened up in many parts. Confused and bewildered, they believed that the end of the third age of the world had already arrived, which, according to the predictions of their wise men in Huehuetlapallan, should end in strong earthquakes, in whose violence many living people would perish, and mankind would suffer the third calamity; but the earthquake ceasing entirely and the sun once again being uncovered perfectly, everyone was found to be whole, without any living persons having perished, and this caused them such great wonder that they noted it in their histories with singular care.

Following these calculations, and adjusted to the comparison of the tables, this event should be placed in the year 4066 of the world, which was indicated with this character as can be seen in the tables, and precisely 166 years after the adjustment of the calendar; and because of the circumstances surrounding this eclipse and earthquake, it was impossible for it to be any other than that which was observed at the death of Jesus Christ Our Lord, having suffered it in the thirty-third year of his age, and so it seems that the incarnation of the Word should be placed in the year 4034 of the world, which the Indians indicated with the same hieroglyph of the House in the number 4, and I have noted it that way in the tables, and with this calculation following the chronological order that they observed, counting the years from one memorable event to another with the assignment of the hieroglyph of the year in which they fell, I have been able to coordinate it perfectly with our years in the year 1519, in which Cortez landed at Veracruz, as will be seen in the discourse of this history.

By this it should not be understood that I take it upon myself to decide on such a questionable point, in which so many great minds have set their pens in such a learned and knowledgeable manner, giving accuracy preference to the Indians over the great number of illustrious talents who have dealt with this subject with great diligence and study in this matter; although it isn't strange for God to have revealed to these small ones what he hid from the wise, as he did with the invention of the leap days; but I do say that among the multitudes of opinions on the age of the world when the Word became incarnate, there is a variation from three thousand and so many years to five thousand and so many, which is almost two thousand years of difference, and this calculation of the Indians is a perfect average between these two extremes. The chronicle of Auberte [the book has "Hauberto"], Father Suarez(1) and the authors he quotes vary by just a few years from the calculations of the Indians; and finally, having to follow the calculation of the Indians according to the historian laws, and their chronological method in assigning their years in which the events occurred, and comparing them to our corresponding years, in order not to fall into the anachronisms that the authors of some of the documents that I have fell into, because of trying to do the count from memory, I assumed the material work of perfecting the tables, and on them I have followed my calculations, precisely observing the hieroglyphs and numbers that the Indians assigned, as will be seen in the discourse of the history by the references that I will be doing for the satisfaction of the curious.

The Gentlemen Boturini, in his mentioned work, says that the first Christian Indians who then perfectly understood their chronology and studied ours with all curiosity left us the knowledge as from the creation of the world until the mentioned birth of Christ, 5199 years had passed, which is the same opinion or calculation of the seventy. Among the monuments that he gathered, I have not been able to find the one that enlightened him with this information, because they wrote most of them without chronology, that is, following the method of the historical charts, referring to the events, assigning only the symbol or hieroglyph of the year in which they occurred, for example, the Flood in the year of one Flint, the suspension of the sun in the year of eight Rabbits, the great earthquake in the year of ten Houses, etc.; but they do not enter into finding out what year of the creation or of the Christian era they correspond to, and the most precise just say the centuries or the years that had passed from one event to another, regularly leaving out the broken years(2). The one who put the most care into the chronology was Fernando de Alba, seeking to compare their eras and reduce their years to ours; but in four manuscripts that I have of his, he varies considerably with a

149

difference of hundreds of years from one calculation to another, and in each one of his narration obvious anachronisms are found at each step. The cause was his having done the counts and calculations from memory(3) and without forming tables; so asserts Boturini himself in his books, and he told me repeatedly that to write the history that he was pondering and that we have in our hands it was necessary to be bound to the tables and work on them, adapting the events with special care to the hieroglyphs of the years; because in assigning these hieroglyphs the Indians were very precise, but not in the number of them that they would assign from one event to another, especially when they were counting by ages or centuries, because then they would regularly omit the extra broken years; and I have experienced it as he was telling about it; therefore, above all, I sought to finish the tables that Boturini himself started in his own hand, and tied to them precisely I have indicated the eras, in which he didn't make the world more than 4033 years old when Jesus Christ was born, and what is more worthy of reflection, Boturini himself, in the mentioned tables that he formed in his own hand, indicates the year in this way: Three Tecpatl, 4033 Nativitatis Domini, from which it appears that he got the same count, and therefore, from the following year, which is the year 4034, he starts to indicate the years of the Christian era in the same way that I do, and it is expressed in the tables; and in the year 4056 he puts this sign in the margin: _ IHS, which means Crucifixion of Jesus, in which time the earthquake occurred, and so I am persuaded that he was mistaken in this assertion from his book, because, as I have already said in other places and he confesses, he wrote from memory and without having access to the documents that he gathered.

Footnotes, Chapter XIV

(1) Suárez In. 3, Part. D. Thomae, volume 1, quaest. 1, art. 6, Disp. 6, sect. 1.

(2) By the expression "quebrados" [broken] are meant the odd years over and above a Mexican age or century.

(3) Echeverría's assertion that Don Ferdinand de Alba Ixtlilxochitl and Boturini had both been guilty of anachronisms, from placing too much dependence on their memory in framing their chronological computations, should be understood of each of them in a different sense. He evidently means that the former writer had fallen into error, from not having formed tables such as he had himself made use of, the better to adjust the signs employed in the

Mexican calendar to our years; and that the latter, when in Spain, could not have been able to consult the paintings which he had left behind him in Mexico.

CHAPTER XV

Of the coming to these lands of a wonderful man to whom they gave the names of Quetzalcohuatl, Cocolcan, and Hueman.

Several years after the great eclipse, in a year that was indicated with the hieroglyph of the Reed in the number one (which according to the tables seems to have been the year 63 of Jesus Christ), a white and bearded man of good stature came to these regions through the northern part, dressed in an ankle-length tunic adorned with red crosses, barefoot, his head uncovered, and a staff in his hand, whom some call Quetzalcohuatl, others Cocolcan, and others Hueman.

They say that he was just and holy, that he taught them a good law, counseling them to overcome their own passions and appetites, to hate vice, and to love virtue; he instituted the forty-day fast, mortification and penitence with shedding of blood, he acquainted them with the cross, promising them, by means of that sign, serenity in the air, the necessary rain, the preservation of their populations, bodily health, and the relief of all their needs. He told them about a triune and one God,(1) taking the opportunity to explain to them this mystery of rocks and triangular poles and other similar figures, of the Virgin birth, and other mysteries that they later mixed with fables and mistakes, as will be seen later on; and crossing the land of Anahuac and the settlements of the Olmecs, he stayed for a time in the city of Chollolan.

Although they do not say the exact number of years that had gone by after the great eclipse until the appearance of this venerable man, they indicate the hieroglyph of the year, which was the Reed in the number 1, and in the suppositions of its having been the eclipse that occurred at the death of Jesus Christ, which we have placed in the year 33 from the incarnation, the first one after it that is indicated with the Reed in the number 1 is that of 63 A.D., 30 years after the eclipse, as can be seen in the tables.

Among all the authors who have written of things of the Indies, there is none who does not talk about this wonderful man, but all with confusion according to the knowledge that they acquired, whether mixed with fables, whether explained with allegories given either by common people or by well-educated people misunderstood by the writers, such that they make him a God, King, Priest, Magician, and finally, in these narrations there are a thousand oddities and contradictions that cause notable revulsion. Therefore, it seems to me that I must declare not only what I find in the authentic monuments, manuscripts, and histories that I have gathered, but also the rule that I follow about this famous man and the foundations that persuade me, although it may seem a digression from the main topics, for not only is it one of the most curious points, but also one of the most necessary points to understand the origin of many of the rites and ceremonies that the Spanish found established among these nations at the time of the conquest, and it is no less important to correct the multitude of errors that most of our writers make in the foundations of some of the cities, and the coming and establishment of several nations.

Father Torquemada,(2) who gathered much ancient information and brought it to light in his Monarquía Indiana [Indian Monarchy] in the same way that it was given by the persons from whom he was informed, without stopping to criticize the difficulties and contradictions that conflict with each other, talks several times in his work of Quetzalcohautl, and says that he was a king of Tollan, a priest, a necromancer, a magician, a liar, superstitious, human and merciful, very honest, very chaste, a pursuer of evil doers, a sufferer of insults, a wise astronomer, a skilled craftsman in works of gold and silver, a very expert farmer who taught them the cultivation of many plants; and finally, adorned with so many good and evil qualities contrary one to another that they do not fit in one individual. And the best part is, that neither his magic nor his wisdom were sufficient to keep him from being deceived and overcome by the sorcerer Titlacuahua, who first persuaded him to take a trip to the kingdom of Tlapallan, and afterwards tried to obstruct his way, without the reason for one or the other being known. Finally the life of this man and his character, according to this author in the different places in which he speaks of him, is a combination of passages that do not fit in one individual, especially if we add the one that also asserts that the remembrance of this man remained so permanent and so venerable that they not only observed the moralities that he taught them and the rites and customs that he introduced, keeping his prophecies very much in mind, the fulfillment of which they were expecting, but also that those who came to reign in Mexico did not receive the kingdom as lords themselves, but as lieutenants of Quetzalcohuatl, it being certain and constant in all the histories of the Indians that he was not king of Tollan, nor was Tollan founded until many years later, and Mexico a great many years more, nor were his four disciples the first founders of the lordship of Tlaxcala, but other very different ones, as will be seen later. And even though some of these passages this author confesses are fables, others he gives as certain and established, equating them with events of sacred and profane history.

Antonio de Herrera says that(3) Quetzalcohuatl, which means god of the air, is made to be the founder of Chollolan,(4) that he came from toward the north by sea and landed at Pánuco with a company of new people who penetrated to Tollan, where they were well received, and not being able to subsist there because of Mexico already being founded and all the land settled, they went on to Chollolan, where they settled and later spread to Huaxaca and Misteca. That the word Quetzalcohuatl, literally translated, means God of the air, there will be no one who is moderately educated in the Mexican language who will say so; but as in later times the Chollotecs worshiped Quetzalcohuatl as the God of the air, that is where Herrera, or those who communicated this information to him, want his name to mean that, and confusing the coming of the Olmecs with that of the Toltecs, and Huemac (another ancient wise person who came with the Toltecs) with Quetzalcohautl, he postpones the founding of Chollolan to that of Tollan and Mexico, and it seems that he gives Quetzalcohautl and his associates the name of Toltecatl, which means craftsman, because in Tollan they started to teach, although he calls Tollan Tula, and instead of saying Toltecatl he says Tulotec.

Quetzalcohautl was neither king nor chief of any nation he came to inhabit, nor a magician, nor a necromancer, sorcerer, or liar, but a venerable, just, and holy man, who with works and words taught the road of truth through the overcoming of ones passions, mortification, fast and penitence. In the worship of just one God he enlightened these natives of the Sublime Mystery of the August Trinity, the coming of the son of God to the World, the Virgin birth, the passion of the Lord and his death on the holy wood of the cross, whose powerful sign he manifested to them, and he was worshiped by them, inspiring a great hope in them of achieving the universal remedy, through him, of all their needs. He made them various prophecies, of which the one of the destruction of the tower of Chollolan, and that of the coming of some white bearded peoples from the east who would take possession of the land,(5) were very notable, and both the one and the other were fulfilled purposely in all their circumstances, as we shall see. For the person who did all this to have been a magician, necromancer or sorcerer, a minister of the devil, is something so repulsive that in itself it becomes unbelievable, and on the contrary, according to the time in which the Indian historians indicate his coming, it seems consistent that it was some apostle or disciple of Jesus Christ, who, after his passion and death, traveled to these parts to spread in them the preaching of the gospel to verify the prophecy of David: Their line is gone out through all the earth, and their words to the end of the world(6) and fulfill the precept of Christ to his apostles: Go ye into all the world, and preach the gospel to every creature.(7) Because one who says "All the World" is not excluding America, which is half of the world's globe, and one who says "every creature" is not excluding the inhabitants of America, who then were a very considerable portion of creatures; and that this precept of Christ to the apostles is to be understood in the generality that it sounds like of the world and creatures is the opinion of St. Gregory, St. Thomas, St. Juan Crisóstomo,(8) Teophilato, Eutimio,(9) the cardinals Hugo and Cayetano,(10) and many other exponents, some of whom assert that in the space of forty years following the death of Christ the apostles preached throughout the world. With the Indians indicating the coming of Quetzalcohuatl thirty years afterwards, it agrees well with this opinion, and all the doctrine that he taught being in agreement with the new gospel law, we must believe that it was one of the holy apostles, and that not as a natural but rather as a miraculous act he walked throughout this new world, and he preached throughout, leaving many traces and signs that survive to our times, as we are going to see.

Footnotes, Chapter XV

(1) Reserving for another place proofs from Clavijero's History of California, of the Indians of that peninsula believing in a Trinity, and in an incarnation of the Son of God, we shall here only observe that the doctrine of a Trinity was known in many parts of America: for example, in Mexico, Yucatan, and Peru; in Nicaragua; amongst the Muyscas, a civilized people of New Granada; in Paraguay, and according to some accounts, even in Chile and amongst the Indians dwelling on the banks of the Orinoco. Statements of this curious fact are to be found in the second chapter of the fourth book of the third part of Oviedo's unpublished General History of the Indies; in the second part of the inedited Noticias Historiales of Pedro Simon; in Acosta's Natural and Moral History of the Indies; in Renessad's Chronicle of Chiapa; in Cogolludo's History of Yucatan; in Torquemada's Indian Monarchy; in the first book of the third volume of the Saggio di Storia Americana by the Abbé Gilii; in Calancha's Chronicle of the Order of Saint Augustin in Peru; and in Garcia's Predicación del Evangelio en el Nuevo Mundo. Echevarría's statement that the Mexicans adored a Trinity in Unity receives great confirmation from the following passage of the first part of an inedited Treatise of Torribio de Benavente, which is preserved in manuscript in the library of the Escorial, who affirms that the people of Tlaxcala, Huexocinco and Chotmla (three states contiguous to Mexico) worshipped one God under three names: "Without the said festivals, there were many others in each province, and they served each demon in their own way with sacrifices and fasts and other diabolical offerings, especially in Tlaxcala, Huexocinco, Chollola, which were lordships in themselves. In all these provinces, which are near each other and came from the same ancestry, they all worshiped and had their God as the main one to whom they gave three names. 'Ancient rites, sacrifices, and idolatries of the Indians of New Spain and of their conversion to the Faith.'" Diego Duran, another ancient Spanish author, whose History of Mexico was given

by Juan de Tobar to Acosta, (although the latter nowhere acknowledges the obligation which he was under to a writer, from whom he appears to have borrowed almost all that he wrote concerning the ancient history of the Mexicans,) confirms in the following passage of that history the previous testimony of Benavente: "It is noteworthy that the present figure was solemnized in the name of the Father, which Tota means, in order that we know that they reverenced the Father and the Son and the Holy Ghost, and said Tota, Teopiltzin, and Yolometl, the words mean our father and our son, and the heart of both, making a festival to each one in particular and to all three in one, where the knowledge is noted that there was a Trinity among these people.

(2) Torquemada Monarquía Ind. Page 3, book 3, chapter 7. Id. Lib. 4, chapter 14.

(3) Herrera dec. 2, book 7, chapter 2. Id. Dec. 5, book 2, chapter 11. [Herrera dec. 2, book 7, chapter 2, folio 219.]

(4) Id. Dec. 3, book 2, chapter 11, folio 79.

(5) The prophecies here ascribed to Quetzalcohuatl must remind us of Christ's famous predictions respecting the destruction of the temple at Jerusalem and the conquest of Judea by the Romans.

(6) Psalms 19:4.

(7) Mark 16:15.

(8) Crisóstomo Hom. 76. Sup. Mat.

(9) Teoph et Euthim. In Math. 24.

(10) Hugo et Caiet. In Math. 28, et Marc. 16.

CHAPTER XVI

The vestiges that are found in New Spain of Quetzalcohuatl denote his having been one of the holy Apostles.

The sovereign sign of the cross, a figure of the crucified, a scandal to the Jews and foolishness to the gentiles according to the Apostle(1), is the insignia and very character of the Christian disciple of Christ and professor of the gospel law, and this was what Quetzalcohuatl manifested and let these natives know, forming crosses in different manners, which he exhibited and placed in many parts for it to be venerated, and this knowledge was found by the Spanish when they arrived in these parts, so constant throughout this new world because of the tradition from fathers to sons, as testified by all our writers. Herrera says(2) that when Grijalva discovered the New Spain, he gave it this name because of the many lime houses and the singing, towers, and crosses that they found in those settlements that they saw. Cortez found a large cross on a beautiful stone wall that was worshiped from very ancient times in Acazamil or Cozumel; and Gomara(3) asserts that this place was considered a common shrine of all the surrounding islands and that there was no town that did not have its shrine of stone or of another material. Crosses were also found in Chollolan, in Tollan, in Texcoco, and in other parts, and generally the sign of the cross was considered the God of the rain among all these natives, because this being such a necessary asset for the success of their planting, Quetzalcohauatl taught them the impetration of god through the cross; and it arose from here that in later times, with those first lights obscured or extinguished, they worshiped it as God of the rain and of the air that conducts it. Finally, they are all in agreement that this man wore a white, ankle length tunic adorned with red crosses, and anyone who took care to extol this sovereign sign and to mark himself with it gives more signs of being a Christian than a gentile, of an apostle than a necromancer, of a saint than of a magician and deceiver.

I am not unaware of the fact that Father Torquemada(4) wants to persuade that the crosses that Francisco de Montejo found when he started the conquest of Yucatan, especially in the province of Totolxiuh, and the one that Cortez found in Acuzamil, were placed there a little before the Spanish arrived there, by a gentile priest named Chilacambal whom they consider as a great prophet, and that this was the one who predicted to them that within a brief time some white, bearded people would go there from the east, who would wear that insignia which their gods couldn't attain, and that this people would rule the land.

But about the inconsistencies and contradictions that this persuasion includes, which Father Gregorio García(5) puts forth in the book that he printed with the title of Predicación del Evangelio en el Nuevo Mundo [Preaching the Gospel in the New World], he adds [book: I add] that it is necessary to prove that this same professor walked all of New Spain and Peru, planting crosses and making the same prophesy, for one and another were found in agreement throughout America, as is seen in all our historians of both kingdoms. But inasmuch as my concern is only New Spain, I will not go out of it to show the vestiges that this venerable man left of the gospel truth.

Father Torquemada(6) himself talks about the miraculous cross of the place of Quautolco that they commonly call Guatulco; and although he says that this was put in this place by Father Martín de Valencia or another of his companions in those early times, this is mere arbitrary conjecture, which Father García refuted with solid reasons in the mentioned place(7); and Father Joachim Brulio, in the History of Peru of his religious order of St. Augustine(8), asserts that this holy cross was venerated in that place since very ancient times. That is confirmed by Father Gregorio Garcia, who adds the miracle that occurred when the heretic Francisco Drake, who landed there, tried to burn it and was unable to do so; for it was thrown into a fire three times and the fire did it no harm; and even though he covered it with fish and tar to get it to burn, he was unsuccessful. This holy cross is venerated at the present time in the city of Guaxacac, to where it was moved by Bishop Juan de Cervantes, and at the Convent of Discalzed Carmelites of Puebla de los Angeles they venerate a cross made of an arm of this one, which was taken there and placed in a chapel of the presbytery by Mr. Antonio de Cervantes Carvajal, a canon of that church and nephew of the mentioned bishop.

Mr. Bartolomé de las Casas, the Bishop of Chiapas, after a serious report was made on the case, asserts in an apology of his, which manuscript is kept in the Convent of Santo Domingo in Mexico, that it is known because of a very ancient tradition of those natives that that cross was brought by a white, bearded man, dressed to the knuckles in a white, ankle-length tunic, that he brought other disciples with him, and that these disciples told their grandparents about the mysteries of the Trinity and the Virgin birth, and they taught them the fast and penitence. These are the same signs that the Indian historians of Quetzalcohuatl give.

And to convince that the worship that they gave to this holy cross was as ancient as the place, and not from the times immediately prior to the conquest, as Father Torquemada suggests, I am going to give irrefutable proof in the very name of the place, for as all [place names] are significant in the Mexican language, many times I have taken advantage of them to resolve my questions, and always with good effects. The true name of this place is Quauhtolco; that is how it is written by the Indian authors and those who know and perfectly possess the Nahuatl language, not Quanhtochco, as fathers Torquemada and García write; the latter is a very different place close to Orizaba and the town of Córdoba, which the Spanish corrupted because they couldn't pronounce it, calling it Guatusco, and they call Quauhtolco Guatulco. Now this name Quauhtolco is a compound of Quautli, which means the wood, from the verb toloa, which means to venerate by bowing the head, and the particle co, which denotes place, and thus Quauhtolco means place where one worships or bows to the pole. And so the worship of the cross was as ancient as its name was in this place, and maybe even more ancient, since it took its name from it.

Father Garcia(9) makes mention of another prodigious cross that was found in the sierra of Meztitlán, and he quotes Esteban de Salazar, a Carthusian monk, who was previously an Augustian monk, as Father Calancha(10) says, whose words he mentioned that are copied from the work of Father Garcia, and afterwards I compared them with the book of Father Salazar entitled Discurso sobre el Credo [Discourse on the Creed], which is the one that Boturini mentions in his catalog of documents that he gathered, and they are these: "On a point of a very high sierra in a very distinguished place, which took its name from the antiquity and sculpture that it has on that peak cut from the mountain, as did all the heavily populated and very wide mountains that they call Meztitlán; because Meztli, in the Nahuatl or Mexican language, means moon, and tetl, stone, crag or cliff, and titlan, on the cliff, so that Meztitlán means the moon over the cliff. On that rocky cliff, at that very high and almost inaccessible place, a cross is cut in relief at the right hand of the river in tau fashion, which is a T, worked in squares like a chessboard, one square of the color of the stone, which is very white, and another of a very perfect blue, one cubit high (as judged by sight from a great distance away), and in front of it a half moon of the same size, on the left hand of the cliff, also carved in relief on it and worked with the same squares and colors. Among that people there are none who have any knowledge about when, or in what manner or by whom, those figures on that cliff were cut and carved, or for what purpose, nor can they see what they mean. Because I myself making a great effort at that very place, which is entrusted to the illustrious gentlemen Francisco de Mérida y Molina [book: the illustrious Franciscan council of Mérida and Molina(11)], and finding very old men in it, including one who, at the very least, from what we were able to learn there, the religious Father Antonio de Mendoza, (who is alive today and is the definitor of that province of New Spain, the son of the illustrious Luis de Marin, of the most principal conquerors of that world, to whom the province of Guazacalco was entrusted, and of María de Mendoza, the aunt of the Count of Aguilar, our highly beloved son in the Lord), was over one hundred forty years old, and I was unable to learn or clarify any more than that it was there from time immemorial, and that it was in his memory and that of his parents and grandparents and progenitors; and the name of the place well shows its antiquity, for as we have said, it was called in their language the moon over the stone, the town being very ancient. But what amazed me the most in such a rare spectacle was that the hue of that most perfect color blue, while exposed to the elements for such a long time, had never faded or gotten worn out."

This marvelous cross still exists today in the same way and the same manner as this author describes it; and some very reliable persons who have seen it have assured me of it, ecclesiastics as well as monks and clerics, who have administered as priests in this sierra, as well as lay persons, and among them was one, the Gentleman Boturini, who made a trip to this place for no other purpose than to see and admire this wonder, and he assured me that the spot where it is at is a very high, steep slope of the hill called Tianguistepetl, a climb so eminent and precipitous and so rough that it is not credible that through human strength and industry anyone could have put it there, as it is carved right in the cliff, and its size is a little more than one cubit, on a background of a very fine blue strewn with white stars, and on the right side it has a shield, on the same blue color, with five white balls representing the five very precious wounds of the Lord, the color so permanent that there has been no water, sun, air, nor elements of any kind that have been able to decrease its beauty in any way. Its antiquity is not disputable, for as the author says, explaining the word Meztitlán, this whole sierra took its name from there, and since very ancient times, distant from the coming of the Spanish, it has been called Meztitlán. So this sovereign sign, so admirable for its workmanship, placement, antiquity, and permanence, proves the preaching of the gospel in these countries since the primitive times of Christianity by some apostle or disciple of Christ [book: the Lord]; and with its being evident through the histories of the Indians that Quetzalcohuatl was the first who let them know the cross, it is likely that it was this apostle or disciple of the Lord who set it there as a reminder of his preaching, or one of his disciples.

Father Gregorio García himself mentions(12), through the account of another monk of his order, that when the Dominicans entered into the province of the Zapotecs in those early times immediately following the conquest, in a place called Quichapa, they found, in the possession of a chief, a Bible of just figures, which were the characters that served them as letters, the meaning of which they knew, because from fathers to sons, they were teaching how to understand those figures; and they had been keeping this book from a very ancient time; and he also mentions(13) that as Father

Alonso de Escalona, of the Order of our Father San Francisco [Saint Francis], was passing through the town of Nejapa, in the province of Huaxaca, the vicar of that convent, who was of the religious order of Santo Domingo, showed him some charts of these Indians of very ancient appearance, which contained some points of our Holy Faith. Among the papers that I have gathered, I have a whole explanation of one of these charts that contains the most principal points of our faith. It begins with the creation of man, his sin, exile from paradise, the flood, the tower of Babel, and this is followed by the incarnation, birth, passion, and death of Christ, and the coming of an apostle who preached the gospel in those early times; and the author of this explanation says that the chart was given to Dr. [book: Bachelor or graduate] Carlos de Sigüenza y Góngora, who was a very well-known individual in Mexico, where his fame endures today because of his great erudition and knowledge in this subject of antiquities of the Indians, and although I have gathered some of his manuscripts, I haven't been able to have this chart in my hands through the efforts that I have made, curious to see whether or not it is from the ancients; because there are many modern ones, that is, subsequent to the conquest, and these prove nothing, and so I am not using this explanation.

Antonio de Herrera, speaking of the things of Honduras(14), tells of a triangular stone that was found in the land of Cerquin, with three deformed faces on each point, which those natives had in veneration from the most remote antiquity; and although the narration that they gave of how that stone came to be there is fabulous and full of mistakes, it is known that those same fables were invented on the Catholic truths that they knew about in the early centuries, and over the course of time they became distorted, as has happened throughout the world, and this has always been how idolatry has spread and multiplied.

Footnotes, Chapter XVI

(1) 1 Corinthians 1:23

(2) Herrera Dec. 2, book 3, chapter 1

(3) Gomara 2, p. c. 15

(4) Torquemada p. 3, book 15, chapter 49.

(5) Book 5, chapter 4.

(6) Torquemada, p. 3, book 16, chaper 28.

(7) García, Predicación del evangelio, book 5, chapter 5.

(8) Brulio, Historia de San Agustín del Perú, book 1, chapter 5.

(9) García, Book 5, chapter 6.

(10) Calancha, Book 2, chapter 2.

(11) It has not been possible to find out what council this might be; and if there is some error here of the copiers, it is not easy to know what it consists of, as it has been difficult to find the book from where the author took this passage. – E.

(12) Book 5, chapter 7.

(13) Book 5, chapter 8.

(14) Dec. 4, book 3, chapter 4.

CHAPTER XVII

The knowledge that they found of the doctrine of Quetzalcohuatl, and the rites and customs that he taught, prove with more efficacy that he was a Holy Apostle.

Besides these vestiges and material signs, others remained from a higher sphere, and they prove with greater efficacy that Quetzalcohuatl was one of the holy apostles or disciples of the Lord, that he preached the gospel in these parts. These are the doctrines, customs, and ceremonies that he taught to these natives, which they preserved in their republics as holy and sacred things, without losing from their memory that it was Quetzalcohuatl who taught them to them. I confirm them in the adoration of the Creator God only, for as we have already said, around these times idolatry had not yet arisen in these countries, and Tloque Nahuaque, or Creator God, was the only object of their adoration, although devoid of all outward worship, because there were no temples, nor did they worship him with outward ceremonies, or sacrifices, or incense, or prayers, so that it was just a knowledge or awareness that all things, and they themselves, were works of the powerful hand of this supreme entity who created them and preserves them, but without their rendering him homage or thanks in any way for these benefits.

Quetzalcohuatl taught them to pray in places separate from all domestic use and intended only to congregate there to worship the Creator God with humility and praises, and to eat together there on certain days, instructing them in the modesty and composure that they should have, and putting the Holy Cross in some of them as a visible object of their adoration, as a figure of the crucified, an instrument of the redemption and a standard that publishes the triumph of the Redeemer. He gave them the knowledge of the ineffable mystery of the Sublime Trinity, explaining to them with those examples and figures provided in their crudeness, such as the triangular stones with the equal and very large faces like the one at Cerquin; and until the arrival of the Spanish in these countries, the memory of the doctrine of Quetzalcohuatl about this mystery was preserved, for as the Bishop of Chiapa, Bartolome de las Casas, mentions in the manuscript that I have already mentioned and which is also referred to by Gregorio García in his work of the Preaching of the Gospel in the New World(1), and Antonio Remesal in the

History of his Province of Dominicos de San Vicente de Chiapa,(2) in Yucatan a principal Indian was found who said, when asked abut his ancient religion and beliefs and that of his compatriots, that they believed that there was a Supreme God in Heaven, that although he was just one, there were three persons. They called the first one Izona, and attributed the creation of all things to him; they called the second Bacab, whom they said was the son of Izona, and had been born of a Virgin names Chibirias, who is with God in the heavens; and the third they called Echuah. Eupoco had Bacab whipped, put a crown of thorns on him, and finally, stretched out and tied to a wood, he took his life. He was dead three days, and then resurrected and rose to the heavens with his father. Afterwards Echuah came to the earth and filled it with whatever was needed. He also said that this doctrine was taught by the lords to his children, and that they had a tradition that it was taught by some men who came to those lands in very ancient times, twenty in number, of whom the main one was named Cocolcan; that they wore beards, long clothing, and sandals on their feet; and that these same people taught them to confess and to fast.

The authority of the bishop of Chiapa who gives this report is very respectable; and although he mentions the narration of a certain cleric named Francisco Hernández, to whom he gave a particular charge to investigate and find out well as much as possible regarding the ancient religion and belief of these natives, we must suppose that he did so with diligence, and at least that he wouldn't feign this fable. Besides the fact that this report is confirmed in Herrera, Salazar, and others, although with some variation, but they all agree that they believed in the existence of a God in three persons, of whom one became man and was born of a virgin, and that this doctrine was taught to them by Cocolcan and his disciples, and this is sufficient for my intent.

Salazar, speaking of the names that they gave to the three persons, believes that with time or because of mispronunciation they were altered and corrupted, and that they were mistaken in the names of the first and second person, because Bacab, which was the name they gave the second, he believes is a corruption of Abba, which means Father; Izona, which was the name they gave the first, he thinks is a corruption of Icon, which means Image, and fits the son better according to St. Paul;(3) and Echuah, which they called the third, seems to be a corruption of Haruach, a Hebrew word that means spirit; and the name of Chibirias or Chiribias that they gave to Our Lady, a corruption of the name of Mary.

Herrera concurs in the coming of Cocolcan and his companions to Yucatán, whom he says came through the west part, three in number, of whom the main one was Cocolcan; but it appears that he puts it many years later, because he says that all three having reigned in Izamal and afterwards founded the city of Mayapan,(4) Cocolcan returned to Mexico, where he had gone by the same road, and there may be a mistake in this, either in those who gave the report or in those who took it, for it could very well have been, and it agrees with the histories of the Indians, that Cocolcan, whom I suppose to be the same as Quetzalcohuatl, for the reasons that I will give later on, or some disciple of his, preached in the settlements of the Olmecs and Xicalancas, which fall to the west with respect to Yucatan, which location was, as we have said, where the territory of Tlaxcallan was later, on the boundary of what was also later the Texcocan empire and kingdom of Mexico; which was not founded until many years later.

Saying that Cocolcan reigned in Izamal should be understood as the respect and veneration with which they looked at him, obeying his precepts with regard to the doctrine and teaching that he gave them, not because in reality he was a king or ruled as such; and this is known with evidence, because they agree in that he was a newcomer and not a native of the country, that he came teaching this doctrine, and afterwards went on to found Mayapan, and so he left them inhabited and educated, he went away, and then they say that he chose one from the lineage of the Cocomes to govern them; that is and should be understood, not as a family known by this name, but of the disciples of Cocolcan, because Cocome is the plural of Cohuatl, or Cocolcan, as we will say later; and thus it means that they chose one of those disciples or followers of Cocolcan to govern them, that they followed and practiced [book: they continued practicing] his doctrine, until these lords or their successors to whom they gave the same name became corrupt and yielded to greed and ambition; which is a very common thing experienced among men at every step, who easily degenerate from the good and sink into evil.

The uses, customs, and ceremonies that were found established throughout New Spain, which by very ancient tradition had to have been introduced by Quetzalcohuatl, are so many and so universal that they alone were sufficient to prove that this was an evangelical preacher who, from those primitive times, instructed them in the law of grace. The knowledge that was found among all these peoples is constant and uniform that he was the one who taught them the forty-day fast that they should observe annually, mortification and penitence, disciplining the back, arms, and calves with burrs and thorns until shedding blood. He exhorted them to give alms and to succor the needs of their neighbor, making them understand that not only should they do so as an act of humanity, but of religion, for love of God and as his gift, without exception of persons; and on this subject there was a festival that was very particular that the Mexicans would celebrate in the month of Hueytecuilhutl in honor of one of their deities named Xilomen, goddess of the tender corn. In it the kings and lords, as well as the other rich gentlemen, would give many poor people food to eat. Not only did it let them know the virtues, but also the vices, seeking to inspire in them hate for the vices, and love for the virtues; and thus, although at the time that he appeared in these regions they already had some manner of government in their republics, more or less, as some nations had become more polished than others, and in general they all had chiefs or lords who commanded them and whom they obeyed and were subject to, who would punish some crimes, many others were left unpunished, because they weren't yet known among them as such, until Quetzalcohuatl let them know, inspiring a great horror in them not only of murder, theft, and the rest which, being prohibited by the natural law, are known by all peoples and nations, but also adultery, lying, unchastity, and drunkenness, persuading them that each man should not have more than one wife, and each woman more than one man, and that once united, they could not separate; and some say that the ceremonies that they used in their marriages, which I will explain later on, were taught to them by Quetzalcohuatl. He also taught them together in a place separated from all bustle and trade to pray and ask the Creator God for the remedy of all their needs, and to go to that place whenever they found themselves afflicted, venerating it as sacred, from which the erection of their temples originated, for the care and assistance of which he instituted priests, whom he instructed in the modesty and composure of truth and circumspection with which they should conduct themselves to be the teachers, directors, and exemplars of the rest. They also assert that in some places he erected schools of virgins, and that those that were found in Mexico and Texcoco, on the arrival of the Spanish, had been erected and were still in existence under the rule or institute that Quetzalcohuatl ordered.

Footnotes Chapter XVII

(1) García, book 5, chapter 9.

(2) Remesal, book 5, chapter 7.

(3) 2 Corinthians 4:4, and Colossians 1:13.

(4) Mayapan was the principal city in Yucatan, the language of which peninsula was named Maya by the Spaniards.

CHAPTER XVIII

Of other customs and rites that were found established in these countries when the Spanish arrived in them.

Other customs and rites were still found among these peoples at the time of the arrival of the Spanish, which, because of being more particular and characteristic of Christianity, prove more effectively that the person who introduced them was an apostle or disciple of Jesus Christ. Baptism is the first sacrament necessary, without which there can be no salvation, and therefore they rightly call it the door of the Catholic Church, to which no one can enter except by it; and it is evident that throughout this country a type of baptism was found to be established. Although it varied in the ceremonies according to the places, substantially they all agreed on this bath of natural water, saying upon the baptized person some forms such as honors and prayers and putting a name upon him, and this they observed as a rite of religion, preserving the memory of Quetzalcohuatl's having taught it to them. Father Remesal affirms that the first Spanish who arrived at Yucatan found that those natives used a type of baptism, to which they gave a name in their language which in our language means being born again. An expression more in agreement with that of Christ in the Gospel cannot be given. They had (he says) so much devotion and reverence for it that no one failed to receive it. They thought that in it they were receiving a pure disposition to be good and to not be harmed by the devils, and to attain the glory that they were hoping for. It was given to them from the age of three years up until twelve, and without it no one got married. They would choose a day for it that was not one of their tragic days, the fathers would fast for three days beforehand and would abstain from the women, the priests would handle the purification of the home, casting out the devil with certain ceremonies, and once these ceremonies were over the children would go one by one, and the priests would give them a little corn and ground incense in the hand, and they in a brazier, and in a cup they would send wine outside the town, with an order to the Indians not to drink it or look back,(1) and with this they believed that they had cast out the devil. The priest would come out dressed in long, solemn clothing with a hyssop in his hand. They would put white cloths on the heads of the children, they would ask the big ones if they had done any sin, and in confessing they would remove them to a

167

place and bless them with prayers, making movements as if to strike them with the hyssop, and with certain water that they had in a bone, they would wet the forehead and the features of the face and between the toes and the fingers, and then the priest would get up and remove the cloths from the children, and certain notifications being done, they were thus baptized and the festival would end in banquets, and in the nine following days the father of the child was not to approach his wife.

In the territories of Texcoco, Mexico, Tlacopan, Culhuacan, and other regions there were certain festivities in which the ceremony was solemnly done of bathing the children and putting names upon them; but when these festivities were not immediate, it was a custom to bathe the children seven days after they were born, standing them on their feet and throwing water on them from the top of the head, and at the same time they would put the name upon them. If it was a boy, they would put an arrow in the right hand and a target in the left, and if it was a girl, in one hand the spindle and in the other the shuttle, or a broom; and two months after birth (which was after forty days),(2) because each month of theirs was twenty days long, the mothers would take them to present them at the temple, where they were received by one of the priests who was the one who was in charge of keeping the count of their calendar or ecclesiastical chart. This priest would present the child to one of their gods as it seemed right to him, and as a surname would give the child the name of that deity,(3) to whom he did certain honors, and they amounted to asking him to give that child a good and peaceful nature, that it not be hard for him to learn what he should learn, for him to be happy in war, for him not to suffer travails and need, and other similar things.

In some towns their bath was not until the tenth day after birth, and in others it was not by infusion but by immersion, submerging the children in ponds, rivers, springs, or fonts full of water; but in all parts they gave them a name in doing this ceremony of the bath; and although in some parts the remembrance had already been lost of the one who introduced these ceremonies or many of them among them, and among the better educated people, as I have said, the knowledge was found that it was Quetzalcohuatl who taught them this ablution or bath of natural water and to give the children a name at the time of performing it; and it seems natural that being an apostle or disciple of the Lord he would carry it out that way, to fill the commandment that the Lord gave to all his apostles when he commanded them to preach the Gospel throughout all the world and to every creature, baptizing them in the name of the Father, of the Son, and of the Holy Ghost, promising eternal salvation through faith and baptism: Whosoever believes and is baptized shall be saved.

Father Torquemade(4) attained the knowledge of this ceremony of the baptism of children, although not as the Indian writers mention it, because he says that it was done four days after the infant was born, but he agrees in the circumstances that in those four days a fire would burn continuously at the house of the mother who gave birth, with great care that it didn't go out, nor be taken outside the house, because they would say that it would bring harm to the child, and on the fourth day they would pass the baby over the flames,(5) giving this ceremony the name of Tlequiquitzinliztli, which Boturini(6) says they had carried down from their ancestors the descendants of Cham; from which it is inferred that he considered the Indians to be descendants of Cham. This day was one of the most solemn and one with the biggest and most lavish feasts(7) that the principal Lords did, and likewise the poor, each one according to his possibility. He also concurs that at the time of doing this washing or type of baptism, they would give the child a name,(8) and even though before birth or just after the parents would assign the baby a name, they wouldn't name him with it until the washing ceremony was done; and even though he says that they would do this following the other nations of the world who thus practiced it, and he brings examples from the Romans, Greeks, and Hebrews, even though by the histories of these peoples it can in no way be gathered that at any time they had communication with those nations, there is no reason to believe that they learned it from them, and it seems more likely that it was taught to them by Quetzalcohuatl himself, who instructed them in the other points of the gospel law, as some of their national historians assert.

No less remarkable is the custom that they found established of confessing to the priests, declaring to them those things that they had as sins, and accepting the penitence that the priests would impose upon them; and the obligation that the priests had, not to reveal the sins that were confessed to them, was so rigorous that if they violated this confidentiality they were severely punished even with the penalty of death.(9) All the Indian historians speak in confirmation of this custom, and Herrera says(10) that the same thing was practiced in Nicaragua, and it is very certain that they did not learn this custom in its full extent from the Greeks and Romans.

That there were priests whose ministry was to offer to the gods the sacrifices and gifts of the people, pray for the people, bless them, care for the temples, reprove vices, live in chastity and be sustained from alms is so well established that without having recourse to the manuscripts of the Indians, all our writers unanimously confirm it. That Quetzalcohuatl was the one who instituted this priestly order, and the first who taught to live in chastity, the men as well as the women who lived a communal life in their monasteries,(11) and they were totally dedicated to the worship of the true God in those early times, and in times after the time of their false deities, not only do the Indian historians say it, but also many of the Spanish, as he also taught them to offer to God the fruits of the earth, flowers, and incense, which custom the Spanish found to be so well established, although the true object of this outward worship was varied and obscured, that even today, restored by the gospel light, they practice it so prolixly that it almost touches on superstition.

There is nothing better known than the offerings that they would make of bread and wine,(12) that is, bread of corn dough because they did not have wheat, and that drink that they used for wine. The Mexicans would celebrate a solemn festival in honor of Centeotl, the God of corn, as it was his bread, and they would do this by forming the body of this God in a human figure of the corn dough in which they would mix some herbs. They would cook it on the day of the feast and take it out in a procession with great solemnity, and around it they would put a large number of pieces from the same dough that the priests would bless with certain formulas and ceremonies, with which they believed that all that dough was converted into the flesh of that God. Once the feast was over, the priests distributed all that bread to the people in very small pieces, and they all ate it, large and small, men and women, rich and poor, who received it with great reverence, humility, and tears, saying that they were eating the flesh of their God, and they would also take it to the sick as for medicine. They would fast the forty [book: four] days beforehand, and they considered it a great sin to eat or drink anything after this bread until a half day had gone by, and they would hide the water from the children so that they wouldn't drink it.(13) This was one of the most solemn festivals that they did, and at the end of it, an elder of authority did a type of sermon, explaining those ceremonies.

No less particular is the other festival that they would make to the great God of heaven, sacrificing a man, whom they would tie to a wooden cross, and there they would kill him with arrow strikes. The next day they would sacrifice another man, putting him on another, lower, cross, but not shooting arrows, but rather breaking his legs(14) with a stick. Many other vestiges were found in their worship as well as in their customs, that give evidential proof of the knowledge that these peoples had of the principal mysteries of the Catholic religion, which we will see throughout the discourse of this history. For now, what has been said is sufficient to show that Quetzalcohuatl, to whom they attribute all the instruction of their ceremonial, worship, and religious practices, could not have been other than some apostle or disciple of Jesus Christ, for the combination of so many things, which, although perverted afterwards either by ignorance or by malice, show so much conformity with Christianity in their origin, leads one to believe that their institutor could have been none other; and it isn't surprising that over the course of time, and lacking in teachers or directors, they would corrupt the sound [book: the holy] doctrine that they learned, abusing the ceremonial, and falling into idolatry. In Europe, the center of Christianity, so close to the head of the Church and to the Vicar of Christ, which has been watchful and tireless in preserving the purity of the religion, so many abuses have been introduced imperceptibly that it has been necessary to hold councils to reform them, and in their decrees it is amazing to see the extravagances and errors to which men had allowed themselves to be led and which it has been necessary to correct.

Herrera(15) says that in the provinces of Coazacoalco and Iluta, they had the custom of circumcising the boys, and Torquemada says that the same use existed among the Totonacas, and some of our writers want to infer from this that these natives were descendants of the Jews. In their histories I have not found any information on this custom; I just find that in one of their festivals that they celebrate to the honor of their famous god Tlaloc, those who did not have posterity and wanted it would cut a small part of the foreskin that they called Metepoliso, and they would offer it as the sacrifice to this God so that he would give them posterity. But even though the information(16) that these authors give may be true, these natives could have gotten the knowledge of this ceremony from the same Quetzalcohuatl, giving them to understand that this was the sign that God gave to his chosen people, that it might be known among all nations, the posterity of Abraham distinguishing themselves in this way, Abraham having been given the promises of the future redemption, which should take place with the coming of the Messiah, who was to be born from his own lineage. He would also let them know that the Messiah himself submitted to this law of circumcision to establish the fulfillment of his promises. And so they could have adopted the use of this ceremony, either out of vanity and a type of nobility to distinguish themselves from other nations, or out of superstition, or through ignorance, after Quetzalcohuatl departed from them, for the governance of the religion having been left in the hands of their priests, the priests would do what they did in other places, and that was to invent new rites, ceremonies, and tricks with which to make themselves respectable and deceive the people, immersing them in an abyss of errors, with which, the true worship being perverted, it degenerated into idolatry. But neither from circumcision nor from other customs in which they are like the Hebrews is it inferred that they descended from them, nor that they learned the ceremonies of outward worship from them, as some say, seeking to persuade that at various times some Hebrews came to these parts, for in their history there is no remembrance of this, and they just attribute to Quetzalcohuatl the first instruction on the subject of religion, worship, and morality. And proof of my opinion on this subject is what Torquemada himself says, that with the little girls they did another indecent ceremony in place of circumcision,(17) and they would not have learned this from the Hebrews, who did not practice it.

Footnotes, Chapter XVIII

(1) It would appear from this passage that the Mexicans felt supersti- tious scruples about looking back, when the occasion of a person's departing was solemn and important: and it is difficult to imagine (on reading, in the concluding paragraph of the third chapter of the ninth book of Sahagun's History of New Spain, that they not only accounted the act itself unlucky, but believed the person to be a great sinner,) that they were wholly ignorant of the tradition of Lot's wife having been turned into a pillar of salt, as recorded in the twenty-sixth verse of the nineteenth chapter of Genesis.

(2) It is extremely remarkable that this was the precise number of days which were to be reckoned, according to the enactment of the twelfth chapter of Leviticus, by Jewish women for the purification after the birth of male chil- dren; at the expiration of which period of forty days they presented themselves and their sons with the gifts at the temple, when an atonement was made for the women by the sacrifice of a lamb and a pigeon −or, if she was poor, of two pigeons; after which offering she became clean.

(3) Echevarría seems to have been led into error here from not recol- lecting that Tezcatlipoca and the goddess Chalchiuitliene were adored by the Mexicans under many names. It deserves likewise to be noticed that the Mexicans were accustomed to give their children the same name as that of the day on which they were baptized; and the signs of the Mexican calendar having been considered by some of the Spanish missionaries objects of reli- gious worship, from the superstitious reverence that the Mexicans entertained towards them, they might be said in this sense to have named their children after some particular deity.

(4) Book 13, chapter 23.

(5) To pass children through the flames was an ancient Hebrew custom, as we learn from many passages of the Old Testament.

(6) Idea de una Nueva Historia General de la América Septentrional [Idea of a New General History of North America], folio 19.

(7) We learn from the fifty-eighth verse of the first chapter of Saint Luke, that rejoicings took place on the birth of Jewish children. These rejoic- ings were renewed on the eighth day after its birth, when the child was circumcised; whence in all probability originated the value which the Jews set on the number eight, which number was equally esteemed by the Mexicans,

and consecrated to the purposes of superstition.

(8) Baptism under the new law was substituted for circumcision under the old; and each rite in its turn became indispensable to salvation. Baptism therefore having thus superseded the old rite of circumcision, it is probable that the primitive Christians would have deemed it incumbent on them to name their children at the time of baptizing them; in this manner conforming with the ancient Jewish precedent, –since we learn from the fifty-ninth verse of the first chapter of Saint Luke that it was a Hebrew custom to name children at the time of circumcising them.

(9) Confession was a religious rite common both in Peru and Mexico; and it was a custom that prevailed in the earliest ages of the Church, although that point is denied by Protestant writers, who contend that it was a fraud of later times, devised for the purposes of promoting spiritual ambition.

(10) Decad. 3, book 4, chapter 7, folio 174, col. 7 and chapter 12, folio 216, col. 2.

(11) The same custom prevailed in Peru.

(12) Chicha, the name which the Peruvians gave to their drink-offerings, nearly resembled [Hebrew writing]; the term applied to the Hebrew drink-offerings in the Pentateuch.

(13) See Herrera, decad. 3, book 2, chapter 17, folio 91.

(14) Crucifixion was a common mode of punishment amongst the ancient Jews, whose penal code annexing the clause "thine eye shall not pity" to some of its enactments, and frequently adjudging criminals to be burnt alive, gave a certain tincture of ferocity to the manners of that people, which was rather heightened than diminished by their being permitted indiscriminately to witness and take a part in public executions, when the sentence to be carried into effect was that of stoning a criminal to death. It is worthy of observation that the refined feelings of modern times are shocked at the bare mention of the Roman ladies going to the theatre to view the combats of gladiators; yet there is something infinitely more revolting in the picture which the imagination forms to itself, of a Hebrew market-place crowded with men, women, and children, all eager to stone an adulterer to death, in order to show themselves zealous followers of the Mosaic law. There was mystery, however, as well as barbarity, in the crucifixions practiced by the Mexicans; and the custom of breaking the legs of a crucified person on one of the festi-

vals, and leaving him in this manner to die upon the cross, reminds us that the Jews broke the legs of those whom they crucified on the eve of the Sabbath day, out of reverence, as it would appear, for that festival. We shall here transcribe a passage from the tenth chapter of the first part of the inedited [unpublished] History of Torribio de Benavente, which fully confirms the account given above by Echevarría; –the sacrifices described are those of the province of Tlaxcala: "In another festival they would raise up a man tied to a very high cross, and there they would shoot arrows at him; in another festival they would tie another man lower, and they would kill him with oak-pole rods the length of a fathom with very sharp points, goading him like a bull; and they used almost these same ceremonies and sacrifices in the provinces of Huexocinco, Tepezca, Zacatlate, in the main festivals, because they all considered Acatachtli[?], which was the large statue that I have said, as the greatest of their gods."

(15) Herrera Dec. 4, book 9, chapter 7, folio 235.

(16) In addition to the authorities cited in the note subjoined to page 334 of the sixth volume of this work, in proof of the existence of the rite of circumcision amongst the Mexicans and other civilized states of America, we shall quote a passage from the second chapter of the fourth book of the third part of Oviedo's General History of the Indies, which can leave no doubt that the practice of that rite was common in Nicaragua; since, had it been confined simply to a few individuals, (as the reply of the Indian would seem to insinuate,) it could scarcely have come to the knowledge of the Spaniards, much less have been a subject of grave inquiry amongst them. The letters I. and F. in the following passage signify Indian and Franciscan; the entire chapter consists of interrogatories and replies. "F. Why do you cut into the generative member? – I. They don't all; just some scoundrels for giving ill pleasure to the women, but it isn't a ceremony of ours. – F. At any time has any people come to this land of Nicaragua, like the Christians, who have told you to do those ceremonies that they command you, or to throw water on top of your heads, or others telling you to cut the head of the penis, or did you learn that the Christians were to come to this land? – I. None of those things had come to our knowledge, and after the Christians came, they have told us that it is good for us to throw water on the head and be baptized." Another Indian nation, named the Yopes, – who inhabited a province not so remotely situated from Mexico as that of Nicaragua, and who worshiped Totec and Tezcatlipoca, – proof that they were of the same religion as the Mexicans, – likewise practiced the rite of circumcision, as we learn from the following passage of a manuscript preserved in the library of the Escorial: "The Yopes, which is a nation of Indians of this land, practiced circumcision, and when asked why, they said

174

that they only knew that their ancestors did it." Torribio de Benavente, in affirming that some supposed the Mexicans to be descended from the Moors, on account of a conformity in certain rites and ceremonies, obliquely perhaps alludes to circumcision, since that was a rite which the Moors and other Muhammadans borrowed from the Jews. But, independent of the existence of this rite among other Indian nations, the Mexican language affords evidence of its long existence amongst the Mexicans; and the Mexican paintings would alone render all other kinds of proof superfluous. The words in the Mexican language which, according to Molina, signify "circumcision" and "to circumcise" are the following: "texipincuayotequiliztli, circumcision; texipinquaruagolequiliztli, circumcision; tlaxipincuayotectli, circumcised; tlazipinquarcuayotectli, circumcised; nite zipinquayotequi, to circumcise or trim around; nite xipinguaryexatequi, to circumcise; nino xipixcuayotequi, to be circumcised; nino xipinguacuayotequi, to be circumcised." "Circumcision," it deserves to be remarked, has as many different names in the Mexican language as "to stone to death,"which renders it probable that that Hebrew ceremony and that Jewish mode of punishment were equally ancient amongst the Mexicans. Acosta and other celebrated writers having laid the greatest stress on the absence of the rite of circumcision amongst the Indians, – disproving the assertion of those who maintained that the Mexicans were descended from the Jews, – we shall not hesitate to lengthen this note by selecting the following passages from Peter Martyr, in which mention is made of that Hebrew rite as common amongst them. "Aliud meo judicio non magis tacendum inteilexi; legum peritus quidam, dictus Corrales, Dariennensiumprator urbantas, inquit, se occarriese cuidam fugitivo ex internis Occidentalibus magnis terris, qui ad regulum repertum a se profugerat. Is legentem cermens praeorern, insilurvit admirabundus,..." [Translator: I'm not sure about all these Latin words; the text I am copying from is hard to read and illegible in many parts, so I'm going to skip all the rest of the Latin. Anyone would be able to copy it from a more legible text, and there may even be an English translation of it somewhere.] Peter Martyr was the first historian who asserted that circumcision was a rite common among the Indians; and the authority of Acosta, although a much later writer, is that which is generally opposed [put forth] on this question to him. Whether, however, the latter author is entitled to unqualified praise for candor, when he declares that the Indians could not be descended from the Jews, because no trace of the rite of circumcision was to be discovered amongst them, will best appear from the following passage of Diego Duran's History of Mexico, which valuable work is preserved in manuscript in the Royal Library at Madrid, and appears to have chiefly assisted Acosta in the compilation of that part of his Natural and Moral History of the Indies, which treated of the history of New Spain, whose words he may be said sometimes almost literally to transcribe. "This festival (of Topi) was a purification of women after child-birth and like circumcision, and in what seemed to be purification of these women, they would offer offerings in the way of the old law for the child as well as for the mothers, where they would offer lambs, turtle doves or young pigeons; here on this day they would offer quails, hens, bread, blankets, etc. This ceremony was done by all the women who had given birth since the last festival the previous year, and the ceremony was in this manner. Those days beforehand they would buy a large quantity of candlewood chips. From these chips they would make a long, thick torch. They would also prepare the offering that they were to take; they would mill a little corn, and done haphaz-ardly and milled wrong by stirring it with toasted pigweed seed, they would knead one flour with the other putting honey in it in place of water, and they would make a bread that was called tamales in their language, and by the very name of this kind of bread it was said tzocoyotl, which is like we say by this diminutive word, bollitos [little buns], which kind of bread was not just made for an offering, but also to eat this day, for it was a ceremony of their religion that no other bread was to be eaten. The mothers of the children who were to be presented at the temple, and they themselves who were to be purified, also busied themselves with weaving blankets and shirts for the women, trusses and robes to dress all those relatives and friends accompanying the women in that station they were doing, and each one did according to his possibility, the rich more, the poor less, each one according to his status. On the eve of the festival, at sunset, the priests of the temple signaled with the conches and horns and drums that they were accustomed to playing and strumming in the solemnities, after which those who were to go out got dressed up, and together they would dress an Indian man whom they had hired for this effect and an Indian woman together; to the Indian man they gave the torch of lit candlewood, and they would put the child on the Indian woman's back. The mother would take her offering herself in her hand and on her back, and with the Indian man going ahead and lighting the way, he would leave the house and they would walk the stations through all the sanctums of the sections of the city in the same way that we use Holy Thursday, and at each sanctum she would leave an offering, and in this way all the women who had given birth went throughout the city so full of torches and luminaries that it was some-thing to see, and so full of people that they couldn't break with each other through the streets. Once they had gone to all the sanctums of the neighbor-hoods, they would come to the great temple, where the main offering took place, presenting themselves to the priests, who would purify them with certain ceremonies and words and they ended up cleansed of that birth. On what we said that this ceremony seemed that on this day the circumcision of children was also done, it seems that way because of what I will say, and it was that on reaching the great temple of Vitzilopochtly, there they would take the child, no matter how small he was, and offer him to the priest, and the priest would take him and, with a stone knife that the mother herself was carrying, they would sacrifice the sheep and the point of the head of his little penis, thus giving him, on the ear as well as on the mentioned place, a very delicate cut that scarcely bled or so seemed, and the females, just the ear. Once the priest was through cutting with that knife, he would throw it in front of the feet of the idol, and the mother would ask for a name for her child, and if it was a lord, they would give him an exquisite name: example, Montezuma means angry Lord, which was the reason they named him that way; the priest considered the physiognomy of the child and the child's face seemed to be [illegible] and sad and angry, or the child was born on a sad and melancholy day and he gave him that name and it was of the other Lords.

(17) This proof is not conclusive, since Ludolfus declares that a similar practice prevailed amongst the Abyssinian Christians. See his Historia Ethiopia [Ethiopian History], folio 274; Alvarez, Historia de las Cosas de Etiopia [History of the Things of Ethiopia], page 27, edit. Antwerp; and Damian a Goes de Ethiopum Moribus[?].

CHAPTER XIX

It seems to have been the apostle Saint Tomas, to whom they gave the names of Quetzalcohuatl, Cocolcan, and Hueman, and who preached in these regions.

The Gentleman Boturini worked a lot to have a work in his hands that was written by the celebrated Carlos de Sigüenza, under the title of Fenix del Occidente [Phoenix of the West], proving that this marvelous man Quetzalcohuatl was the apostle Saint Tomas, which never went to press; but his efforts to obtain it were fruitless. Still, he did not lose the hope of finding it, taking other steps of which he instructed me when I went to New Spain in the year 1750; and even though I put them into practice with the greatest exactness, I have not been able to find anything other than the information that I already had that he wrote this [book: another] work; but no one who has seen it, much less who can enlighten me to be able to find it. I do not doubt that if I had obtained it, it would fully satisfy the curiosity and good taste of my readers; because I feel that because of the vast erudition of its author, especially in the antiquities of the Indians, that it would be a complete work. But notwithstanding my lacking this support, making use of the monuments that I have in my hands, I venture to affirm that this wonderful man was the apostle Saint Tomas; and the proofs that these documents supply seem to me to be convincing.

The first proof that is presented is in the meaning of the very name Quetzalcohuatl, which, translated literally, means peacock snake, because it is composed of the two words Quetzallin, which means the peacock, and Cohuatl, the snake. It is necessary to know that all the names of persons among these people were allegorical and significant, relating to a natural gift or defect, a particular event or feat of the individual, as is seen in the names of the Emperors of Texcoco, such as Netzahualcoyotl, which means fasting vixen,(1) relating to the events of his youth;(2) and in the kings of Mexico, such as Moteuhzuma(3) severe lord, and so with the rest; and this is the reason why most of them, especially the lords and principle people, had several names; because as newborns their parents would give them a name allusive to the time or circumstances of their birth, but afterwards, because of the various events of their lives, because of their deeds, or because of other events, they would take or the people would give them other names, which were either added to the first name, or they would change the name entirely. It should also be advised that they would apply the word Quetzalli allegorically to mean any species of excellent plumage, because of this being one of the most highly esteemed kinds among them, and therefore being that of the peacock, which, as the richest plumage, was what they used to adorn the head. That is why they also gave this name to persons of talent, to explain their judgment and capacity, and for that reason some authors translate the name Quetzalcohuatl as snake of rich plumage, understanding that they meant very wise man or man of much talent or highly esteemed.

But the Bachelor Luis Becerra Tanco,(4) in the books that he printed with the title Felicidad de México en la aparicion de Nuestra Señora de Guadalupe [Happiness of Mexico in the Appearance of Our Lady of Quadalupe], says that in the name Quetzalcohuatl, the surname that the apostle had was preserved, being a true translation of it. This was Didymus, which in Hebrew(5) means twin; and in the native [book: Nahuatl] language the word Cohuatl, which in a natural sense means snake, also allegorically means twin, by allusion to the idea that snakes always give birth to children in pairs,(6) and it is evident that in this language that today they call Mexican there is no word with which to explain the concept of twin other than that of cohuatl or coatl, which is shortened, and in plural they say cocoa or cocome. The Spanish themselves have adopted this word just as much in our times, Spanishizing it, and those who are born with two or more from one birth they call coates, and the common person only understands it by this word, and in no way by the word twin, which absolutely has no use in these countries.

Though this seems inarguable and obvious, no more so is what we know through the gospel, that the apostle Saint Tomas had the surname of Didymus, [omitted from book: a word that in Hebrew means twin. Didymus is Greek and means twin, and Tomas means the same thing in Hebrew, from the root "tham," which means "geminare" {twin}, and thus twins in Hebrew is said "thesnim," see Saint Geronimo in the Hebrew Questions. This note is from Doctor Mier, a Mexican,] and so for the Indians to translate it into their language, they called it [book: call him] cohuatl, adding quetzalli as an adjective, meaning very wise or very excellent or very highly esteemed coate [twin], and all this they meant to signify in the rich plumage, which, as I have said, was used among them for adornment of the head, and thus they would use it to symbolize wisdom, talent, dignity [book: deity], and everything most excellent; and anyone who has an average instruction in the Mexican language knows how familiar these allegorical expressions and phrases are in [book: among] them, of which not a few examples will be seen in the course of this history.

To prove that the true name that they gave to this man was that of

Cohuatl, and that Quetzalli was just an epithet of veneration and esteem, it is sufficient to see that they constantly called all his disciples Cocomes, which is the plural of Cohuatl, in the way the followers of Mohamad were called Muhammadans, those of Luther, Lutherans, and those of Christ, Christians; and it will not be found that anyone calls them Quetzallis, or Quetzame, which is the true plural of Quetzalli, because this was an epithet of esteem and veneration that they gave to this man, but his own name, from which his disciples took their name, was Cohuatl; and I say the same thing about the other name that they gave him of Hueman, because it was also a surname of esteem and not his own name, and so for that reason they didn't give his disciples a name alluding to it.

But worthy of reflection, and a new and robust proof of having been the Apostle Saint Tomas to whom they gave the name of Quetzalcohuatl, is the information given to us by the authors of the Holy Cross of stone that was found in Meliapor, in the sepulcher of the Holy Apostle, a copy and illustration of which are given by Father Atanasio Kirker in his China Ilustrada, Father Lurema in the life of San Francisco Javier, Gregorio García in his mentioned book of the Preaching of the Gospel, and other authors; for in it, over the holy cross(7) a peacock is seen, as if descending, and having the cross in its beak, which is the same bird Quetzalli(8) from whose beautiful plumage the natives of this kingdom took the allegory that we have mentioned, in the name of Quetzalcohuatl that they gave to the Holy Apostle. It cannot be denied that this is a symbol or hieroglyph that wants to denote or mean something, because whether it was the saint himself who put it there (if he was the one who planted the cross there) or, more likely, his disciples after his death to indicate his sepulcher, there is no room for doubt that the placement of the figure of this bird had some purpose, some reason, and [book: or] some meaning. What could this be? My inadequacy cannot find anything else other than that this hieroglyph was a mute tomb inscription declaring the name of the hero who was buried there, because of the famous epithet that they gave him as wise, prudent, great, and powerful, all comprised in the allegory of the peacock that the natives of this kingdom invented, calling him Quetzalcohuatl.

The name Cocolcan has the same etymology as the word Cohuatl, snake, and wants to denote or signify the chief or head of the Cocomes. It could have been the same saint that went to Yucatan with his companions, or one of his disciples who went as the head and superior of the rest, to whom they gave this name for that reason, and who, after the city of Mayapan [book: Maiopan] was founded, returned by the same western road over which he had gone; and with the lords of Yucatan considering that the government was not well except in the hands of one of these Cocomes, they say that they elected one of those of this lineage as their lord, that is, of those who followed the doctrine and were disciples of Cocolcan, and the government remained in them until, degenerating from that school and doctrine of their master, and abandoning themselves to vices, they lost the esteem and veneration of the people.

A few years before the arrival of the Spanish, the master Gil González(9) says that a priest of their idols, named Chilamcambal, who among them was very venerated, prophesied it; and it is noteworthy that the word Cambal also means Twin in the language of the Indians of the Philippines, where many vestiges of the preaching of Saint Tomas are also found, and there they were able to give him this name by translation of Didymus, and that he would take one of his disciples who in later times had gone to these parts announcing the same doctrine, from where this gentile priest was able to learn it, boasting of that name to make himself respectable, and proffering those predictions of the Holy Apostle as his own, which, as we will see later on, were so well known throughout this New World.

They also gave him the name of Hueman, made up of the words Huey, meaning large, and Maitl, meaning hand, that is, he with the large hands; either because in this way they were expressing his great power because of the wonderful works they saw him perform, or because in fact he had large hands, as is seen today in several places where he left them imprinted and stamped, of which historians speak in this kingdom as well as in Peru and Brazil. The two hands that are seen in the place that they call Santa Maria Mege of the doctrine of Xocotitlan, in the jurisdiction of Ixtlahuacan, are particular, painted and perfectly stamped as a white plaster in some black cliffs, with neither time nor the efforts of many who have attempted it being able to erase them. No less so is the hand stamped in a little bridge close to Tlalnepantla in the vicinity of Mexico, which by ancient tradition they mention as have been stamped there by Quetzalcohuatl, going to Chollolan, and in memory of this case a town was founded there which is called Tlemaco, which means the stone of the hand. In other places prints are also found stamped and imprinted, the size of which, having to correspond to those of the hands, denote that these hands were large. I note in passing that the similarity, or rather the identity, of the names Hueman and Huemac has been a cause for our authors to have confused Hueman, that astronomer or diviner who came out of Huetlapallan with those who came to found Tollan, which we will discuss later, with Quetzalcohuatl or Cocolcan, because really the name is the same, and so some Indian authors call this astronomer Hueman and Huemantzin, which is reverential, to denote his great wisdom and power; and so I am more inclined to the opinion of those who say that they gave this name to Saint Tomas because of the great works that they saw him perform, because this is more in conformity with the nature of these nations and with their way of explaining.

In the information that I give in Chapter 16 [XIV in book], regarding the holy cross of Quauhtolco, Brulio affirms that not only was it venerated from very ancient times, but that its natives had as a tradition from their fore-fathers that the apostle Saint Tomas had placed it and positioned it there in that spot, and that his image and very name they preserved on the historical charts and paintings that they were using in place of letters, and in many other parts the remembrance of the true name Thomé, or Tomás, was preserved in New Spain as well as in Peru and the kingdom of Chile, as can be seen in Calancha,(10) Ovalde,(11) and many others.

Finally, it is proven by reason to have been Saint Tomas, because in the supposition that we made to have to fulfill the precept of Jesus Christ to preach the gospel in this very considerable part of the world and to this very large number of creatures, the obligation for its fulfillment had to fall upon one of the holy apostles; and since it had not been any of the other eleven, because the respective country in which all of them preached is known, it follows that it was Saint Tomas. That the apostles were those who were to fulfill this precept we established in Chapter 15 [book: XI] , with the authori-ties that I quote there, and reason persuades it, because if eleven apostles were designated to preach the gospel in the other parts of the world that are included in that half of the globe, why wasn't one to be designated to preach it in America, which extends throughout almost all of the other half, popu-lated with such a large number of creatures likewise partakers of the fruit of redemption? That it wasn't any of the other apostles is confirmed by the account of their lives, and because there is no author who says so. Then, inas-much as there are so many reasons of congruity in the names, in the time, in the doctrine that he preached, in the customs and ceremonies that Quetzalcohuatl taught, we must believe that this was the apostle Saint Tomas, who may have been accompanied by some other disciples who helped him in his apostolic ministry; but I am persuaded that these were the natives of the country who first joined him and followed his doctrine, who, although few, were the fruit of his work, the consolation of his difficulties, and the first fruits that he rendered to God of the large number of creatures who then inhabited these vast regions.

Footnotes Chapter XIX

(1) The Mexican coyotl was properly neither a wolf, a fox, nor a dog, but a different variety of the species to which those animals belong; it was fierce and carnivorous; the Spaniards named it a fox from some similitude in its habits to that animal.

(2) This proper name might be interpreted, the fasting wolf. It

commemorated both the personal prowess and the religious habits of the monarch who bore it, who was accustomed to fast, tasting very little food for forty days together; his son, for a similar reason, might have received the appellation of Nezahualpilli.

(3) Clavijero writes Moteuczoma, and interprets it as indignant Lord. – E.

(4) Becerra Fel. de México fol. 55, 1685 edition in Mexico.

(5) In Greek it should say, because Didymus is a Greek word.

(6) A serpent is an oviparous animal, and Echevarría seems here to be mistaken in assigning to the serpent a quality that belonged to the goddess Cihuacohuatl, which proper name, literally signifying the female serpent, might have led him into the error of supposing that the tradition of Cihuacohuatl, the Mexican Eve, always giving birth to twins, referred to the serpent.

(7) The figure of a bird is sculptured upon the cross which M. Dupaix discovered in the temple of Palenque. The dove, it is scarcely necessary to observe, was an ancient symbol of the Holy Ghost; and the apostles are commanded in the New Testament to assimilate themselves both to doves and serpents. On the supposition that this most beautiful of American birds, the huitzilin, the green feathers of which were named quetzalli, and highly prized by the Mexicans, was substituted in the New World for the dove, both the proper name Quecalcoatl and the symbol of the green-feathered serpent would seem to contain a double allegory.

(8) A respectable individual assures me that Mr. Pablo de la Llave, well known for his dedication to natural history, told him that the Quetzalli is not the peacock, but another bird, very beautiful indeed, and of very colorful plumage, which is sufficient to support the author's conjectures. – E.

(9) Teatro de la Iglesia de Indias, folio. 203.

(10) Calancha, Historia del Perú, book 2, chapter 2.

(11) Ovalde, Historia de Chile, book 8, chapter 7.

CHAPTER XX

Of two famous prophesies that Quetzalcohuatl made when he preached in Chollolan.

Around this time the city of Chollolan was the most famous and numerous settlement of the land of Anahuac. It was in its greatest height and splendor, and was renowned and applauded for its high tower, which, as I have said, its inhabitants had built for the glory of their nation and as a monument to declare to those in the future that this had been the first settlement of the Olmecs, and where the founders of the other settlements of this nation had originated. Its outline was round, having in its plane a little more than a thousand yards of diameter, and it rose in a pyramid shape, we don't know to what height; but undoubtedly it was great, as manifested by the ruins that still remain in our times. Its construction deserved the name of hill better than tower, because it was solid of loose rock and large adobes of earth, one layer of these and another layer of rock pressed and compacted with earth, and the ascent, as perceived from the lower remnant of it (which is what is still in existence in the place and manner in which it was built), seems to have gone around its contour through a type of terrace. In one of the charts that Boturini gathered on maguey paper, this hill is seen drawn in the mentioned pyramid shape, with four divisions that served as landings, and they surrounded everything, with sufficient space to walk around them; they say that outside it was covered with a very hard white mortar, of which no trace has remained to this day.

This tower was situated in the middle of the town, which is on a beautiful and fertile plane, although at the present time the tower or hill is almost outside the town, because of how much the surrounding area has decreased, as because of the inhabitants having gone further north, for traces still remain of how far their settlement extended on the opposite side. The splendor of this city was contributed to more than a little by its having been the first in which it is said that houses were built for its dwellers to live in; because situated on a plane where caves were lacking and there were no slopes in which to carve them out, they were obligated by necessity to seek shelter and defense from the inclemency of the weather. For all these reasons its population was very numerous, and even though nothing is known about their government, they had to have had one to keep such a multitude of people in harmony.

These were the ones whom the Apostle Saint Tomas sought, to instruct them in the gospel truths; and finding such a copious harvest field in this city, they say that he stayed there three months preaching and teaching the new law of Jesus Christ. But the time had not yet come for the holy seed to bear fruit, and so with the saint seeing the rebelliousness and hardness of those hearts difficult to yield up in a short time, and having accomplished his mission, he decided to leave them. But first he predicted to them that the time would come in which all would embrace the new law that he was preaching to them, and that in a year that would be indicated with the hieroglyph of a reed, some white, bearded men would come from the East over the waters of the sea, who would strip them of their dominion of the land, and ruling over all the land, they would make them embrace the law of the gospel; and as signs that this, his prophecy, would be perfectly fulfilled, he made them another one, telling them that a few days after his departure from the city, their famous tower would be destroyed, which happened exactly as he predicted it to them, for eight days after the saint had left the city, a very strong earthquake(1) was felt, which brought down the great tower, the ruins remaining in existence until our days as a perpetual reminder of the event that he announced to them, in several fragments, of which there are two so large that they form two little hills immediately at the main base that was left unmovable, and this is about two hundred yards tall. One can only imagine how much must have been destroyed and ruined by the continuation of so many centuries.

The destruction of this tower was, for these peoples, one of the most memorable events, because of the fame of the tower, as well as Quetzalcohuatl's prediction having been fulfilled in its ruin, [omitted from book: which was a sign that] in the same way the one that he made about the coming of those peoples from the East [omitted from book: would be fulfilled] who would become the lords of the land; and as this prophecy had been made in all the other settlements where he had gone, its fulfillment interested everyone, and since then they were persuaded that the time would come in which it would take effect, and they always waited for its fulfillment. Therefore, when the Spanish arrived in these parts, they found this knowledge to be constant and uniform throughout all the towns of the New Spain, as all the historians assert unanimously; and it was not a small reason for the happiness of their conquests, for the Indians, firmly believing that the prophecy of Quetzalcohuatl could not fail to be fulfilled, they lost enthusiasm for the defense, and in large part the ease with which a small number of Spanish conquered a multitude of them, as the historians of the conquest mention at every step, must be attributed to this.

For although in these times of which I am speaking the great empire of

Texcoco had not yet arisen, nor the other monarchies that later occupied these lands, the northernmost countries and their maritime coasts were already very populated; there were already many settlements on the coasts of the heart of Mexico to Yucatan, in the kingdom of Peru, and it is evidenced through Toltec history that Quetzalcohuatl traveled through all those settlements of the north, teaching the same doctrine and making the same prophecy to them, the knowledge of which was brought by the founders of those monarchies, and finding it corroborated here with the event of Chollolan, they were more firmly persuaded that some day its fulfillment would arrive, and although time introduced some variation into this also, trying to interpret the prophecy as will be mentioned later on, the substance of it, which boils down to announcing the coming of the white people from the East who would dominate the land, remained constant, as is seen by the histories.

In view of this event, these people formed a high concept of Quetzalcohuatl, and started to honor and venerate his memory by putting into practice many of the doctrines that he had taught them, the observance of which they always maintained without forgetting that it had been Quetzalcohuatl who had taught them to them, although later, in the course of time, they introduced some abuses into them. The main one that they make mention of in these times is the worship of the Holy Cross, for which they built a magnificent temple over the base that remained intact of their famous tower,(2) which the Spanish found still in existence with a wooden cross placed in it; and this is the first temple of which I find a report in the histories of the Indians. Nor before this do I find any information that they worshiped any divinity, nor venerated any material idol, nor recognized any Gods other than Tloque Nahuaque or creator of all things. They gave various names to the Holy Cross; those that I find to be most frequent are these three: Quiahuitziteotl,(3) which means the God of wood; Chicahualizteotl, which is interpreted the strong and powerful God; and Tonacaquahuitl, which is interpreted as God of the rains; but its genuine meaning in the Nahuatl language is the pole of fertility or of abundance, an allegory very particular to this language to mean that through this pole they would attain the rains that fertilized their seed planting; and so this was the most common and general name that they gave it; because Quetzalcohuatl having taught them that this sovereign sign had virtue to attract the rains to their sewn fields, and they having experienced this benefit through it, they worshiped it as a powerful deity to succor them in this need, which was of unique [book: great] importance to them; and its worship having spread afterwards into the other kingdoms and monarchies that were founded subsequently, it was always worshiped and known as the god of the rains, with ignorance perverting the true object of the worship, and this was the reason the conquerors have found such a large number of crosses in these countries.

In successive times, with the Toltec nation dominating, the Chololtecs, who were of the same Olmecs now mixed with the Toltecs, again erected their famous tower, and they say that they made it higher than the first time(4), but it was again ruined one night when they least expected it, with no earthquake, hurricane, nor any other cause to attribute it to preceding its destruction, and so it caused so much terror in them that from that time forth they did not dare to attempt its rebuilding again. On the chart or painting of this tower which I talked about at the beginning of this chapter, an inscription is found in the Mexican language, placed there undoubtedly by those first neophytes who learned how to write in our characters, and applauding the Chololtecs, it says that their ancestors did it to save themselves from another flood. It gives the city the name of Tollan Chollolan, and says that that tower is a precious monument of the Toltec nation; but in reality it was the Olmec nation that built it, and realistically they were also the ones, although now mixed with the Toltecs, who restored it. The author of the inscription adds that the archangel Saint Michael was the one who knocked it down this second time(5), and that some people saw him tear it down. Now it is seen that in those times they neither knew Saint Michael nor had his name even reached their ears; and so even though the information may be true (though I have not found in any other author) of having seen persons in the air tearing it down, we must be persuaded that this expression of the author of the inscription is no more than a pious discourse, founded on the fact that the bishopric of Tlaxcallan, now of the Puebla de los Angeles, is under the guardianship and protection of Saint Michael, who with singular wonders has tried to manifest himself as its protector since the early times of its Christianity.

Footnotes, Chapter XX

(1) Ollín[?], or the sign of the Earthquake, was dedicated to Quecalcoatl, perhaps on this account.

(2) This is a very curious passage, as it is here expressly declared that the famous temple of Cholula, which the Spaniards found in a complete state of preservation on their arrival in the New World, and which, dedicated to Quecalcoatl, was frequented by pilgrims from all parts of New Spain, had been built in honor of the cross, and contained a wooden cross when the Spaniards first visited it.

(3) This proper name is compounded of quiahuitl, rain, and teotl, god, and signifies "the god of rain,' an interpretation which Echevarría has erroneously given to Tonacaquahuitl; which latter term being compounded of

tonacayo, defined by Molina to be "human body, or our flesh," and qu[illeg-ible]tl or quahuitl, which, according to the same author, signifies "wooden tree or pole," may be interpreted 'the tree of life or of our bodies.' Don Ferdinand de Alba Ixtlilxochitl, in the first chapter of his History of the Chichimecan Empire, mentions these amongst the names by which the cross was adored in ancient times in New Spain; but as he does not assign its signi-fication to each name separately in the order in which he writes them, but explains their meaning collectively, it is not unlikely that this was the cause of Echevarría confounding the signification of Quiahuitzteotl[?] with that of Tonacaquahuitl.

(4) The temple of Cholula, like the temple of Jerusalem, was said to have been twice built; and it is singular that after its second destruction the same superstitious notion should have prevailed about any attempt to rebuild it.

(5) This tradition supposed the destruction of the second temple of Cholula to have been a judgement on the people of Cholula for their sins.

CHAPTER XXI

EMIGRATION OF THE TOLTECS

The Toltecs rebel in their old fatherland, and leave in exile from it to settle the land of Anahuac.

The ancient and primitive city of Huehuetlapallan, the court of the Chichimec empire, was not only very famous in these times, but with many companies of people having gone out of it who populated all that country, founding cities and places in their region, all the inhabitants of them recognized it as the head and cradle of their elders, and it had given its name to all that region, and although historians do not give us any particular information of their mode of government, they tell us that it was monarchial and that in the great city of Huehuetlapallan the supreme Chichimec emperor resided, and in each one of the settlements there was a lord or regulus to which its inhabitants were subject; but this ruler recognized the Chichimec Emperor as the supreme lord.

Among the great settlements that existed, very numerous and renowned was the city of Tlachicatzin, founded by one of those companies of people who left Huehuetlapallan, to whom they gave the name of Toltecatl, because of their great ability, industry, and skill, for the cultivation of the fields as well as for the exercise of the arts that they learned and attained, the invention of which they attributed to them.

Whether they took the name Toltecatl from the Nahuatl language, or whether the language got it from them, is not easy to find out. The common thing among these peoples was to take the name of their chiefs, and it seems likely that because of its leader being named Toltecatl, the whole nation would take the name, and that afterwards, because of the nations having excelled in ingenuity and ability, they would apply the name Toltecatl to every skilled craftsman, as there are many examples of this in this history.

Two great lords named Chalcaltzin and Tlacamihtzin lived in the city, descendants of the house and main family of the Toltecs, who, trusting in the large following that they had, incited a rebellion against their natural lord. They don't say who this was, whether the Chichimec Emperor or the regulus of their Toltecatl nation; but because of the course of history I am inclined to believe the first; and although they don't tell the reason for the rebellion either, it is easy to be persuaded that it was ambition, and wanting to be freed from subordination to the empire, flattered by the praise that they had in this city as well as in other settlements of the region.

There were so many people who followed them, that once their supporters took up arms, they maintained the war for thirteen years, with various events, until finally they felt it necessary to yield to the greater power and leave their city. Although exiled from it, they kept the war going for eight more years, until in the year of twelve reeds they saw the need to abandon the undertaking, fleeing however they could to escape the punishment that threatened them. A considerable number of persons followed their party, on this occasion as well as in the subsequent years, so that although they do not describe it in detail, their multitude is perceived because they kept settling until they reached Tollan; for not only the men were following, but also the women and families of all of them.

Besides the two main lords, they mentioned five others who were also of the principal nobility, and relatives of theirs, whose names they preserved for us, and they are Checatl, Cohuatzon, Mazacohuatl, Tlapalhuitz, and Huitz. They all continued their journey without stopping until they were sixty leagues away from Tlachicatzin, on the south, to where they were joined by many other relatives and family members, particularly from another large city called Tlaxicoluican. And in a place that Checatl discovered and that seemed right to plant their crops, they decided to stay and settle, giving the new settlement the name of Tlapallan, either to emulate the Chichimec empire, the court of which had this name, or to preserve the memory of that first settlement that their progenitors founded when they settled in these countries, and which they always looked upon with much affection, calling it their old fatherland. This other, new Tlapallan they later called Tlapallanconco, which means the little Tlapalan, to distinguish it from the old one.

They say that this Toltec rebellion occurred more than six hundred years after the correction of their calendar, in a year that was indicated with the hieroglyph of a reed, which according to the tables seems to have been the year 4616 of the world, which is the first one found in it indicated with this hieroglyph, counting the six hundred years after the correction of their calendar, and it corresponded with the year 583 of Jesus Christ; and the civil war having lasted thirteen years until their departure from Tlachicatzin, they place this departure in the year of a flint, which precisely corresponds to the year 596 of the Christian era, and adding the other eight years that they continued the war until their last flight, it seems that their flight must be placed in the year 604, and the founding of Tlapalanconco in the same year.

The Indian authors, although all assert that six hundred years had gone by since the correction of the calendar and they agree on the hieroglyphs of the years in which these disturbances occurred, as annotated by the ancients on their charts, they vary a great deal in their comparison with the corresponding years in our calculations, because in my report no one did the work of forming tables, and doing the count from memory, they made considerable mistakes. These are manifested by the narration itself that they make of the events; for interpreting the charts in that simple style of their authors, the figures of which denote the number of ages, centuries, or years that had passed from one event to another, they indicate the character of the year in which the event which they are referring to occurred, regularly omitting the intervening broken [Translator: see the previous footnote on "años quebrados," or broken years] years. And the interpreters try to indicate the corresponding year in our calculations without the help of the chronological tables, and for this reason they fall into these errors at each step.

We are given curious and singular information of a type of vow that these people made at the time of leaving their fatherland as fugitives. This vow was for the men not to know their women for the space of twenty-three years, which they fulfilled perfectly. It is a very unique thing among such a multitude of people for there not to have been a single one who would break it. I figure that the reason that they had for this could have been that of freeing themselves from the bother and care of pregnant(1) women and little children on the trip they were undertaking for the purpose of populating new regions, it seeming to them that in the space of twenty-three years they would then be able to have fixed settlements and establishments. Although the historians say that they made a vow,(2) it should be supposed that this was a commitment among themselves, or a determination of their principal chiefs, whom they blindly obeyed; and some authors even add with Fernando de Alba that they imposed this precept with rigorous penalties to anyone who broke it. But their government and prudence in this resolution to make their pilgrimage less bothersome is worthy of admiration, as is their constancy and chastity in fulfilling it, without there being anyone among such a large multitude who would break it, according to the assertion of their writers. It is true that, if as the historians themselves assert, those principal lords who ruled them imposed rigorous penalties on transgressors, these penalties were undoubtedly in large part the restraint that contained them; but this does not make it less worthy of admiration.

So far all the reports that these historians give us are just an overview, because the historical charts that they interpret are not truly ancient history of their first origin, but rather some notes or commentaries that serve as a preface to the history of the Toltecs that they themselves wrote; and so everything that they mention up to the rebellion, which is where they take the beginning of the history of their nation and the founding of their kingdom, are very scant reports which they give of their pilgrimage through Asia to

America, of their multiplication, settlements, and governance in the 2,379 years that went by since the founding of their first city of Huetlapallan until the rebellion of the Toltecs; and they only bring them as suppositions or preliminary to starting to relate their history. But it is sufficient to understand that all the settlers of this new world which is called America came from those seven families that joined together in the dispersion of Babel, that they came from the North, crossing rivers or arms of the sea, and sailing along its banks in rafts of reeds or light wood, as they are accustomed to doing in many places today; that the first place that was settled was the northern part of America, which goes from the Tropic of Cancer on the North from the height of 24 degrees to 75, including the remote provinces of Sinaloa, Taraumara, Chihuahua, Sonora, California, Pimeria, and the others that follow of gentiles, where so far the Catholic religion has not entered, as testified to today by the innumerable crowd inhabiting them, as asserted by those who have entered them, and that just as they kept multiplying, they kept leaving in companies to inhabit the rest of all this continent, as far as the other [book opposite] part to the South, some by land, like these Toltecas, and some others that we shall see, and the others by sea sailing its beaches, like the Olmecs, Xicalancas, and other nations who inhabited the coast of Yucatan. But regarding their government and customs in those primitive times, however, in all the manuscripts that I have become familiar with, I have not been able to investigate nor understand any other thing than that which I have written.

Nor does it seem to me that I can go any further on the subject in such remote antiquity, because the most able among them who were these Toltecs, and the historical charts which are the only sources from which I was able to get this information, do not give us any other than what I have expended here. That is not the case for subsequent times, for as will be seen, they sought to preserve the memorable events of their history in great detail, and following the example of the Toltecs, the other nations that settled these lands did the same thing, after the destruction of the first Toltecs kingdom.

Before closing this chapter, I want some reflection on the fact that, as we have seen in Chapter I, there were seven families who, in the dispersion of the tower of Babel, joined together because they understood each other's language, to come to settle these regions; but also there were seven main Toltecs families who left Tlachicatzin in this rebellion to settle the land that is called New Spain today, and that, as we will see later on, there were also seven families of the Mexitzin nation, who founded the city of Mexico. This uniformity in the number of families has been the origin of the multitude of confusions, mistakes, and errors incurred by our historians who wrote based on the narrations that the Indians gave them, from whom they found out about the origin, customs, kings, and other events of their antiquity. Because if it was of the Texcocans, their origin referred to the seven primitive families who founded Huehuetlapallan, because these nations always considered themselves as Chichimecs and descendants of them; if a Toltec or Aculhua was giving information, he would mention his origin as going back to these seven Toltec families who came to settle. And if a Mexican or Michoacan was reporting, he would refer his origin to the seven families of their founders who left the caves of Chicomostoc, and judging them all to be the same nation, they also believed the history of all these nations to be the same, mixing the events, and they filled their own history with confusion.

I already mentioned in Chapter II that the Gentlemen Boturini, in his mentioned work, confuses these seven Toltecs families who left Tlachicatzin to settle these lands of New Spain, with the other seven who joined together in the dispersion of Babel and journeyed so many years to these regions, and he expressly says that seven Toltecs who were present at the construction of that tower, seeing that they did not mutually understand the others, departed with their wives and children, etc.; the explanation of which can confuse anyone who is not versed in this history; because the seven families from Babel were the progenitors of all the innumerable multitude of peoples who settled these regions, dividing themselves after many years into various nations, of which only one was the one to which they gave the name of Toltecatl, and a branch of this nation was the one that came to settle the New Spain, guided and led by the seven chiefs whom I have named, whom I suppose came with their families, but different from those first seven who, because of being of the same language, joined together in the dispersion of Babel. Because these families journeyed through Asia until coming to settle in America, and because others left the city of Tlachicatzin in the northern part of the same America because of rebellion and as fugitives and came to settle in the New Spain. Confusing one with another is an obvious error opposed to the very history of these natives.

Some authors are persuaded that in the number seven these peoples were trying to denote an indefinite multitude, as we see the septinary number used in the sacred letters to denote multitude, and Boturini himself was inclined toward this opinion, but I do not find reasons on which to base it, because in the entire history I do not find that they take advantage of the number seven, being that in these settlements and founding of cities, wars, deaths, and other similar events, it was usual that if not in all, in some they would use this explanation to denote multitude of inhabitants, of soldiers, of rebels, of dead, etc., and thus I am persuaded that it is mere conjecture, because of the uniformity that is found of the seven families in the three events noted.

Footnotes, Chapter XXI

(1) "Woe unto them that are with child, and to them that give suck in those day!" were words uttered by Christ in reference to the flight of the Jews from Jerusalem, as we learn from St. Matthew, in the nineteenth verse of the twenty-fourth chapter of his Gospel; from which expressions it might be inferred, that pregnant women and sucking children were reckoned by the Jews amongst the worst evils of a forced flight, which might have led them to adopt the expedient alluded to in the text.

(2) A vow was what the Jews considered most binding. The twenty-seventh chapter of Leviticus entirely relates to vows; and its first ordinance reminds us that the same very singular custom of self-devotion for the religious service of the temple, and to obtain favour in the eyes of the Deity by such a mark of zeal, prevailed amongst the Mexicans as well as the Jews. In the eleventh verse of the first chapter of the First Book of Samuel we read, that Hannah the mother of Samuel "vowed a vow," in order to obtain a son from God. And the emperor Nezahuaicoyotl[?] is recorded to have vowed, that he would fast forty days in order to obtain a victory. Mexican and Jewish parents likewise were accustomed to bind themselves by a vow, that they would offer their children for the service of their respective temples, when they should attain a fit age; and both nations considered the breach of a vow to be a sin of the most atrocious kind.

CHAPTER XXII

By counsel of the astronomer Huemantzin, the Toltecs decide to go settle the land of Anahuac. They undertake their voyage, which they describe in all detail, and the settlements that they founded on the road until reaching Tolantzinco.

After the Toltecas stopped and founded Tlapallanconco, they dedicated themselves to the cultivation of the land, sowing the fields of their area to provide sustenance for that numerous people, which was increasing each day with the new companies of people who were coming there from the city as well as from other settlements of their same nation. The government resided in the seven principal lords, who, conferring among themselves, decided what was best for the subsistence and good order of that great crowd which was entirely subordinate to them. Thus they maintained themselves for three years; but at the end of those three years, seeing the considerable increase of people, with more people being added every day, which was making good order and governance difficult in one single settlement, the seven lords met to consult among themselves on the measures that they should take to divide that numerous group into different populations.

A venerable old man named Hueman attended the meeting, Huemantzin in the reverential style of the Nahuatl language, of whom I said in Chapter XIX that some authors have confused him with Quetzalcohuatl, because both were given the name of Hueman, which means he of the large hands, and allegorically, he who has much power, talent, and wisdom.

This old man Hueman was highly esteemed and respected by everyone, not just because of his age, but because of his prudence, maturity, and wisdom, especially in astronomy and the divinatory art. This man, then, told them that it didn't seem appropriate for them to remain in that place, nor to extend their settlements in it; because with their enemies being so close, they were always exposed to living without peace, and with arms in hand to defend themselves from their insults. That he had observed in their histories that all the great works and calamities that their elders had suffered had occurred in the year indicated with the hieroglyph of the flint, which was a disastrous sign to them, and this was confirmed by the fact that their last misfortune and departure from their fatherland had been in a year of this same character. But that he had also observed that after the misfortunes, later great prosperity occurred, especially in the years indicated with the second hieroglyph, which is the house, and it was an announcement of happiness. That he was venturing to promise happiness to them if they would follow his counsel to leave that land, and undertake their voyage to the eastern lands, in which the giants had lived for many years, because he knew because of his learning that its climate should be milder, its lands very fertile and abundant, and its extent great to be able to found a prosperous and happy monarchy in it. That because of the distance they would be free from the insults of their enemies; that that country was not subject to the evil influences of the heavenly body that was pursuing them; and that although he also knew by his learning that another great misfortune was still threatening them, its fulfillment was very distant, and with time its harmful aspects could change; and if not, they and their descendants could, in the meantime, achieve up to the tenth level of a happy empire. And finally, that the giants who had been the inhabitants of those lands were known to have been entirely destroyed; and thus there was no opposition whatsoever to fear.

The reasoning of the old man moved the spirits of the lords in such a way that they immediately agreed to follow his counsel, and it was resolved to undertake the trip, staying at the places that seemed best for them to plant and provide what they needed for their sustenance, leaving settlements in all those places to protect them in case of a quick retreat. For this reason they did not agree to completely abandon Tlapallanconco, but rather they decided to keep some families of plebeian people in it. The lords declared their decision to the people, and finding in them a quick and blind obedience, they then determined to undertake their march and, in fact, they started it in the year of twelve reeds, which in the tables corresponds to the year 607, eleven years after the departure from their fatherland.

For twelve straight days they walked towards the dawn, without making any mention, until the darkness of night made them stop and take some rest and sustenance. They went about six leagues each day, which was not few in such a mixed throng of women and children(1) and people carrying provisions on their shoulders. After twelve days they reached the land of Hueyalan, which seemed good and fertile to them, and so they decided to stay. They make the discoverer of it to be Cohuatzon, one of the five who joined the two principals, and he would happen to give it the name of Hueyalan, which means large sandy area. They stopped here for close to four years, planting their fields, and taking up their voyage again, leaving a settlement in Hueyalan, they walked for twenty straight days toward the west, and at the end of those twenty days, another of the five captains, named Mazacohuatl, discovered the land of Jalisco on the shores of the sea; it seemed good and fertile to them, and they decided to dwell in it, which they did, and they founded the city of Xalixco, which is still in existence in our days, and it seems that its founding should go back to the year of 610, or 611, with respect to their assertion to have stayed in Hueyalan about four years. They dwelled in Jalisco, for eight years, and having left a competent population in it and the surrounding area, they continued their trek along the shores and beaches of the sea; and having gone twenty days straight, they stopped on the coast that they called Chimalhuacan Atenco, where they stopped for close to five years.

While here, the time of the twenty-three years of their vow, or commitment, was fulfilled, and the men started to multiply; and having left sufficient population, they continued their trek in the year of a rabbit in which they counted twenty-seven years since the departure from their fatherland, which according to the tables corresponds to the year 622; they walked for eighteen days always seeking the East until arriving at Toxpam, of which they make someone named Metzotzin the discoverer. They stopped in it for another five years, and the last of them again undertook their travels, and having walked for twenty days they arrived at the coasts and beaches that they called Quiyahuitztlan Anahuac, where they found it necessary to form rafts to cross some large rivers, or arms of the sea. They make Tlacamihtzin the discoverer of it, one of the two principal lords, to whom they also give the name of Acapichtzin, perhaps because of having discovered these beaches and arms of sea, because until this occasion they don't give him this name, which sounds or can be interpreted as the discoverer of the reed fields, perhaps because of having found some on these beaches, in which they suffered not a few discomforts; but, nevertheless, they stayed on them for six years, cultivating the immediate lands, the fertility of which made the other discomforts tolerable to them.

After six years they decided to continue their trek, moved by the persuasions of the wise Hueman, and they walked for eighteen days, until arriving at the land of Zacatlan, of which they make Chalcatzin the discoverer, the other one of the principal lords who was governing them. They decided to stop there, and after a short time a son was born to Chalcatzin, whom he named Zacapantzin, which they interpret over the grassland, and in memory of this they decided to found a settlement there, giving it the name of Zacatlan, which means grassland or meadow covered with grass. Others say the opposite, that is, that because of having given the settlement the name of Zacatlan, he named the son Zacapantzin. The year in which this happened they indicated with the hieroglyph of a reed, and they say that in it they counted one Xiuhtlalpilli or century from the beginning of their war, which they started in a year of the same character, and comparing it with the tables, it seems that the founding of this settlement should be set in the year 4668 of the world, and 635 of the Christian Era.

They stopped at this settlement for seven years, and in the eighth, which was indicated with the hieroglyph of eight rabbits, they again undertook their trek, and having walked for eighteen days, they arrived at the land of Tutzapan, which they interpret Tuzal, a word very much used and made Spanish today, which means land where moles nest, the mole being a well-known animal called Tutzan or Totzan in the Nahuatl language, and it is known by this name in this country where the name of mole is not used. They make the discoverer of Tutzapan to be Checatl, the same man who discovered the land of Tlapallanconco, one of the five captains who joined them, and they say that he founded the settlement of Tutzapan, and they say that a son was born to him in the last year of the seven years that they stopped in it, and he gave him the name of Totzapantzin. The year in which this child was born they indicate with the hieroglyph of a flint, which, according to the tables, corresponds to the year 4681 of the world and 648 of the Christian Era, and they remember that in that year one century was completed since the departure from their fatherland, in a year of the same character, as we have asserted.

In the same year [book: a century was fulfilled in which] they again undertook their trek, and they walked twenty-eight days straight without a certain course, until reaching the land of Tepetla, of which they make the discoverer to be Cohuatzon, one of the five captains, and the same one who had discovered the land of Hueyxalan. They stayed in Tepetla for seven years, and at the end of the seven years they again took up their trek, and having walked for eighteen days, they arrived at Mazatepec, of which the discoverer was Mazacohuatl, another of the five captains, who called it Mazatepec from his name. They were there for eight years, and at the end of the eight years they continued their walk for eighteen days straight until reaching a place to which they gave the name of Ziuhcohuatl, because of its discoverer having been Ziuhcohuatl, another of the five captains to whom they also gave the names of Tlapalhuitz and Tlapalmetzin. They stayed here another eight years, and then they continued their walk for twenty days straight until reaching Itztachuexuca, a very fertile land that Metzotzin discovered, and in which they stopped the longest, because they assert that they had dwelled in it for twenty-six years.

They recall that in the sixteenth year, which was indicated with the hieroglyph of a reed, one age was fulfilled, which is 104 years since their wars had started in their fatherland; and according to the tables their count is exact; because the sixteenth year of their stay in Itztachuexuca, according to the previous eras, was the year 687 of Christ, which was indicated with the hieroglyph of a reed.

Now tired of walking and pleased with the goodness of the country, they had little desire to continue the trek, if it weren't for the astronomer Hueman repeating his urge, assuring them that now their sufferings would last a very little time, because the happy and fortunate country that he had predicted to them was not very far away, where they would attain a prosperous empire and would live satisfied and happy with as many comforts as they could imagine. With these persuasions, he got them to move from there after twenty-six years and continue their trek for another eighteen days straight, in which they reached Tolantzinco; and although the astronomer was persuading them to walk a little more, he couldn't get them to, because Acapichtzin having discovered the land of Tolantzinco, it pleased them so much that they determined to make their seat and perpetual dwelling in it, there founding the main settlement and capital city of their kingdom.

Then they set their hand to building a house of wood so large that once it was completed, all the people fit in it. But this was no cause for the astronomer to cease trying to dissuade them from the intent, declaring to them that this still wasn't the place in which, according to his learning, he had foreseen that the court of their empire was to flourish, and from where they were to become owners of all the land and extend their settlements throughout all the land; but with everything, he did not succeed at the time in getting them to move, and they remained in Tolantzinco for sixteen years; but after a short time families started to leave, who were forming various settlements, extending throughout the contours where they found land provided for their fields, these new colonies continuing always to be subject and subordinate to the government of the chiefs, which, with the bulk of the nation, remained in Tolantzinco, the founding of which they note in a year indicated with the hieroglyph of eleven reeds, which seems should be fixed, according to the tables, in the year 697 of Christ.

Footnote, Chapter XXII

(1) [From book] At first sight it seems that there is a contradiction here; for if they were taking children, how is this reconciled with the vow of chastity that they made and kept so scrupulously? But on carefully reading what precedes, it will be seen that they had been traveling for three years, not counted from their departure from Tlachicatzin, but from their last flight, which is when the vow should be supposed to have been made; and therefore they could take children up to two and a half years old. – E.

CHAPTER XXIII

They leave Tolantzinco, go to Tollan and found this city, which was later the court of their kingdom.

The bulk of the nation remained in Tolantzinco for sixteen years with their chiefs and captains, who were governing all the settlements from there, which settlements were being formed each day, extending throughout the land until, persuaded by the wise Hueman, they decided to move to another piece of land, not far from the banks of a river; and with effect in a year that they indicate with the hieroglyph of a house, which, according to the expression of their wise Hueman, was a prosperous sign that was announcing happiness to them, they moved to it, and with all diligence started building their city, with houses and streets, in which, dividing the families, they lived more comfortably; and of course making this settlement the capital of their empire, and the center of their Toltecatl nation, they gave it the name of Tollan.

In it, some say that they started to make their first houses of mud and stone, the art of making them already being known to them, and Fernando de Alba says that this construction invention was already very ancient among them even before leaving from their fatherland. The founding of this city of Tollan, which is still in existence in our days in its same ancient location, twelve leagues to the north of Mexico City, and known by the name of Tula, they say was in a year indicated with the character of a house, and so it should be set, according to the tables, in the year 713 of Christ, which was indicated with this hieroglyph, as is manifested in them. This famous city was the court of the Toltec kings, as will be seen further on, and up to the present time it is a considerable settlement, and the natives of these kingdoms keep in remembrance the knowledge of its ancient opulence.

It is not easy to find out the road that these peoples followed, nor the leagues that they walked from the city of Tlachicatzin to Tolantzinco; because not having a certain destination or a known route, they would wander now in some parts, now in others; and at least asserting, as their interpreters assert, that they were walking six leagues each day, and calculating the days that they walked from Jalisco to Tolantzinco, it amounts to one hundred ninety-six days, which, at the rate of six leagues a day, makes one thousand one hundred seventy-six leagues; and it is evident that from Tolantzinco to Jalisco, and even to Culuacan, which is more to the North, it wouldn't have been much more than three hundred leagues; but it is not surprising, with these people following uncertain courses, in which we must believe that the road that they would make one day they would undo another day, and even though they would spend days and multiply leagues, they did not make much progress toward the place at which they were coming to stop. All the way, and especially in the places where they stayed, they were leaving settlements, so that when they arrived at Tolantzinco it should be supposed that all the land through which they had come was now settled, not just with the settlements that they had made at the places where they stayed, but at many other places where they went after leaving those same stopping places, extending throughout the continent, from the coasts of the Southern Sea, those of the Mexican heart, through the provinces that are now known by the names of Chihuahua, el Parral, la Nueva Vizcaya, and Parras; because Ciuhcohuatl and Hueyxalan, which they now call Huexutla, are next to Pánuco and Tampico, maritime settlements on the coast of the Northern Sea, and it may still be that some companies had already entered the province of Texas and Florida, because besides the multiplication that we must suppose they experienced in the one hundred years that the trip lasted, they give us the information that many companies of people at various times left, following them, from the same parts of the North and region of Huehuetlapallan, of which some settled and inhabited the coasts of the South without reaching Tollan, others arrived, and many others passed by until occupying the area of this new world to the Strait of Magellan, and maybe beyond, if the land that Francis Drake discovered is populated, and they found a way to cross the straight to those lands, as they crossed the sea of California and the other straits, sea arms, and large rivers that they went over; thus for the first inhabitants to have arrived from the field of Sennaar to the region of Huehuetlapallan, as for this Toltecatl nation until reaching Tollan.

The extended life of these people is noteworthy, because at least the two principal lords, Chalcatzin and Tlacamihtzin, the five additional captains, and the astronomer Hueman, who assert to have arrived at Tollan, and were living in the year 713, it had been one hundred thirty years since they rebelled against their sovereign, which was the cause of their departure; and even if they were just twenty years old then, they must have reached or surpassed one hundred fifty years. For one or another to live to such an advanced age is not uncommon; but for all of them to live so long is something significant, and Fernando de Alba expressly says of the astronomer that he was already over one hundred eighty years old when they arrived in Tollan. But it is evident that not only in these times, but also in many other later times, they give us information of persons with very long lives; because they say of Icoatzin, who at the time was reigning in the Chichimec empire, that he governed for one hundred eighty years; his successor Motzeloquixtzin, one hundred fifty-six; Tlamacatzin, who succeeded him, one hundred thirty-three; Xolotzin, the first emperor who reigned in these parts after the Toltecs, governed one hundred twelve years; and many others who will be seen in the course of this history, and the Toltecs kings themselves, all of whom reigned for fifty-two years, and some survived many more, for the reason that will be said further on.

It is not difficult for me to believe that the sovereign providence that was guiding them and sending them to settle these very vast regions would preserve their lives for such a long time, as it willed to extend the life of the patriarchs and first inhabitants of the Universe; and we must suppose that just like these principal lords, there would be a great many others in such a numerous gathering of people who would likewise attain a very long life. And truly this should not be very difficult to those who have traveled somewhat through these kingdoms, for it is very common in these times to find many Indians of advanced age. I have known and now know many, including a woman who is over one hundred, and she is as strong and robust as any other woman of twenty, and the experience is evident that in general the Indians live long lives, and if they didn't break their health with their excesses and abuses that they give to it, many would reach a very advanced age.(1)

Footnote, Chapter XXIII

(1) The eleven chapters which follow of the first part of Echevarría's History of the Origin of the Indians of New Spain, and the entire of the second part, which chiefly relates to the ancient History of the Mexicans, are here omitted, because the original Histories of Tezozomoc and Ixtlilxochitl which treat of the same subject will be found in the ninth volume of the present work. To the merits of the former of these Histories Echevarría bears honorable testimony, in the following passage of the twelfth chapter of the second part of his History of the Origin of the Indians, which we transcibe at greater length because it makes mention of some other native Indian historians whose works have escaped the ravages of time, and, we might also add, the flames of the Inquisition. "The two most famous historians of the Mexican nation, who have interpreted their charts with the most clarity and order, are Fernando de Alvarado Tezozomoc, a descendent of the kings of Azcaputzalco, who wrote in the years around 1598, an enormous volume with the title of Crónica Mexicana; and Don Domingo de San Anton Muñon Chimalpain Ququhthuamitzin, who wrote in his Nahuatl language with the title of Crónica Mexicana, and the same work in our language with the title of Mexican History, around the year 1626. The two most famous in the Teochichimec

history are Don Domingo Muñon Camargo, a Tlaxcaltec mestizo, who wrote with the title of Crónica Tlaxcayan around the year 1585, and Juan Buenaventura Zapata y Mendoza, a chief of Tlaxcallan of the head of Quiyahuiztlan, who wrote in his Nahuatl language with the title of Crónica de la muy noble y leal Ciudad de Tlaxcayan por los años de 1589 [Chronicle of the very noble and loyal City of Tlaxcayan around 1589]."We may here remark, as a fact very deserving of attention, that for nearly half a century after the conquest of Mexico by the Spaniards, the ecclesiastical authorities discouraged all researches into the history and religion of the ancient Mexicans; and when at the expiration of that long period greater latitude was given to inquiry, the recollection of many important events had been already swallowed up in the gulf of oblivion.

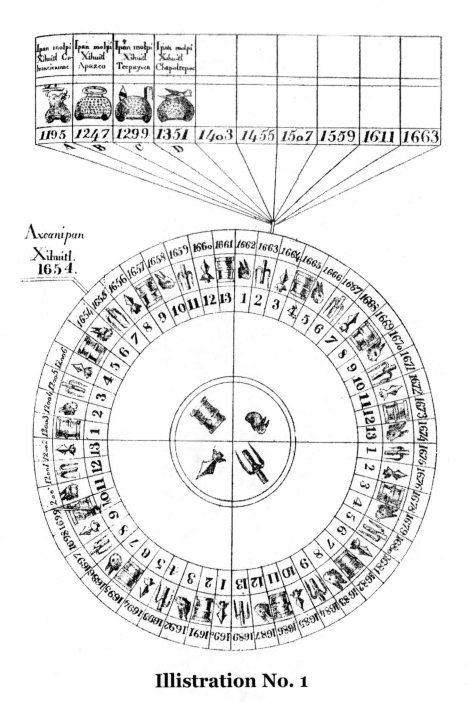

Illistration No. 1

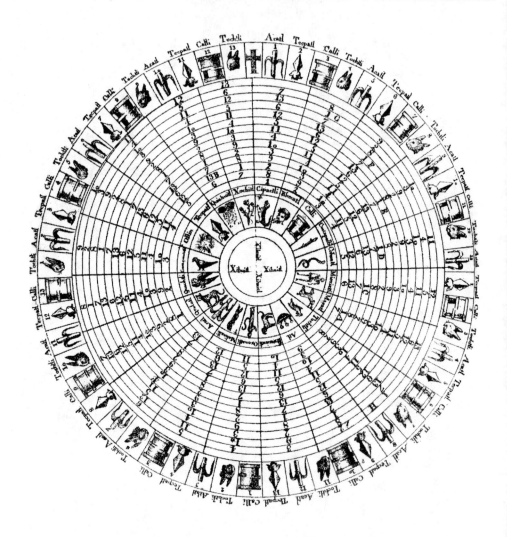

Illistration No. 2

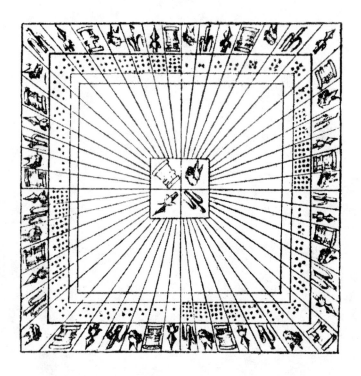

Illistration No. 3

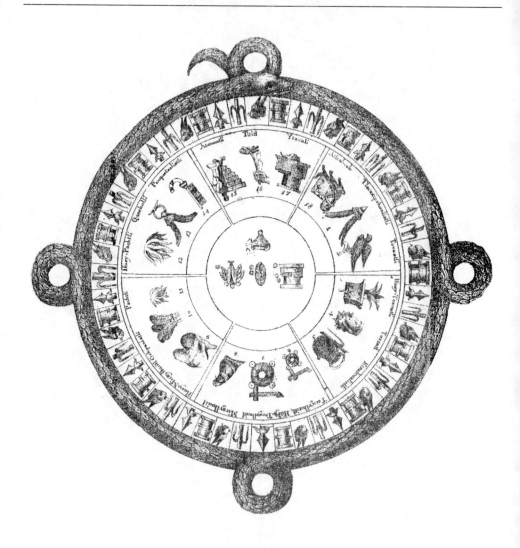

Illistration No. 4

Illistration No. 5

Illistration No. 6

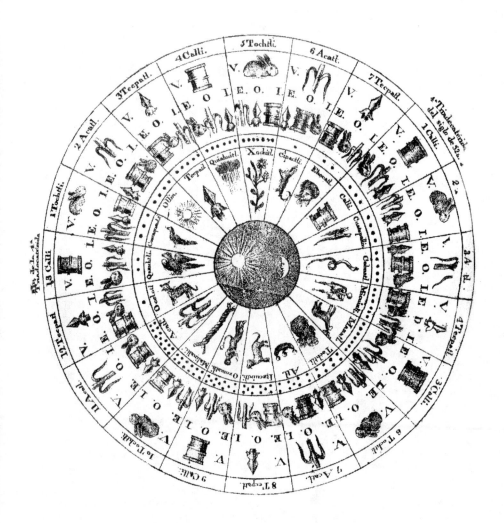

Illistration No. 7

INDEX

(Numbers indicate pages where cited information can be found)